The ROCK LISTS Album

JOHN TOBLER/ALAN JONES

Plexus, London

Text copyright © 1982 by John Tobler and Alan Jones
This edition copyright © 1982 by Plexus Publishing Limited
Published by Plexus Publishing Limited
30 Craven Street
London WC2N 5NT

Tobler, John
   The rock lists album
   1. Rock music   Statistics
   I. Title   II. Jones, Alan
   784.5′4′0212   ML3534

   ISBN 0–85965–049–9
   ISBN 0–85965–048–0 Pbk

Jacket design by Bob Ughetti
Book design by Robin Allen

Manufactured in Great Britain

CONTENTS

1. LABELS

SUN RECORDS RECORDING ARTISTS

Sun Records started in Memphis, Tennessee, in February 1952. Its most fruitful period occurred during the mid-1950s, when an array of the finest rock'n'roll artists of all time were contracted to Sun simultaneously. Some of the names on the list will be familiar, but many of the others should not be underrated.

1. Jackie Boy and Little Walter
2. Johnny London
3. Walter Bradford and the Big City Four
4. Handy Jackson
5. Joe Hill Louis
6. Willie Nix
7. Rufus Thomas
8. Dusty Brooks and his Tones
9. D. A. Hunt
10. Jimmy DeBerry
11. The Prisonaires
12. Little Junior Parker and the Blue Flames
13. The Ripley Cotton Choppers
14. Dr Ross
15. Little Milton
16. Billy Emerson
17. Earl Peterson, Michigan's Singing Cowboy
18. Howard Serratt
19. James Cotton
20. Doug Poindexter and the Starlite Wranglers
21. Raymond Hill
22. Harmonica Frank
23. Buddy Cunningham
24. Elvis Presley
25. Malcolm Yelvington
26. The Jones Brothers
27. Slim Rhodes
28. Johnny Cash
29. The Five Tinos
30. Carl Perkins
31. Eddie Snow
32. Roscoe Gordon
33. Smokey Joe
34. Maggie Sue Wimberley
35. Charlie Feathers
36. Jimmy Haggett
37. Warren Smith
38. Roy Orbison and the Teen Kings
39. Billy Lee Riley and the Little Green Men
40. Sonny Burgess
41. Jerry Lee Lewis and his Pumping Piano
42. Ernie Chaffin
43. Glenn Honeycutt
44. Rudi Richardson
45. Roy Harris
46. Mack Self
47. Edwin Bruce
48. Dickey Lee and the Collegiates
49. Jack Clement
50. Ray Smith
51. Gene Simmons
52. Tommy Blake
53. Vernon Taylor
54. Jimmy Isle
55. Onie Wheeler
56. Jerry McGill and the Top Coats
57. Johnny Powers
58. Sherry Crane
59. Will Mercer
60. Tracy Pendarvis
61. Texas Bill Strength
62. Tony Rossini
63. Wade Cagle and the Escorts
64. Harold Dorman
65. Shirley Sisk
66. Anita Wood
67. The Four Upsetters
68. The Teen Angels
69. David Houston
70. Billy Adams
71. Randy and the Radiants
72. The Jesters
73. Bill Yates and his T-Birds
74. Gorgeous Bill Carleen
75. Load of Mischief

The more astute reader may wonder why such names as Charlie Rich, Bill Justis, Johnny Carroll, Thomas Wayne and Carl Mann are omitted from this list. The answer is that in America, at least, these artists were on other labels affiliated with Sun (eg Phillips International) but were not actually Sun recording artists.

RED BIRD/BLUE CAT RECORDING ARTISTS

Red Bird and Blue Cat were twin labels started during the mid-1960s by Jerry Leiber, Mike Stoller and George Goldner, all of whom had impressive music business connections. The labels were active between 1963 and 1966, when Leiber and Stoller sold their shares in the business to George Goldner, soon after which the labels became dormant.

1. The Dixie Cups
2. The Jelly Beans
3. The Latin Quarters
4. The Lovejoys
5. Jersey Red

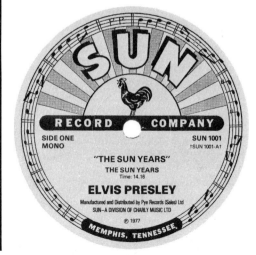

6. Chi-Chi MacCauley
7. The Rockaways
8. The Honeyman
9. The Butterflys
10. Alvin Robinson
11. The Shangri-Las
12. Barry Mann
13. The Tradewinds
14. Roddie Joy
15. Jimmy Rice
16. Jeff Barry
17. Steve Rossi
18. Ellie Greenwich
19. Andy Kim
20. Sidney Barnes
21. Murray the K
22. Ral Donner
23. The Ad-Libs
24. Bessie Banks
25. Bruce Forsyth (the same)
26. Evie Sands
27. Dickie Goodman
28. John Hammond
29. The Young Generation
30. The Four Evers

ARTISTS SIGNED TO IMMEDIATE RECORDS

Immediate Records, the brainchild of erstwhile Rolling Stones manager Andrew Loog Oldham, was active between 1965 and 1970, when lack of finances caused it to enter liquidation. While the record industry is obviously not an easy place to survive, the label's artist roster contains so many famous names (not to mention the involvement of Messrs. Jagger and Richard as A&R men/producers) that its demise is all the more surprising.

1. The McCoys (including Rick Derringer)
2. Nico
3. The Poets
4. The Strangeloves (including Richard Gottehrer)
5. Glyn Johns (the record producer)
6. Fifth Avenue
7. Gregory Phillips

8. The Masterminds
9. The Factotums
10. Van Lenton
11. John Mayall (with Eric Clapton)
12. The Golden Apples of the Sun
13. Barbara Lynn
14. Mick Softley
15. The Mockingbirds (including Graham Gouldman)
16. Chris Farlowe
17. Jimmy Tarbuck
18. The Variations
19. Joey Vine
20. Fleur De Lys
21. Charles Dickens (!)
22. Goldie (aka Genya Ravan)
23. Tony Rivers and the Castaways
24. The London Waits
25. The Turtles
26. Twice As Much
27. P. P. Arnold
28. Apostolic Intervention
29. Nicky Scott
30. Mort Shuman (the songwriter)
31. Small Faces
32. The Marquis of Kensington
33. Murray Head
34. Australian Playboys
35. Warm Sounds
36. The Nice
37. Rod Stewart
38. Billy Nicholls
39. Duncan Browne
40. Michael d'Abo
41. Fleetwood Mac
42. Amen Corner
43. Sam Cooke

THE DECCA TAPES – THE AUDITION THE BEATLES FAILED

In 1962, the Beatles were looking for a British record deal, and on the first day of that year, the group performed an audition for Decca Records which was recorded. Although the full results of the full session have never been legally released, numerous bootlegs of the recordings have subsequently surfaced, and the listing below represents the contents of one such bootleg.

1. Like Dreamers Do*
2. Money
3. Till There Was You
4. Sheik Of Araby
5. To Know Him Is To Love Him
6. Take Good Care Of My Baby
7. Memphis
8. Sure To Fall
9. Hello Little Girl*
10. Three Cool Cats
11. Crying, Waiting, Hoping
12. Love Of The Loved*
13. September In The Rain
14. Besame Mucho
15. Searchin'

* Items marked with an asterisk(*) have not (so far) been released on official Beatles records.

ARTISTS SIGNED TO APPLE RECORDS

Apple Records was the label set up by the Beatles in 1968, and, like most record companies owned by artists, after a very promising start it began to crumble in much the same way as its owners did at the same time.

1. The Beatles (actually signed to Parlophone, but allowed to release their own records with Apple labels)

2. Mary Hopkin
3. Jackie Lomax
4. Black Dyke Mills Band
5. The Iveys (later known as Badfinger)
6. Trash (later known as White Trash)
7. Brute Force
8. Billy Preston
9. Plastic Ono Band (actually signed to Parlophone – see 1)
10. Radha Krishna Temple
11. Hot Chocolate
12. Doris Troy
13. James Taylor
14. Ronnie Spector
15. Bill Elliott and the Elastic Oz Band
16. Ravi Shankar
17. Yoko Ono and the Plastic Ono Band
18. Chris Hodge
19. Sundown Playboys
20. Elephant's Memory
21. Lon and Derek Van Eaton
22. John Lennon
23. Paul McCartney
24. George Harrison
25. Ringo Starr
26. Wings
27. Modern Jazz Quartet
28. John Tavener

THE 2 TONE SINGLES LIST

2 Tone was the phenomenon of 1979–80, a label based in Coventry and boasting an artist roster of bands playing derivations of ska music, and with one exception, integrated and multi-racial bands. With the break up during October 1981 of the Specials, founders and owners of the label, the label lost all its credibility, although by that time nearly all the original 2 Tone bands had either signed with other labels or split.

TT1	The Special AKA	Gangsters
TT2	The Selecter	The Selecter (released as B side of TT1)
TT3	Madness	The Prince/Madness
TT4	The Selecter	On My Radio/Too Much Pressure
TT5	The Specials	A Message To You Rudy/Nite Klub
TT6	The Beat	Tears Of A Clown/Ranking Full Stop
TT7	Elvis Costello and the Attractions	I Can't Stand Up For Falling Down/ Girls Talk

(Pressed, but not released on 2 Tone. Eventually replaced by . . .

TT7	The Special AKA	Too Much Too Young EP
TT8	The Selecter	Three Minute Hero/James Bond
TT9	The Bodysnatchers	Let's Do Rock Steady/Ruder Than You
TT10	The Selecter	Missing Words/Carry Go Bring Come
TT11	The Specials	Rat Race/Rude Boys Outa Jail
TT12	Bodysnatchers	Too Experienced/East Life
TT13	The Specials	Stereotype/International Jet Set
TT14	The Swinging Cats	Mantovani/Away
TT15	Rico	Sea Cruise/Carolina
TT16	The Specials	Do Nothing/Maggie's Farm
TT17	The Specials	Ghost Town EP
TT18	Rhoda with the Special AKA	The Boiler/Theme From The Boiler
TT19	Rico with the Special AKA	Jungle Music/Rasta Call You
TT20	The Apollinaires	The Feeling's Gone/The Feeling's Back

(List supplied with the help of Bert Muirhead, *Hot Wacks* Magazine.)

STIFF TOURING PARTIES

Stiff Records, founded in the mid 1970s, have used many original methods to promote their wares. One of the most successful was their semi-legendary series of tours featuring a selection of their artists. Happily, in many cases these tours provided a launching pad for future stardom.

1977 tour
1. Elvis Costello and the Attractions
2. Ian Dury and the Blockheads
3. Nick Lowe's Last Chicken in the Shop
4. Wreckless Eric and the New Rockets
5. Larry Wallis' Psychedelic Rowdies
6. Dave Edmunds

1978 Tour
1. Lene Lovich and the Musicians Union
2. Mickey Jupp and the Cable Layers
3. The Records
4. Jona Lewie and Two's Company
5. Rachel Sweet
6. Wreckless Eric and the Four Rough Men

1980 Tour
1. Tenpole Tudor

2. Joe 'King' Carrasco and the Crowns
3. The Equators
4. Dirty Looks
5. Any Trouble

STIFF RECORDS SLOGANS

1. Where perfection is no accident
2. Money talks, people mumble
3. We're the best, ignore the rest
4. Even our socks smell of success
5. We lead where others follow but can't keep up
6. Stemming the poverty of 20th century culture
7. Made the way they don't make them anymore
8. If you don't use it you'll lose it
9. If it doesn't smell it'll never sell
10. There's no business like business
11. Where the fun never sets
12. Uneasy listening
13. If it's Lene's you'll Lovich
14. The vinyl is final
15. Larger than life and more fun than people
16. The shape of things that Win
17. Surfing on the new wave
18. For miracles you can rely on
19. Upstairs for thinking, downstairs for dancing
20. You can tell a company by the artist it keeps
21. Forget the platinum – buy one
22. The address that spells success
23. Keep up if you can
24. Our record is extremely good
25. Hit records for missing people
26. We are limited because we keep the best company
27. Where others fear to tread
28. Hits with less fattening centres
29. Round records for square people
30. First in the field last in the ditch
31. If you can't be sure be Stiff
32. Never give up when you can give in
33. A hit in the hand is worth two in the can
34. If it ain't Stiff it ain't worth a Fuck

(A Nigel Dick super-list.)

A LIST OF STIFF PREFIXES

BUY 1 The majority of Stiff singles have this catalogue prefix – though obviously it had most impact with the first one!

BUY IT 1 12-inch singles

SEEZ 1 Most Stiff albums are in the 'SEEZ' range. It is a strong rumour that this catalogue group would have been 'SEIZE' but none of the early Stiff employees knew how to spell!

GET 1 Once again the aggressive marketing face of Stiff Records shows itself. All 'GETs' were cut price compilations and packed brimful with quality.

FIST 1 There was only ever one of these. FIRST 1 perhaps – another typing error!

USE 1 All American versions of English LPs as issued by Stiff America.

LENE 1 One of those great interview discs designed for American DJs. There was only one of these for Lene Lovich.

GOMM 1 Ditto above for one of the Brinsley mafia whose solo LPs were released by Stiff America -- Ian Gomm.

TRUBZ 1 We at Stiff always abbreviate our artists carefully thought out *noms de guerre*. This is the abbreviation for the great Any Trouble for whom this was the official live bootleg.

MAIL 1 A UK Subs album sold exclusively through the mail order depot.

OAK 1 Stiff goes down the Palace Theatre. The cast of *Oklahoma!* were recorded live for this LP. Once again an illiterate did the typesetting.

ABRA 1 — Well, this one was licensed from Magic Records.

SINK 1 — The album was called Start Swimming – work the rest out for yourself.

YANK 1 — There never was a YANK 1 but this series of 2 records featured exclusively American groups.

LAST 1 — First in a line of EPs. Every artist who had a 'LAST' released left Stiff under mysterious circumstances soon after!!

LOT 1 — A great record by Johnnie Allan but I've got no idea why the prefix.

DEV 1 — Devo

BOY 1 — More De-vo-lution from the Booji-Boys.

OFF 1 — Four singles from the One-off series. If they're successful we'll sign them up. If they're not we'll cast them back into the gutter from whence they came! We did.

LEW 1 — Lew Lewis.

HORN 1 — Davey Payne – saxophone man for the Blockheads.

SMUT 1 — A special Dirty Looks record.

ERIC 1 — A special Wreckless Eric disc. Not very inspired this one.

MAD 1 — Well, most of those Nutty Boys are.

OWN 1 — Persuasive selling technique for Stiff America singles.

CROWN 1 — By Joe King Carrasco and the Crowns.

BROKEN 1 — Borrowed from Dave Stewart's Broken record label which released this his first hit – 'What Becomes Of The Broken

Hearted'.

WED 1 — Scandalous Australian record by 2 DJs released in time for the Royal Wedding.

SAVE 1 — Royalties from this record are destined for the 'Save the Children Fund'.

ZBUY
ZSEEZ etc — Z means cassette – obvious isn't it?

FREEB — Disgusting record company ploy to make friends, usually resurrected at Christmas. It's very simple – Stiff press up the records and give them away for nothing. Needless to say it's wildly successful.

UPP — Someone missed out on the 'J' – it's that typewriter again. It was Mickey Jupp.

Compiled by the warm and extremely wonderful Nigel Dick, or, as his rubber stamp would have it, 'The Dick at Nigel's Desk'.

LENE LOVICH
"FLEX"
the new album out now on Stiff Records
cat.no. seez 19
cassette zseez 19

f l e x

ERIC & CO TREADING IN THINGS NO MAN HAS EVER TROD IN BEFORE. (AND COMING BACK FOR MORE)

B L O CKHEAD

THE SON OF STIFF TOUR 1980

STIFF'S GREATEST HITS

The ten Stiff singles which have achieved greatest UK sales, in descending order:

1. Hit Me With Your Rhythm Stick – Ian Dury and the Blockheads
2. Stop The Cavalry – Jona Lewie
3. Baggy Trousers – Madness
4. It's My Party – Dave Stewart and Barbara Gaskin
5. Embarrassment – Madness
6. My Girl – Madness
7. Lucky Number – Lene Lovich
8. One Step Beyond – Madness
9. Return Of The Las Palmas 7 – Madness
10. Pretend – Alvin Stardust

STIFF'S GREATEST STIFFS

The ten Stiff singles which have achieved the lowest UK sales, in ascending order:

1. Dust On The Needle – Thunderbolts
2. Put Some Water In – Sprouthead Uprising
3. Trial By Television – The Mexicano
4. You Talk Too Much – Otis Watkins
5. Thunderbird – Nigel Dixon
6. Romeo – Ernie Graham
7. Made In Germany – Michael O'Brien
8. Couldn't Believe A Word – 45s
9. Saxophone Man – Davey Payne
10. Gimme Your Heart – Subs

ARTIST OWNED RECORD LABELS

1. Apple (The Beatles)
2. Threshold (The Moody Blues)
3. Rocket (Elton John)
4. T. Rex (Marc Bolan)
5. Ring O (Ringo Starr)
6. Dark Horse (George Harrison)
7. Rolling Stones (Guess who!)
8. Swan Song (Led Zeppelin)
9. Beserkely (Earthquake)
10. I-Spy (Secret Affair)
11. 2-Tone (The Specials)
12. Witch (Polly Brown)
13. Lone Star (Willie Nelson)
14. Go Feet (The Beat)
15. Shelter (Leon Russell)
16. Sounds Of The South (Al Kooper)
17. Eel Pie (Pete Townshend)
18. Public (Patrick Campbell-Lyons)
19. Extracked (John Otway)
20. Takoma (John Fahey)

PRODUCER OWNED LABELS

1. Philles/Phil Spector International –
   Phil Spector
2. Dreamland – Nicky Chinn and
   Mike Chapman
3. Red Bird/Blue Cat – Jerry Leiber and
   Mike Stoller
4. RAK – Mickie Most
5. Surrey Sound – Nigel Gray
6. Good Earth – Tony Visconti
7. Shelter – Denny Cordell
8. Planet – Richard Perry

Mickie Most

MICKIE MOST'S RAK HITS

Mickie Most is one of the world's most successful record producers, and since 1969/70, he has owned what must be the world's most consistently successful independent record label, RAK. Most has been quoted as saying that of every one hundred singles released, only six will be hits. Just how well he has used that information in terms of releases on his own label can be seen by the listing below of the hits among the first hundred releases on RAK.

Artist	Title
Julie Felix	If I could (El Condor Pasa)
Herman's Hermits	Bet Yer Life I Do
Hot Chocolate	Love Is Life
CCS	Whole Lotta Love

Artist	Title
Julie Felix	Heaven Is Here
Peter Noone and Herman's Hermits	Lady Barbara
John Paul Jones	The Man From Nazareth
CCS	Walkin'
Hot Chocolate	You Could Have Been A Lady
New World	Rose Garden
Peter Noone	Oh You Pretty Thing
New World	Tom Tom Turnaround
Hot Chocolate	I Believe In Love
CCS	Tap Turns On The Water
New World	Kara Kara
New World	Sister Jane
Duncan Browne	Journey
Hot Chocolate	You'll Always Be A Friend
Kenny	Heart Of Stone
Mud	Crazy
New World	Roof Top Singing
Hot Chocolate	Brother Louie
Suzi Quatro	Can The Can
Mud	Hypnosis
Kenny	Give It To Me Now
CCS	The Band Played The Boogie
Hot Chocolate	Rumours
Suzi Quatro	48 Crash
Mud	Dyna-Mite
Suzi Quatro	Daytona Demon
Cozy Powell	Dance With The Devil
Mud	Tiger Feet
Suzi Quatro	Devil Gate Drive
Hot Chocolate	Emma
Mud	The Cat Crept In
Arrows	A Touch Too Much
Cozy Powell	The Man In Black
Suzi Quatro	Too Big
Mud	Rocket
Cozy Powell	Na Na Na
Suzi Quatro	The Wild One
Kenny	The Bump
Mud	Lonely This Christmas
Arrows	My Last Night With You
Suzi Quatro	Your Mama Won't Like Me
Tam White	What In The World's Come Over You
Mud	The Secrets That You Keep
Kenny	Fancy Pants

Suzi Quatro

Which makes no less than 48 hits out of the first hundred singles released on RAK, eight times the average applicable to others, according to Mickie Most.

2. PRODUCERS

ACTS PRODUCED BY ROY THOMAS BAKER

1. Nazareth
2. Man
3. Richard Myhill
4. Lindisfarne
5. Hustler
6. Queen
7. Jet
8. Bob Calvert
9. Be-Bop Deluxe
10. Gasolin'
11. Lone Star
12. Starcastle
13. Pilot
14. Lewis Furey
15. Ian Hunter
16. Peter Straker

17. Dusty Springfield
18. Reggie Knighton
19. The Cars
20. Journey
21. Ron Wood
22. Foreigner
23. Hilly Michaels
24. Alice Cooper
25. Santana

Roy Thomas Baker started out as an engineer for Decca at the age of sixteen. In 1968 he began an association with Trident Studios which brought him fame via his discovery and production of Queen.

ACTS PRODUCED BY CHINN AND CHAPMAN

Although it is actually Mike Chapman who supervises in the recording studio, his erstwhile partner, Nicky Chinn, often received partial production credit since many of the songs which were recorded by the following acts were jointly written by Chinn and Chapman.

1. The Sweet
2. Mud
3. Suzi Quatro
4. Smokie
5. Exile
6. Nick Gilder
7. Blondie
8. Rick Derringer
9. Tanya Tucker
10. Pat Benatar
11. The Knack
12. Spider
13. Shandi
14. Nervus Rex
15. Holly Penfield
16. Michael Des Barres

ACTS PRODUCED BY STUART COLMAN

Stuart Colman's early musical career centred around his role as bass player with Pinkerton's Assorted Colours, a group he joined following their sole hit, 'Mirror Mirror'. He subsequently became Britain's number one rock'n'roll disc jockey, hosting Radio One's *It's Rock'n'Roll* for several

Stuart Colman

years, before moving to his current highly rated *Echoes* programme on BBC Radio London. 1981 saw his emergence as one of Britain's top record producers.

Act	Label
Brian Copsey and the Commotions	Chrysalis
Rikki and the Cufflinks	MCA
Billy Fury	Polydor
Marshall Doktors	Rewind
The Inmates	WEA
Tommy 'J'	RAK
The Jets	EMI
Paul Kennerley	A&M
Pete Sayers	Country Roads
Shakin' Stevens	Epic
The Stroke	CBS

Among the hit records produced by Stuart are 'Marie Marie', 'This Ole House', 'Green Door', 'You Drive Me Crazy', 'It's Raining' and 'Oh Julie' by Shakin' Stevens, plus the LPs 'This Ole House' and 'Shaky', 'Yes Tonight Josephine' and 'The Honeydripper' by the Jets.

40 ARTISTS PRODUCED BY GEORGE MARTIN

1. Beatles
2. Bee Gees
3. Goons
4. Little River Band
5. America
6. Neil Sedaka
7. Jeff Beck

Paul McCartney and George Martin

Rolf Harris

8. Peter Sellers and Sophia Loren
9. Cleo Laine
10. Cilla Black
11. Shirley Bassey
12. Ringo Starr
13. Temperance Seven
14. Stackridge
15. Peter Ustinov

16. Aerosmith
17. Rolf Harris
18. George Burns
19. Mastersingers
20. Robin Gibb
21. Paul McCartney
22. Matt Monro
23. John Williams
24. Fourmost
25. Frankie Howerd
26. Sea Train
27. American Flyer
28. Spike Milligan
29. Billy Preston
30. Stan Getz
31. Dianne Steinberg and Stargard
32. Brenda Arnau
33. Bernard Cribbins
34. Steve Martin
35. David and Jonathan
36. Peter Frampton
37. Flanders and Swann
38. Gerry and the Pacemakers
39. Ultravox
40. Billy J. Kramer and the Dakotas

ACTS PRODUCED BY GEORGE 'SHADOW' MORTON

1. The Shangri-Las
2. Janis Ian
3. The New York Dolls
4. Vanilla Fudge
5. Mott the Hoople
6. The Beatlettes
7. Shadow Morton
8. Holly and the Italians
9. The Goodies
10. The Nu-luvs

A protégé of Leiber and Stoller, George Morton acquired his 'Shadow' epithet from his legendary ability to vanish without anyone noticing. His career has been spasmodic, but the hits he produced remain classics.

ACTS PRODUCED BY CHRIS THOMAS

It would be difficult to deny that any record producer who can successfully work with both the Sex Pistols and Paul McCartney is at the very least versatile. Chris Thomas has worked with both those acts, and quite a few others besides...

1. Climax Blues Band
2. Nirvana
3. Procol Harum
4. Mick Abrahams Band
5. Christopher Milk
6. John Cale
7. Roxy Music
8. Badfinger
9. Sadistic Mika Band

Kokomo

10. Kokomo
11. Bryan Ferry
12. Krazy Kat
13. Sex Pistols
14. Frankie Miller
15. Chris Spedding
16. Tom Robinson Band
17. Wings
18. Pretenders
19. Pete Townshend
20. Elton John

Incidentally, Chris also mixed 'Dark Side Of The Moon' by the Pink Floyd...

AN RGM PRODUCTION

Joe Meek was a wayward genius probably best remembered for creating three chart topping singles ('Johnny Remember Me' by John Leyton, 'Telstar' by the Tornados, and 'Have I The Right?' by the Honeycombs), although these were but the cream topping a substantial cake of nearly fifty UK hits between 1960 and 1965. Inevitably, he also worked with many acts without scoring hits, and the list below contains a number of interesting names among the unknowns. 'RGM' stands for Robert George Meek (his real name), and since his tragic death in 1967 (Joe is believed to have committed suicide on the anniversary of the death of his idol, Buddy Holly), RGM productions have steadily increased in value. Check your loft, eh?

The RGM Appreciation Society can be found at 37A, St Mary's Road, London, SE15.

1. Michael Cox
2. John Leyton
3. Mike Berry
4. The Outlaws
5. The Tornados
6. The Honeycombs
7. The Blue Men
8. Peter Jay and the Jaywalkers
9. Rodd and the Cavaliers
10. Joy and Dave
11. Yolanda
12. Ricky Wayne
13. The Fabulous Flee-Rekkers
14. George Chakiris
15. Carol Jones
16. Don Fox
17. Rex and the Minors
18. Pat Reader
19. Barbara Lyon
20. Laura Lee
21. Heinz
22. Danny Rivers
23. Davy Kaye
24. Don Charles
25. Geoff Goddard
26. Pamela Blue
27. Joe Meek Orchestra
28. Freddie Starr and the Midnighters
29. Tony Victor
30. The Cryin' Shames
31. Screaming Lord Sutch
32. Roger LaVern and the Microns
33. Sounds Incorporated
34. The Millionaires
35. The Saxons
36. Glenda Collins
37. Tom Jones (the same)
38. The Dowlands
39. Iain Gregory
40. The Moontrekkers
41. The Saints
42. Gerry Temple
43. Houston Wells and the Marksmen
44. The Stonehenge Men
45. Andy Cowell
46. Charles Blackwell Orchestra
47. Chad Carson
48. Gunilla Thorne
49. Flip and the Dateliners
50. Eddie Silver
51. Chris and the Students
52. Cliff Bennet and the Rebel Rousers
53. The Chaps
54. Neil Christian
55. Shade, Joey and the Nightowls
56. David John and the Mood
57. Wes Sands
58. Jason Eddy and the Centremen
59. Jenny Moss
60. The Cameos
61. Gene Vincent
62. Deke Arlon and the Offbeats
63. The Syndicats
64. Valerie Masters
65. The Shakeouts
66. Davy Morgan
67. The Hotrods
68. Charles Kingsley Creation
69. The Four Matadors
70. Diane and the Javelins
71. The Buzz
72. Tommy Steele
73. Peter, Chris and the Outcasts
74. Terry White and the Terriers
75. The Lindys
76. Ray Dexter and the Layabouts
77. Peter Cook
78. Jess Conrad
79. Les Paul and Mary Ford
80. The Checkmates
81. Dick Emery
82. Gene Pitney
83. The Original Checkmates
84. The Beat Boys

RECORDS PHIL SPECTOR CLAIMS TO HAVE PRODUCED

1. Donna – Ritchie Valens (this was recorded at Gold Star Studios in Los Angeles at roughly the same time as was 'To Know Him Is To Love Him' by the Teddy Bears, a group of which Spector was a member)
2. Save The Last Dance For Me – The Drifters
3. On Broadway – The Drifters
4. Spanish Harlem – Ben E. King
5. Lavender Blue – Sammy Turner

(All the last four tracks were recorded while Spector was 'apprenticed' to Jerry Leiber and Mike Stoller in New York during the early sixties).

6. Deep Purple – Nino Tempo and April Stevens
7. Whispering – Nino Tempo and April Stevens
8. Nature Boy – Bobby Darin
9. You Must Have Been a Beautiful Baby – Bobby Darin
10. Elvis Is Back LP – Elvis Presley.

(Numbers six to ten above boast little documentary evidence to prove that Spector was involved, although in every case there is at least a possibility that he may have been involved.)

List supplied by Keith Beach of the UK Phil Spector Appreciation Society.

Phil Spector

PHIL SPECTOR'S BIZARRE B-SIDES

Phil Spector was a supreme tactician among record company executives, although on more than one occasion, his revolutionary ideas appeared to backfire on him. Whether the concept behind the list which follows was successful is difficult to establish – in order to ensure that radio programmers would be in no doubt as to which side of a record was intended to be the A side, many of his most famous singles were released with totally instrumental B sides. Although the artist credit was identical to that on the A side of the record, these B sides were nothing more or less than hastily thrown together jam sessions performed by Spector's regular backing musicians, many of whom later found fame in their own right. Often these musicians, plus friends, relatives and associates of Spector, also found their names in the titles of these strange B-sides . . .

Phil Spector

The Drifters

Artist	B side title	Referring to
Bob B. Soxx	Flip And Nitty	Phil Spector and Jack Nitzsche
Bob B. Soxx	Dr Kaplan's Office	Spector's psychiatrist or lawyer?
Bob B. Soxx	Annette	Annette Mirar, Spector's first wife
Crystals	Brother Julius	Shoeshine boy outside Goldstar Studio where many Spector hits were made
Ronettes	Tedesco And Pitman	Tom Tedesco and Bill Pitman (session musicians)
Darlene Love	Nino And Sonny (Big Trouble)	Nino Tempo and Sonny Bono (session musicians)
Ronettes	Miss Joan And Mister Sam	Joan Berg, Spector's secretary, and Sam, his chauffeur
Darlene Love	Harry And Milt Meet Hal B.	Harold Battiste, Milton? and Hal Blaine, (session musicians)
Crystals	Harry (From W.Va.) and Milt	As previous entry
Ronettes	Big Red	One of Spector's bodyguards
Ronettes	Bebe And Susu	The mothers of the Ronettes
Crystals	Irving (Jaggered Sixteenths)	?
Bonnie and the Treasures	Bramwell, Robitaille And Carr	Tony Bramwell (Spector's UK representative), Deura Robitaille (Spector's secretary), Roy Carr (rock writer)
Treasures	Pete Meets Vinnie	Peter Anders and Vinnie Poncia, songwriters
Veronica	Larry L.	Larry Levine, studio engineer
Veronica	Chubby Danny D.	Danny Davis, longtime Spector associate

List compiled by Keith Beach of the UK Phil Spector Appreciation Society. Any help in filling the gaps would be appreciated . . .

ACTS PRODUCED BY TONY VISCONTI

1. Tyrannosaurus Rex (including T. Rex)
2. David Bowie
3. Strawbs
4. Badfinger
5. Legend
6. Marsha Hunt
7. Osibisa
8. Mary Hopkin
9. Gentle Giant
10. Gasworks
11. Ralph McTell
12. Tom Paxton
13. Carmen
14. Sparks
15. Surprise Sisters
16. Omaha Sheriff
17. Thin Lizzy
18. Radiators
19. Steve Gibbons Band
20. Zaine Griff
21. Hazel O'Connor
22. Boomtown Rats
23. Stranglers
24. Afraid of Mice
25. Photos

Tony Visconti was born in Brooklyn on 24 April 1944 and began producing records after moving to Britain in the late sixties. He is best known for producing David Bowie and Marc Bolan.

David Bowie

BRIAN WILSON'S NON-BEACH BOY PRODUCTIONS

Artist	Titles	Date
Rachel and the Revolvers	The Revo-Lution/Number One	August 1962
Bob and Sheri	The Surfer Moon/Humpty Dumpty	October 1962
The Honeys	Shoot The Curl/Surfin' Down the Swanee River	May 1963
	Pray For Surf/Shoot The Curl	August 1963
	The One You Can't Have/From Jimmy With Tears	December 1963
	He's A Doll/Love Of A Boy And Girl	April 1964
	Tonight You Belong To Me/Goodnight My Love	February 1969
Sharon Marie	Runaround Lover/Summertime	November 1963
	Thinkin' 'Bout You Baby/Story Of My Life	June 1964
Paul Peterson	She Rides With Me/Poorest Boy In Town	March 1964
The Castells	I Do/Teardrops	March 1964
Gary Usher	Sacramento/That's Just The Way I Feel	June 1964
Glen Campbell	Guess I'm Dumb/That's All Right	May 1965
Ron Wilson	I'll Keep On Loving You/As Tears Go By	October 1968
American Spring	American Spring (LP)	October 1972
	Shyin' Away/Fallin' In Love	June 1973
California Music	Why Do Fools Fall In Love?/Don't Worry Baby	September 1975

... and three that got away:
an unreleased LP by the Redwoods (later Three Dog Night): late sixties
an unreleased country LP by Fred Vail (BBs first promoter), late seventies
an unreleased single by Marilyn Wilson (Brian's wife), 'Honeycomb', early 1976.

(List compiled by Andrew C. Doe.)

The Beach Boys

3. WRITERS & COMPOSERS

**SONGS WRITTEN BY JERRY LEIBER
AND MIKE STOLLER
AND RECORDED BY
ELVIS PRESLEY**

1. Hound Dog
2. Love Me
3. Loving You
4. Hot Dog
5. Jailhouse Rock
6. Treat Me Nice
7. I Want To Be Free
8. Baby, I Don't Care
9. Don't
10. Santa Claus Is Back In Town
11. King Creole
12. Trouble
13. Steadfast, Loyal And True
14. Dirty Dirty Feeling
15. She's Not You
16. Just Tell Her Jim Said Hello
17. Three Corn Patches
18. Girls Girls Girls
19. Bossa Nova Baby
20. Little Egypt
21. Fools Fall In Love
22. If You Don't Come Back
23. Saved

**SONGS WRITTEN BY BOUDLEAUX
AND FELICE BRYANT
AND RECORDED BY
THE EVERLY BROTHERS**

The Hits
1. Bye Bye Love
2. Wake Up Little Susie
3. All I Have To Do Is Dream
4. Bird Dog
5. Devoted To You
6. Problems
7. Love Of My Life
8. Take A Message To Mary
9. Poor Jenny
10. ('Til) I Kissed You
11. Like Strangers

*and the B-sides and
Album Tracks*
12. Brand New Heartache
13. You Thrill Me
14. Love Hurts
15. Oh True Love
16. Always It's You
17. So How Come (No-One Loves Me)
18. Donna Donna
19. A Change Of Heart
20. Rocky Top
21. Just In Case
22. Sleepless Nights
23. Some Sweet Day
24. Nashville Blues
25. Don't Forget To Cry
26. You're The One I Love
27. Follow Me

Elvis Presley

SONGWRITERS OF CLIFF RICHARD'S CHART TOPPING SINGLES

1.	Living Doll	Lionel Bart
2.	Travellin' Light	Tepper/Bennett
3.	Please Don't Tease	Bruce Welch/Peter Chester
4.	I Love You	Bruce Welch
5.	The Young Ones	Tepper/Bennett
6.	The Next Time	Kaye/Springer
7.	Summer Holiday	Welch/Bennett
8.	The Minute You're Gone	Mike Gately
9.	Congratulations	Bill Martin/Phil Coulter
10.	We Don't Talk Anymore	Alan Tarney

Felice and Boudleaux Bryant

17

HITS WRITTEN BY JIMMY WEBB

Title	Artist and year of release	Highest chart position UK	Highest chart position US
All I Know	Art Garfunkel (1973)	–	9
By The Time I Get To Phoenix	Glen Campbell (1967)	–	26
	Isaac Hayes (1969)	–	37
	Mad Lads (1969)	–	84
	Glen Campbell/Anne Murray (1971) (Medley with 'I Say A Little Prayer')	–	81
Carpet Man	Fifth Dimension (1968)	–	29
Didn't We	Richard Harris (1969)	–	63
	Barbra Streisand (1972)	–	82
Do What You Gotta Do	Nina Simone (1968)	2	83
	Four Tops (1969)	11	–
First Hymn From Grand Terrace	Mark Lindsay (1969)	–	81
Galveston	Glen Campbell (1969)	14	4
	Roger Williams (1969)	–	99
The Girls' Song	Fifth Dimension (1970)	–	43
Honey Come Back	Glen Campbell (1970)	4	19
MacArthur Park	Richard Harris (1968)	4	2
	Waylon Jennings/Jessi Colter (1969)	–	93
	Four Tops (1971)	–	38
	Donna Summer (1978)	5	1
Paper Cup	Fifth Dimension (1967)	–	34
Up, Up And Away	Fifth Dimension (1967)	–	7
	Hugh Masekela (1967)	–	71
	Johnny Mann Singers (1967)	6	91
Where's The Playground Susie	Glen Campbell (1969)	–	29
Wichita Lineman	Glen Campbell (1968)	7	3
	Sergio Mendes Brasil '66 (1969)	–	95
Worst That Could Happen	Brooklyn Bridge (1969)	–	3
The Yard Went On Forever	Richard Harris (1968)	–	64

Fifth Dimension

BEATLES SONGS WHICH WERE HITS FOR OTHER ARTISTS IN THE UK

1. All My Loving – The Dowlands
2. Bad To Me – Billy J. Kramer and the Dakotas
3. Can't Buy Me Love – Ella Fitzgerald
4. Come Together – Ike and Tina Turner
5. Day Tripper – Otis Redding
6. Discobeatlemania – D.B.M.
7. Do You Want To Know A Secret – Billy J. Kramer and the Dakotas
8. Eleanor Rigby – Ray Charles
9. Fool On The Hill – Shirley Bassey
10. From A Window – Billy J. Kramer and the Dakotas
11. Get Back – Rod Stewart
12. Girl – St Louis Union; Truth
13. Golden Slumbers/Carry That Weight – Trash
14. Goodbye – Mary Hopkin
15. Got To Get You Into My Life – Cliff Bennett; Earth, Wind and Fire
16. Hard Day's Night – Peter Sellers
17. Hello Little Girl – Fourmost
18. Here Comes The Sun – Steve Harley and Cockney Rebel
19. Here, There And Everywhere – Emmylou Harris
20. Hey Jude – Wilson Pickett
21. I Saw Her Standing There – Elton John Band featuring John Lennon
22. I Should Have Known Better – The Naturals
23. I Wanna Be Your Man – Rolling Stones
24. I Wanna Hold Your Hand – Dollar
25. If I Needed Someone – Hollies
26. I'll Keep You Satisfied – Billy J. Kramer and the Dakotas
27. I'm In Love – Fourmost
28. It's For You – Cilla Black
29. It's Only Love – Gary 'US' Bonds
30. Like Dreamers Do – The Applejacks
31. Long And Winding Road – Ray Morgan
32. Love Of The Loved – Cilla Black
33. Lucy In The Sky With Diamonds – Elton John

34. Michelle – Overlanders; David and Jonathan
35. Nobody I know – Peter and Gordon
36. Nowhere Man – Three Good Reasons
37. Ob-La-Di, Ob-La-Da – Marmalade; Bedrocks
38. Please Please Me – David Cassidy
39. Something – Shirley Bassey
40. Stars on 45 – Star Sound
41. Step Inside Love – Cilla Black
42. That Means A Lot – P. J. Proby
43. We Can Work It Out – Four Seasons; Stevie Wonder
44. When I'm 64 – Kenny Ball
45. With A Little Help From My Friends – Joe Cocker; Joe Brown; Young Idea
46. Woman – Peter and Gordon
47. World Without Love – Peter and Gordon
48. Yesterday – Matt Monro; Marianne Faithfull; Ray Charles
49. You've Got To Hide Your Love Away – Silkie

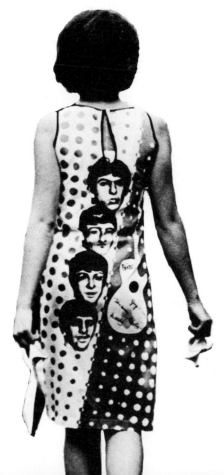

50 SONGS RECORDED BUT NOT WRITTEN BY THE BEATLES (and not necessarily officially released)

Title	Composer
1. Till There Was You	Meredith Willson
2. Slow Down	Larry Williams
3. Matchbox	Carl Perkins
4. Bad Boy	Larry Williams
5. Roll Over Beethoven	Chuck Berry
6. Money	Bradford/Gordy
7. Please Mr Postman	Gorman/Holland
8. Twist And Shout	Medley/Russell
9. Boys	Dixon/Farrell
10. Long Tall Sally	Johnson/Penniman/Blackwell
11. Rock'n'Roll Music	Chuck Berry
12. Kansas City	Leiber/Stoller
13. Dizzy Miss Lizzy	Larry Williams
14. Everybody's Trying To Be My Baby	Carl Perkins
15. Anna	Arthur Alexander
16. Chains	Goffin/King
17. Baby It's You	David/Williams/Bacharach
18. A Taste Of Honey	Scott/Marlow
19. Hippy Hippy Shake	Chan Romero
20. Sweet Little Sixteen	Chuck Berry
21. Lend Me Your Comb	Wise/Weisman/Twomey
22. Your Feet's Too Big	Benson/Fisher
23. Mr. Moonlight	Roy Lee Johnson
24. Besame Mucho	Velasquez/Skylar
25. Reminiscing	Curtis Ousley
26. Nothin' Shakin'	Frazier/Owens
27. To Know Her Is To Love Her	Phil Spector
28. Little Queenie	Chuck Berry
29. Falling In Love Again	Hollander/Connelly
30. Be Bop-A-Lula	Vincent/Davis
31. Hallelujah I Love Her So	Ray Charles
32. Red Sails In The Sunset	Kenneddy/Williams
33. Talkin' About You	Ray Charles
34. Shimmy Shake	Smith/Land
35. I Remember You	Mercer/Schertzinger
36. Ain't She Sweet	Ager/Yellen
37. Words Of Love	Buddy Holly
38. Act Naturally	Morrison/Russell
39. Honey Don't	Carl Perkins
40. You Really Got A Hold On Me	Smokey Robinson
41. Devil In Her Heart	Richard B. Drapkin
42. Sheik Of Araby	Snyder/Wheeler/Smith
43. Take Good Care Of My Baby	Goffin/King
44. Memphis	Chuck Berry
45. Sure To Fall	Perkins/Cantrell/Claunch
46. Three Cool Cats	Leiber/Stoller

47. September In The Rain	Dubin/Warren
48. Searchin'	Leiber/Stoller
49. Carol	Chuck Berry
50. Clarabella	Frank Pingatore

C'EST CHIC: THE HITS OF NILE RODGERS AND BERNARD EDWARDS

The focal point of Chic is the songwriting and producing team of Nile Rodgers (born New York City, 19 September 1952) and Bernard Edwards (born Greenville, North Carolina, 31 October 1952). In the last five years they have been responsible for some of the most innovative and distinctive disco music ever created, both with their Chic sidekicks and with a galaxy of other artists. They are amazingly prolific. Rodgers and Edwards have written and produced over 130 songs since 1977 and continue to work at a frenetic pace. Their latest collaborations with Carly Simon, Fonzie Thornton and Odyssey have still to be released as this book goes to press but will doubtless improve their hit ratio still further.

The Rodgers and Edwards hitlog ranked in order of highest UK chart position:

Title – Artist	Highest pos UK singles chart	Highest pos US singles chart
1. Upside Down – Diana Ross	2	1
2. Rapper's Delight – Sugarhill Gang	3	36
3. I Want Your Love – Chic	4	7
4. Good Times – Chic	5	1
5. My Old Piano – Diana Ross	5	109
6. Dance, Dance, Dance (Yowsah, Yowsah, Yowsah) – Chic	6	6
7. He's The Greatest Dancer – Sister Sledge	6	9
8. Le Freak – Chic	7	1
9. We Are Family – Sister Sledge	8	2
10. Everybody Dance – Chic	9	38
11. I'm Coming Out – Diana Ross	13	9
12. My Forbidden Lover – Chic	15	43
13. Lost In Music – Sister Sledge	17	–
14. Spacer – Sheila B. Devotion	18	–
15. My Feet Keep Dancing – Chic	21	–
16. Why – Carly Simon	24	74
17. Backfired – Debbie Harry	32	46
18. Got To Love Somebody – Sister Sledge	34	64
19. Rebels Are We – Chic	–	61
20. Soup For One – Chic	–	80

All songs written and produced by Nile Rodgers and Bernard Edwards except 'Rappers Delight', produced by Sylvia Robinson. Early copies of this record credited Robinson and the Sugarhill Gang as composers. After objections from the Chic Organization, Robinson and the Sugarhill Gang – who actually did write the lyrics – waived all writers' royalties and agreed to designate all future pressings as 'based on "Good Times" by Nile Rodgers and Bernard Edwards'.

SONGS WRITTEN BUT NOT OFFICIALLY RELEASED BY BOB DYLAN

Percy's Song – Fairport Convention
Si Tu Dois Partir – Fairport Convention
Jack Of Diamonds – Fairport Convention: Ben Carruthers (who co-wrote it)
I'll Keep It With Mine – Fairport Convention; Nico
Long Distance Operator – The Band
Don't Ya Tell Henry – The Band
Mama You Been On My Mind – Joan Baez
Farewell Angelina – Joan Baez
Love Is Just A Four Letter Word – Joan Baez
Troubled And I Don't Know Why – Joan Baez
The Walls Of Redwing – Joan Baez
Only A Hobo – Rod Stewart
I'd Have You Anytime – George Harrison (who co-wrote it)
Playboys And Playgirls – Pete Seeger
Who Killed Davey Moore – Pete Seeger
Wanted Man – Johnny Cash
Catfish – Kinky Friedman
Golden Loom – Roger McGuinn
Up To Me – Roger McGuinn
Champaign Illinois – Carl Perkins
Sign Language – Eric Clapton
Seven Days – Ron Wood; Joe Cocker
Wallflower Days – Ron Wood
Wallflower – Doug Sahm
Lay Down Your Weary Tune – The Byrds; Coulson, Dean, McGuinness and Flint
Eternal Circle – Coulson, Dean, McGuinness and Flint
Get Your Rocks Off – Coulson, Dean, McGuinness and Flint
The Death of Emmett Till – Coulson, Dean, McGuinness and Flint
Sign On The Cross – Coulson, Dean, McGuinness and Flint
I Need a Woman – Ry Cooder

(List by Patrick Humphries.)

IT AIN'T ME, BABE: SONGS WRITTEN BY BOB DYLAN WHICH BECAME HITS FOR OTHERS

Title	Artist	UK	US	Year
		Highest chart pos.		
All Along The Watchtower	Jimi Hendrix Experience	5	20	1968
All I Really Want To Do	Byrds	4	40	1965
	Cher	9	15	1965
Blowin' In The Wind	Peter, Paul and Mary	13	2	1963
	Stevie Wonder	36	9	1966
Don't Think Twice, It's All Right	Peter Paul and Mary	–	9	1963
	Wonder Who?	–	12	1965
Hard Rain's Gonna Fall	Bryan Ferry	10	–	1973
I Shall Be Released	Tremeloes	29	–	1968
	Box Tops	–	67	1969
If Not For You	Olivia Newton-John	7	25	1971
If You Gotta Go, Go Now	Manfred Mann	2	–	1965
It Ain't Me, Babe	Johnny Cash with June Carter	28	58	1964
	Turtles	–	8	1965
It's All Over Now, Baby Blue	Joan Baez	22	–	1965
Just Like A Woman	Manfred Mann	10	–	1966
Knockin' On Heaven's Door	Eric Clapton	38	–	1975
Mighty Quinn	Manfred Mann	1	10	1968
Mr. Tambourine Man	Byrds	1	1	1965
*Si Tu Dois Partir	Fairport Convention	21	–	1969
This Wheel's On Fire	Julie Driscoll and Brian Auger	5	–	1968
Times They Are A-Changin'	Peter, Paul and Mary	44	–	1964
	Ian Campbell Folk Group	42	–	1965
You Angel You	Manfred Mann's Earth Band	54	–	1979

Bob Dylan

* French version of 'If You Gotta Go, Go Now'.

SONGWRITERS WHOSE WORK BOB DYLAN HAS RECORDED

Name	Song Title	Dylan LP Title
Eric Von Schmidt	Baby, Let Me Follow You Down	Bob Dylan
Blind Lemon Jefferson	See That My Grave Is Kept Clean	Bob Dylan
Jesse Fuller	You're No Good	Bob Dylan
Bukka White	Fixin' To Die	Bob Dylan
Jerry Jeff Walker	Mr Bojangles	Dylan
Joni Mitchell	Big Yellow Taxi	Dylan
Trader	A Fool Such As I	Dylan
E. Davies/J. Peterson	Lily Of The West	Dylan
G. Weiss/Hugo Peretti	Can't Help Falling In Love	Dylan
P. LaFarge	The Ballad Of Ira Hayes	Dylan
C. A. Null	I Forgot More Than You'll Ever Know	Self Portrait
Gordon Lightfoot	Early Mornin' Rain	Self Portrait
Curtis/Gilbert Becaud/Delano	Let It Be Me	Self Portrait

P. Clayton	Gotta Travel On	Self Portrait
Richard Rodgers/ Lorenz Hart	Blue Moon	Self Portrait
Paul Simon	The Boxer	Self Portrait
Boudleaux Bryant	Take Me As I Am (Or Let Me Go)	Self Portrait
Robbie Robertson	Yazoo Street Scandal	Basement Tapes
Robbie Robertson/ Richard Manuel	Katie's Been Gone	Basement Tapes
Richard Manuel	Orange Juice Blues	Basement Tapes
Robbie Robertson/ Richard Manuel	Ruben Remus	Basement Tapes
Rick Danko/Robbie Robertson	Bessie Smith	Basement Tapes
Robbie Robertson	Up On Cripple Creek	Before The Flood
Robbie Robertson	Endless Highway	Before The Flood
Robbie Robertson	The Night They Drove Old Dixie Down	Before The Flood
Robbie Robertson	Stage Fright	Before The Flood
Robbie Robertson	The Shape I'm In	Before The Flood
Robbie Robertson/ Richard Manuel	When You Awake	Before The Flood
Curtis Mayfield	People Get Ready	Renaldo And Clara

BOB DYLAN'S CO-WRITERS

In a long and distinguished career as a songwriter, Bob Dylan has usually preferred to work alone. The following is a complete record of cuts on which he has collaborated with other writers, then officially released in his own right.

Co-Writer	Title	Dylan LP Title
Richard Manuel	Tears Of Rage	Basement Tapes
Rick Danko	This Wheel's On Fire	Basement Tapes
Jacques Levy	Joey	Desire
Jacques Levy	Romance In Durango	Desire
Jacques Levy	Black Diamond Bay	Desire
Henry Thomas	Honey, Just One More Chance	The Freewheelin' Bob Dylan

BEACH BOY ALBUMS YOU'LL NEVER HEAR

1. Smile (1966)
One of the most notorious of all rock enigmas, 'Smile' was originally scheduled for release in December 1966. Capitol executives were so confident about this schedule, they prepared a sleeve, accompanying booklet, radio promo spot, and even a release number – T2580. They must have been unpleasantly surprised when they discovered that the album consisted of hundreds of hours of largely incomplete backing tracks to unconnected segments and melodic snatches. Many of the segments had as many as 23 different takes – a result of Brian Wilson's unsuccessful attempt to transfer his musical vision to recording tape. Although

there are dozens of recognized 'Smile' titles, there is no definitive track listing since the album's structure changed on a daily basis according to Brian's moods and whims.

There is endless speculation about 'Smile's' continuing non-appearance. It can't be ascribed to a single overriding cause, but there are several front-runners: Brian's paranoia and instability, the departure of Van Dyke Parks as a collaborator, the resistance of the other Beach Boys to the new and uncommercial material, business pressures, drugs, and, the old standby, the release of the Beatles' 'Sgt Pepper'. Over the years, some of the more commercial melodies, though *not* the original tracks, have emerged on subsequent Beach Boys albums. The more experimental and esoteric material (which listeners rave about), such as the legendary 'Fire Music', remain in the can.

The Beach Boys

2. Lei'd In Hawaii (1967)
Recording and filmed on 25/26 August 1967, this live concert album features Brian on bass and vocals, a rare event in those days which soon became even rarer. Made during the post 'Smile' depression/drug phase of the band, it is reportedly very poor.

3. Live At Michigan University (1967)
Produced by Brian, this Fall 1967 concert is said to be a very good performance.

4. The Fading Rock Group Revival (1970)
An album no one will ever hear because it doesn't exist! In a jocular mood, Bruce Johnston informed a credulous NME reporter in 1970 that the band's last Capital LP would be 'The Fading...' and has had to deny the album's existence in interviews ever since.

5. Add Some Music (1970)
Severing a stormy relationship with Capitol, the Beach Boys sailed straight into another one with Warners-Reprise. The first album submitted to the company was returned with a note suggesting it could be stronger and that a few track changes might be in order. Repressing a strong desire to tell the company to forget it, the band *did* remove nine tracks and substituted seven new compositions. The company beamed, changed the album title to 'Sunflower', released it, and were not amused when, despite critical acclaim, 'Sunflower' proved to be the band's worst selling album to date. Of the rejected tracks, four have since appeared on disc, although the five better ones remain unreleased.

6. Landlocked (1970)
Warner's must have wondered what kind of jerks they'd signed when the 'Landlocked' master arrived a year later after 'Sunflower' stiffed. For it contained the majority of the songs rejected from that LP, bolstered by some new compositions in a similar vein. Not surprisingly, the company bounced the album straight back to the band, this time with a note that Van Dyke Parks had had a good idea, so why not call the new album 'Surf's Up' and include the legendary 'Smile' track? Despite Brian's understandable resistance, this view prevailed and only three 'Landlocked' tracks made it to Surf's Up. Of the ditched tracks, 'Big Sur' emerged two years later on 'Holland' in a radically remixed form, and 'San Miguel' showed up on a 1981 compilation. Unfortunately, the impressive production number, 'Loop De Loop', remains confined to the tape racks.

7. Adult Child (1977)
Following the resurgence of public interest in the Beach Boys in 1976 and the return of Brian Wilson to work in 1977, Warners received the double shock that the band was moving to Caribou Records and that 'Adult Child' would be the final album the Warners contract demanded. Ill-disposed to give Warners an all-new LP as a parting gift, the band fleshed out Brian's post-'Love You' submissions which included tracks from as far back as 1969. In fact, one cut was an 'Add Some Music' reject! These tracks, together with out-takes from the 1976 '15 Big Ones' sessions made for a less than even album. Once again, the best material remains

The Beach Boys

JAN & DEAN

unreleased; of particular interest are 'It's Over Now' and 'Still I Dream Of It', two of Brian's very personal songs which rank among the best of his ballads.

8. Merry Christmas From The Beach Boys (1977)
Still trying to give Warners their final LP, the Beach Boys went to Iowa to put together a new Christmas LP, the last one having been released in 1964. The company bounced the product again, and not without reason – once again the band had resorted to re-cycling old material. They added Christmassy lyrics to backing track for 'Peggy Sue' cut at the '15 Big Ones' session, unsuccessfully re-worked 'Help Is On The Way' (a song rejected from 'Landlocked' and 'Adult Child'), and re-recorded 'Child Of Winter', again to its detriment. Though Brian and Dennis did come up with one impressive new song apiece, the mood was generally tired and uninspired. Two of the cuts have since come to light, 'Peggy Sue' on MIU and 'Go And Get That Girl' on 'Celebration'.

Two members of the Beach Boys are also hanging on to unreleased albums. Following his critically successful 'Pacific Ocean Blue', Dennis Wilson recorded 'Bamboo' in 1979. Mike Love is also sitting on a couple of LPs; 'First Love', which is pretty good, and 'Country Love', which is awful. 'Looking Back With Love', which Mike finally released in late 1981 is surprisingly enjoyable.

List submitted by Andrew G. Doe, a leading authority on the life, times and music of Brian Wilson and the Beach Boys.

ARTISTS WHO HAVE RECORDED SONGS BRIAN WILSON GAVE AWAY

1. Rachel and the Revolvers (1962): With long-time collaborator Gary Usher, Brian co-wrote 'The Revolution' and 'Number One'. These were his first record productions.

2. Jan and Dean (1963–65): Jan and Dean had better results from the informal collaborations of the mid-sixties than the Beach Boys did. They copped the titles below when the rest of Brian's gang weren't looking. Brian co-wrote all the following:
    Surf City
    Drag City
    Deadman's Curve
    New Girl In School
    Gonna Hustle You
    Sidewalk Surfin'
    Ride The Wild Surf
    She's My Summer Girl
    Surf Route 101
    Surfin' Wild
    Move Out Little Mustang
Brian sang on many, if not most of these songs. Although 'Move Out Little Mustang' appears on an Jan and Dean LP, it's actually performed by Sloan and Barri.

3. The Honeys (1963–64): Brian wrote 'Hide Go Seek', 'He's A Doll', and 'The One You Can't Have' all by himself for his wife, sister-in-law and their cousin. He also produced all their singles with a stunning lack of success.

4. Sharon Marie (1963–64): Together with Mike Love, Brian came up with 'Runaround Lover', 'Thinkin' 'Bout You Baby' (which is melodically identical to 'Darlin'') and 'Story Of My Life'.

5. Gary Usher (1964): Brian co-wrote 'Sacramento' with Gary, a song that ranks with the leading contenders for the most uninspired Brian Wilson production ever.

6. The Castells (1964): 'I Do', a rather fine Brian Wilson production, is Brian's re-write of his own 'Country Fair'.

7. The Hondells (1964): As well as co-writing 'My Buddy Seat' with Gary Usher, Brian did a little vocalizing on this record.

8. Paul Petersen (1964): Roger Christian was Brian's partner on 'She Rides With Me', another good production marred by bad mastering.

9. Annette Funicello (1964–65): Roping in both Usher and Christian, Brian dashed off 'Surfer's Holiday', 'Muscle Hustler' and 'Muscle Beach Party'. These songs are featured on eminently forgettable beach movie soundtracks.

10. Frankie Avalon (1964): The Wilson/Usher/Christian team came up with 'Runnin' Wild' for Annette's movie pal.

11. Sunsets (1964): 'My Little Surfin' Woodie' was another Wilson/Usher/Christian opus, as was . . .

12. Superstocks (1964): 'My First Love'.

13. Glen Campbell (1965): After working as a session man and touring with the Beach Boys in early 1965, Campbell was interested in launching a solo career. So he asked Brian to produce 'Guess I'm Dumb', a song Brian had co-written with Russ Titleman. Needless to say, this was not the record that made Campbell a star.

14. Dino, Desi and Billy (1970): Brian co-wrote 'Lady Love' with Billy Hinsche, one-third of the trio that included Dino Martin and Desi Arnaz Jr. Billy later joined the Beach Boys for several years.

15. American Spring (1971–73): A re-activated two-thirds of the Honeys received 'Sweet Mountain' and 'Shyin' Away' from Brian and David Sandler.

16. David Cassidy (1975): Cassidy and Gerry Beckley of America managed to squeeze 'Cruise To Harlem' out of Brian during his reclusive period.

17. Celebration (1978–79): The 'Almost Summer' theme was originally a Brian Wilson composition entitled 'Highschool', but when the film title was changed, Al Jardine and Mike Love had to rework the lyrics.

18. Shaun Cassidy (1978): Originally written for American Spring, Cassidy 'borrowed' the Wilson/Rovell/Pamplin song, 'It's Like Heaven'.

One other Brian Wilson song not released by the Beach Boys has made it to vinyl. 'Do Ya?' was written by Wilson, Rovell and Pamplin and recorded by American Spring. It appears only on test pressings of the unreleased compilation album La Radio. At the last census, the entire world population of LA Radio was three copies.

(List by Andrew G. Doe.)

Frankie Avalon and Annette Funicello

The Beach Boys

SONGS WRITTEN BY BRUCE SPRINGSTEEN, BUT NEVER RECORDED BY HIM

1. Fire – Robert Gordon, The Pointer Sisters
2. Because The Night – Patti Smith
3. The Fever – Southside Johnny, Dean Ford, Alan Rich
4. Jeannie Needs A Shooter – Warren Zevon
5. If I Was The Priest – Allan Clarke
6. Rendezvous – Greg Kihn
7. This Little Girl; Your Love; Dedication – Gary 'US' Bonds
8. Talk To Me; Hearts Of Stone; Trapped Again; You Mean So Much To Me Baby; Little Girl So Fine; Love On The Wrong Side Of Town; When You Dance – Southside Johnny and the Asbury Jukes
9. From Small Things Big Things Come – Dave Edmunds

List by Patrick Humphries.

Bruce Springsteen

GRAHAM GOULDMAN'S EARLY HITS

Before he became a founding member of 10CC, Graham Gouldman was an enormously successful songwriter, as can be seen from this list of the hits he wrote during the 1960s.

		Highest Positions	
Title	Artist	US Chart	UK Chart
Heart Full Of Soul	Yardbirds	9	2
Listen People	Herman's Hermits	3	–
For Your Love	Yardbirds	6	2
Look Through Any Window	Hollies	32	4
Bus Stop	Hollies	5	5
No Milk Today	Herman's Hermits	35	7
East West	Herman's Hermits	27	37
Pamela, Pamela	Wayne Fontana	–	11
Evil Hearted You	Yardbirds	–	3
Tallyman	Jeff Beck	–	30

1978 HITS WRITTEN BY THE BEE GEES (BARRY, ROBIN AND MAURICE GIBB)

			Highest Positions	
Title – Artist	Bee Gee Composer(s)	Co-writer(s)	UK	US
How Deep Is Your Love – Bee Gees	B, R, M	–	3	2
Stayin' Alive – Bee Gees	B, R, M	–	3	1
Night Fever – Bee Gees	B, R, M	–	1	1
Too Much Heaven – Bee Gees	B, R, M	–	3	2
(Love Is) Thicker Than Water – Andy Gibb	B	Andy Gibb	–	1
Shadow Dancing – Andy Gibb	B, R, M	Andy Gibb	42	1
An Everlasting Love – Andy Gibb	B	–	10	5
(Our Love) Don't Throw It All Away – Andy Gibb	B	Blue Weaver	–	9
If I Can't Have You – Yvonne Elliman	B, R, M	–	4	1
More Than A Woman – Tavares	B, R, M	–	7	32
Grease – Frankie Valli	B	–	3	1
Warm Ride – Rare Earth	B, R, M	–	–	39
Emotion – Samantha Sang	B, R	–	11	3
Ain't Nothing Gonna Keep Me From You – Teri De Sario	B	–	52	43
Words – Rita Coolidge	B, R, M	–	25	–
Night Fever – Carol Douglas	B, R, M	–	66	–
Stayin' Alive – Richard Ace	B, R, M	–	66	–

Six songs written by some or all of the Bee Gees reached No. 1 in America in 1978. Four of these were written jointly by Barry, Robin and Maurice (including one with Andy Gibb). One ('Grease') was written by Barry alone and one by Barry in partnership with younger brother Andy. The common factor in these and the other eight American hits listed above is the songwriting of Barry Gibb. 'Night Fever' spent eight weeks at No. 1, one week more than 'Shadow Dancing'. 'Stayin' Alive' held the top spot for four weeks, '(Love Is) Thicker Than Water' and 'Grease' for two each and 'If I Can't Have You' was top for just seven days.

4.GROUPS OF GROUPS

DOOWOP GROUPS

1. The Heartbeats
2. The Angels
3. The Harptones
4. The Echoes
5. The Devotions
6. The Teenagers
7. The Chantels
8. The Cleftones
9. The Dubs
10. The Moonglows
11. The Eldorados
12. Lee Andrews and the Hearts
13. The Crests
14. The Cadillacs
15. The Vibrations
16. The Monotones
17. The Nutmegs
18. The Spaniels
19. The Turbans
20. The Five Satins
21. The Magnificents
22. The Mello Kings
23. The Harptones
24. The Tune Weavers
25. The Dreamweavers
26. The G Clefs
27. The Four Esquires
28. The Sparkletones
29. Shep and the Limelites
30. The Edsels

PSYCHEDELIC GROUPS – UNITED KINGDOM

1. Pink Floyd
2. Soft Machine
3. Procol Harum
4. Haphash and the Coloured Coat
5. Spooky Tooth
6. Blodwyn Pig
7. Sam Gopal's Dream
8. Elmer Gantry's Velvet Opera
9. Dr Marigold's Prescription
10. Constable Zippo and his Electric Commode Band
11. Sam Apple Pie
12. Smokestack Crumble
13. Rupert's People
14. Dead Sea Fruit
15. Opal Butterfly
16. Warm Sounds
17. Glass Menagerie
18. Rainbow Ffolly
19. Pink Fairies
20. Hydrogen Jukebox
21. Third Ear Band
22. The Open Mind
23. Nirvana
24. Heavy Jelly
25. Crocheted Doughnut Ring
26. Skip Bifferty
27. The Fresh Windows
28. Dantalian's Chariot
29. Wimple Winch
30. Strawberry Children
31. Blossom Toes
32. Apostolic Intervention
33. Jason Crest

Miss Christine of the GTO's

34. Orange Bicycle
35. The Lemon Tree
36. Fleur-de-Lys
37. The Acid Gallery
38. Jaxon's Dogfood
39. Boeing Duveen and the Beautiful Soup
40. Dream Police
41. Battered Ornaments
42. The Nice

PSYCHEDELIC GROUPS – SAN FRANCISCO

1. Crome Surcus
2. The Only Alternative and his Other Possibilities
3. Quicksilver Messenger Service
4. Day Blindness
5. Country Joe and the Fish
6. Moby Grape
7. Maby Grope
8. Magnesium Waterlily
9. Blue Cheer
10. Mint Tattoo
11. Notes From the Underground
12. Electric Flag
13. Mad River
14. Tripsichord Music Box
15. Jefferson Airplane
16. Mystery Trend
17. South Bay Experimental Flash
18. Acid Symphony
19. Mystic Knights of the Sea
20. Bethlehem Exit
21. Chocolate Watchband
22. Harbinger Complex
23. Celestial Hysteria
24. Frumious Bandersnatch
25. Prince Albert and the Cans
26. Blue Crumb Truck Factory
27. Ballpoint Banana
28. Magick Powerhouse of Oz
29. Dream Merchants
30. Indian Pudding and Pipe Band
31. Glass Thunder
32. Gossamer Kyte

PSYCHEDELIC GROUP NAMES – THE REST OF THE UNITED STATES

1. The Trippers
2. Captain Beefheart and His Magic Band

3. Mystic Eye
4. Leathercoated Minds
5. Mystic Astrological Crystal Band
6. Crystal Revelation
7. Sound Sandwich
8. Scarlet Letter
9. Lothar and the Hand People
10. Subterranean Monastery
11. Tangerine Zoo
12. Neurotic Sheep
13. Daily Flash
14. Strawberry Alarm Clock
15. Peanut Butter Conspiracy
16. Moving Sidewalks
17. Stereo Shoestring
18. Shiva's Headband
19. West Coast Pop Art Experimental Band
20. Love
21. The Doors
22. String Cheese
23. Spirits Rebellious
24. Thirteenth Floor Elevators
25. Kaleidoscope
26. Velvet Underground
27. Captain Glasspack and His Electric Mufflers
28. W. C. Fields Memorial String Band
29. Iron Butterfly
30. The Mesmerising Eye
31. Sacred Mushrooms
32. The Id
33. Children of the Mushroom
34. Balloon Farm
35. Waterproof Candle
36. International Submarine Band
37. Marshmellow Steamshovel
38. Zinc Toenail
39. Caretakers of Deception
40. Infinite Staircase
41. Earth Opera
42. Clear Light
43. Peppermint Trolley Company
44. Lemon Pipers
45. Incredible Broadside Brass Bed Band
46. Higher Elevation
47. The Glass Wall
48. Merrell Fankhauser and His Trusty HMS Bounty
49. Fever Tree
50. Autosalvage

(Lists compiled by Colin K. Hill of *Bucketful of Brains* fanzine.)

GROUPS WHO ARE KNOWN EQUALLY FOR THEIR INITIALS AND FULL NAMES

1. CSN&Y – Crosby, Stills, Nash and Young
2. SHF Band – Souther, Hillman and Furay Band
3. BTO – Bachman Turner Overdrive
4. BB&A – Beck, Bogert and Appice
5. TRB – Tom Robinson Band
6. OMITD – Orchestral Manoeuvres in the Dark
7. MGs – Memphis Group (as in Booker T and the MGs)
8. ACNE – Kevin *A*yers, John *C*ale, *N*ico and *E*no
9. BB&Q Band – Brooklyn, Bronx and Queens Band
10. SB&Q – Sutherland Brothers and Quiver
11. FF&Z – Fishbaugh, Fishbaugh and Zorn
12. ELO – Electric Light Orchestra
13. ELP – Emerson, Lake and Palmer
14. AWB – Average White Band
15. PiL – Public Image Limited

MEMBERS OF THE DRIFTERS

1. Clyde McPhatter
2. David Baughan
3. Johnny Moore

Johnny Moore

4. Bobby Hendricks
5. Gerhart Thrasher
6. Andrew Thrasher
7. Charlie Hughes
8. Bill Pinckney
9. Tommy Evans
10. Ben E. King
11. Rudy Lewis
12. Charley Thomas
13. Doc Green
14. Elsberry Hobbs
15. Willie Ferbee
16. Johnny Lee Williams
17. Eugene Pearson
18. Johnny Terry
19. Rich Sheppard

20. William Brent
21. Don Dendridge
22. Bill Fredericks
23. Butch Leake
24. Milton Turner
25. Don Thomas
26. Clyde Brown
27. Grant Kitching
28. Billy Lewis

The Drifters first formed in 1953, and despite occasional lapses, have been functioning ever since, although with an ever-changing cast. At least two names on the list are now dead, McPhatter and Rudy Lewis, while probably the longest serving member has been Johnny Moore (1955–57 and 1964–80).

MEMBERS OF THE FOUR SEASONS

1. Frankie Valli
2. Bob Gaudio
3. Tommy DeVito
4. Nick Massi
5. Joey Long
6. Charlie Calello
7. Bob Grimm
8. Gary Wolfe
9. Dimitri Callas
10. Al Ruzicka
11. Paul Wilson
12. Clay Jordan
13. Bill Deloach
14. Lee Shapiro
15. Gerry Polci
16. Don Ciccone
17. John Paiva
18. Jerry Corbetta
19. Larry Lingle

The Four Seasons were formed in the mid-1950s, and apart from occasional brief periods, have always been led by Frankie Valli. They were originally known as the Four Lovers and also scored several hits under the name the Wonder Who. Of 45 American hits between 1956 and 1977, Frankie Valli has appeared on all but two. Of the other members, Bob Gaudio became a significant record producer and songwriter and Don Ciccone was an original member of another hit-making group called the Critters.

MEMBERS OF THE SHADOWS

The Shadows

1. Terry Smart
2. Ken Pavey
3. Ian Samwell
4. Norman Mitham
5. Hank B. Marvin
6. Bruce Welch
7. Jet Harris
8. Tony Meehan
9. Brian 'Licorice' Locking
10. Brian Bennett
11. John Rostill
12. John Farrar
13. Alan Jones
14. Alan Hawkshaw
15. Geoff Atherton
16. Cliff Hall
17. Alan Tarney
18. Dave Lawson
19. Dave Richmond

The Shadows, the most successful British chart act of all time, were known as the Drifters until 1959. It seems peculiar that they apparently had no knowledge of the American group the Drifters, who had already had six American hits before the Shads caught up with them and changed their name.

MEMBERS OF THE YARDBIRDS

1. Keith Relf
2. Paul Samwell-Smith
3. Chris Dreja
4. Jim McCarty
5. Eric Clapton
6. Tony 'Top' Topham
7. Jeff Beck
8. Jimmy Page
9. Robert Plant*
10. John Paul Jones*
11. John Bonham*

* Reunited as the New Yardbirds, who later, with Jimmy Page, became Led Zeppelin.

MEMBERS OF FAIRPORT CONVENTION

1. Shawn Frater
2. Judy Dyble
3. Ashley Hutchings
4. Simon Nicol
5. Richard Thompson
6. Martin Lamble
7. Ian Matthews
8. Sandy Denny

9. Dave Swarbrick
10. Dave Mattacks
11. Dave Pegg
12. Roger Hill
13. Tom Farnell
14. David Rea
15. Trevor Lucas
16. Jerry Donahue
17. Paul Warren (roadie, who drummed on one European tour.)
18. Bruce Rowland
19. Bob Brady
20. Dan Ar Bras
21. Roger Burridge

ANCILLARY
22. Rick Grech (fiddled on some BBC sessions in 1969)
23. Ralph McTell (Guitar on 'Rosie' and onstage at 80/81 Reunions)
24. Marc Ellington (sang on 'Unhalfbricking')
25. Timi Donald
26. Gerry Conway
27. Linda Peters (helped on 'Rosie')

List by Patrick Humphries, who is the author of a book about Fairport Convention entitled *Meet On the Ledge*.

MEMBERS OF FLEETWOOD MAC

1. Peter Green
2. Mick Fleetwood
3. John McVie
4. Jeremy Spencer
5. Bob Brunning
6. Danny Kirwan
7. Christine McVie
8. Bob Welch
9. Bob Weston
10. Dave Walker
11. Stevie Nicks
12. Lindsey Buckingham

MEMBERS OF WINGS

1. Paul McCartney
2. Linda McCartney
3. Denny Laine
4. Henry McCullough
5. Joe English
6. Jimmy McCulloch
7. Geoff Britton
8. Steve Holly
9. Lawrence Juber
10. Denny Seiwell

Paul McCartney

BYRD DROPPINGS

(Groups spawned by the original five members of the Byrds)

1. Flying Burrito Brothers (Chris Hillman)
2. Crosby, Stills and Nash (David Crosby)
3. Dillard and Clark (Gene Clark)
4. Manassas (Chris Hillman)
5. Firefall (Michael Clarke)
6. Souther, Hillman and Furay (Chris Hillman)

The Byrds

7. Crosby, Stills, Nash and Young (David Crosby)
8. Thunderbyrd (Roger McGuinn)
9. Crosby and Nash (David Crosby)
10. McGuinn, (Gene) Clark and Hillman

ROXY MUSIC BASS PLAYERS

Roxy Music, despite being one of the most popular bands in the world, have spent the majority of their nearly ten years existence without a permanent bass player. Whether this is by design or by accident is not clear . . .

1. Graham Simpson
2. Rik Kenton
3. John Porter
4. Sal Maida
5. John Wetton
6. Chris Thomas
7. John Gustafson
8. Ricky Wills
9. Gary Tibbs
10. Alan Spenner
11. Neil Jason

UNSUCCESSUL GROUPS WHICH INCLUDED MORE THAN ONE LATTER DAY STAR

1. The Gods: This Hatfield based group of the mid-1960s included at various times Mick Taylor, later a Rolling Stone, Greg Lake, who joined King Crimson and Emerson, Lake and Palmer, and Ken Hensley, a founder member of Uriah Heep.

2. The Rising Sons: A Los Angeles band with a floating membership which included Taj Mahal, still a solo star, Ry Cooder, also a present day bandleader, and Ed Cassidy, who remains one of the two founder members playing with Spirit.

3. The Outlaws: Another sixties group, who were frequently used as session musicians as well as in their own right by the late and legendary producer, Joe Meek. Among their members were Chas Hodges, now of Chas and Dave, and Ritchie Blackmore, later in Deep Purple and now a star in his own right as leader of Rainbow.

4. The Roosters: A shortlived blues group from the early sixties in Britain whose members included Tom McGuinness, a member of the Manfred Mann Band during their heady days of hitmaking, and currently guitarist with the Blues Band, and Eric Clapton.

5. Peter B's Looners: Again from the sixties R&B era in Britain, this band included Mick Fleetwood (of Mac fame) and Peter Green, who later joined John Mayall and subsequently founded Fleetwood Mac, although he left the group some years ago. Peter B (Bardens) himself didn't do badly, joining Camel and also enjoying spells with Them, and more recently with one of Van Morrison's bands.

6. The Flowers of Romance: Probably the least able band in this list, the Flowers personnel included the late Sid Vicious and 1981 guitar hero Marco Pirroni, Adam's right hand Ant. Incidentally, Public Image Limited recorded an album called Flowers Of Romance, and the fact that current PiL-er Keith Levene was also a Flower may be relevant ...

7. Bryndle: A Los Angeles group of fledgling superstars, among those who later emerged to solo success (at least in America), were Andrew Gold, Karla Bonoff and Wendy Waldman.

8. The Au Go Go Singers: A coffee house folk group which included Stephen Stills and Ritchie Furay, who both subsequently joined Buffalo Springfield, before Stills formed Crosby, Stills and Nash and so on, and Furay formed Poco before allowing himself to become involved in the Souther Hillman Furay (SHF) Band.

9. The London S.S: This legendary rehearsal group (no-one can remember them actually playing a real gig), included at various times Mick Jones, Paul Simonon and Topper Headon, (later three quarters of the Clash), Tony James, who went on to found Generation X, and Rat Scabies, well known hooligan and Damned drummer.

10. El Riot and the Rebels: Birmingham boys Ray Thomas and Mike Pinder were later founder members of the Moody Blues, while a third ex-Rebel, John Lodge, joined the Moodies some years later.

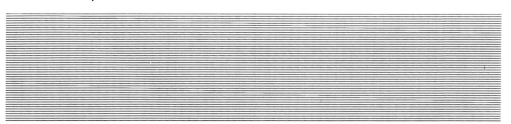

LARGEST CHARTMAKING ACTS

US

In 1958 the Mormon Tabernacle Choir scored an American top twenty hit with a rousing version of 'The Battle Hymn Of The Republic'. The 375 member choir was directed by Richard P. Condie and accompanied by the Philadelphia Orchestra under conductor Eugene Ormandy.

UK

For the 1979 hit 'Tusk' the five member Fleetwood Mac was supplemented by the 260 members of the USC Trojan Marching Band. Rather than being crammed into a recording studio, the band recorded their contribution live at Dodger Stadium, Los Angeles.

Chuck Berry's biggest hit 'My Ding-A-Ling' was recorded at the 1972 Arts Festival in Lanchester, England. Audience participation played a major part in the success of the record. Alas, the size of the audience and the extent of its participation is not recorded.

GROUPS OF WHICH ROD STEWART HAS BEEN A MEMBER

1. Jimmy Powell and the Five Dimensions
2. Long John Baldry and the Hoochie Coochie Men.
3. The Soul Agents
4. Steampacket
5. Shotgun Express
6. Jeff Beck Group
7. The Faces

GUITARISTS CONSIDERED TO REPLACE MICK TAYLOR IN THE ROLLING STONES

When lead guitarist Mick Taylor decided to leave the Rolling Stones in 1974, his place in the group was coveted by superstars and unknowns alike. Before it was finally decided in April 1975 that the new incumbent should be Ronnie Wood, numerous guitarists were auditioned, suggested or rumoured to be favourites for the post.

1. Jimmy Page
2. Chris Spedding
3. Harvey Mandel
4. Jeff Beck
5. Robert Johnson
6. Ry Cooder
7. Wayne Perkins
8. Rory Gallagher
9. Peter Frampton
10. Bobby Tench
11. Wilko Johnson
12. Steve Marriott
13. Leslie West
14. Shuggie Otis
15. Joey Molland
16. Ronnie Wood

Stuart Sutcliffe

FIFTH BEATLES

There were of course only four Beatles to all intents and purposes, although from time to time, the press, or in some cases, the individual himself, would bestow the epithet 'Fifth Beatle' on someone closely connected with the Fab Four.

1. Pete Best: The drummer replaced by Ringo Starr before it all happened.
2. Stuart Sutcliffe: The group's original bass player, who died pre-fame.
3. Brian Epstein: The manager.
4. Neil Aspinall/Mal Evans: Pre-fame friends, post-fame supports.

5. Murray Kaufman (Murray the K): Significant New York disc jockey when the Beatles first hit the colonies.
6. George Martin: Faithful producer and gentleman.
7. Klaus Voorman: Friend from Hamburg, bass player (ex-Manfred Mann) and painter, mooted to replace Paul McCartney in the late 1960s. The only German fifth Beatle.
8. Billy Preston: The only black fifth Beatle, who played keyboards on 'Let It Be'.
9. Yoko Ono: Mrs John Lennon, and the only Japanese fifth Beatle.
10. Derek Taylor: Publicist, eccentric and gentleman.
11. Maharishi Mahesh Yogi: Indian guru, later immortalized as 'Sexy Sadie'. The only Indian fifth Beatle.
12. John 'Duff' Lowe: Pianist on the earliest discovered Beatle recording, who refused to sell the single remaining copy to Paul McCartney for a reported £5,000.
13. Jimmy Nicol: Ringo's replacement on a European and Far East tour, while the drummer was enjoying a bout of tonsillitis in 1964.
14. Andy White: Session drummer who replaced Ringo on one of the two recordings of 'Love Me Do', when the latter was an 'unknown quantity' to George Martin.

Diana Ross

CHARTMAKING CONFIGURATIONS FEATURING DIANA ROSS

With the exception of Jonathan King, Diana Ross has charted in more guises than anyone else in the history of the British and American charts. These are the label credits which have hidden or revealed her identity, in chronological order

1. Supremes	from 1962
2. Diana Ross and the Supremes	from 1967
3. Diana Ross and the Supremes and the Temptations	1969
4. Diana Ross	from 1970
5. Marvin Gaye and Diana Ross	1974
6. Diana Ross and Michael Jackson	1978
7. Diana Ross, Marvin Gaye, Smokey Robinson and Stevie Wonder	1979
8. Diana Ross and Lionel Richie	1981

SINGING DRUMMERS

1. Don Henley (Eagles)
2. Levon Helm (Band)
3. Mike Felix (Migil 5)
4. Karen Carpenter (Carpenters)
5. Ringo Starr (Beatles)
6. Kevin Godley (10CC)
7. Ted Bluechel (Association)
8. Dennis Wilson (Beach Boys)
9. Robert Wyatt (Soft Machine)
10. Moulty (Barbarians)

PUNK ROCK GODFATHERS

These acts have generally been regarded as the most influential on the burgeoning punk new wave scene of the late 1970s.

1. The Velvet Underground
2. New York Dolls
3. Iggy Pop and the Stooges
4. David Bowie
5. The Doors
6. The Rolling Stones
7. Thirteenth Floor Elevators
8. Alice Cooper
9. Captain Beefheart
10. The Seeds
11. Love

PERFORMERS AT THE MONTEREY INTERNATIONAL POP FESTIVAL 16–18 JUNE 1967

1. The Mamas and the Papas
2. The Who
3. Jimi Hendrix
4. Eric Burdon and the Animals
5. Beverley Martyn
6. Buffalo Springfield
7. The Paupers
8. Ravi Shankar
9. Hugh Masekela
10. Otis Redding
11. The Mar-Keys
12. Booker T and the MGs
13. Paul Butterfield Blues Band
14. The Electric Flag
15. The Byrds
16. The Association
17. Johnny Rivers
18. Simon and Garfunkel
19. The Blues Project
20. Canned Heat
21. Big Brother and the Holding Company (with Janis Joplin)
22. The Steve Miller Blues Band
23. The Grateful Dead
24. Quicksilver Messenger Service
25. Country Joe and the Fish

Monterey is acknowledged as the first of the major pop festivals and has been much imitated but never equalled.

PERFORMERS AT THE 1970 ISLE OF WIGHT FESTIVAL

Held near Freshwater, Isle Of Wight, from 19 August to 23 August, 1970, the Isle Of Wight Festival has become known as 'The Last Great Festival', a reasonably accurate description in terms of the remarkable array of talent which performed over the five days.

1. Rosalie Sorrels
2. Judas Jump
3. Kathy Smith
4. Redbone
5. Kris Kristofferson
6. Mighty Baby
7. Supertramp
8. Black Widow
9. Everyone with Andy Roberts
10. Howl
11. Groundhogs
12. Tony Joe White
13. Fairfield Parlour
14. Lighthouse
15. Arrival
16. Melanie
17. Procol Harum
18. Chicago
19. The Voices of East Harlem
20. Taste
21. Family
22. Cactus
23. Cat Mother and the Allnight News Boys
24. Mungo Jerry
25. John Sebastian
26. Miles Davis
27. Free
28. Emerson, Lake and Palmer
29. The Doors
30. Joni Mitchell
31. Ten Years After
32. The Who
33. Sly and the Family Stone
34. Good News
35. Ralph McTell
36. Tiny Tim
37. Donovan
38. Pentangle
39. Heaven
40. Richie Havens
41. Leonard Cohen
42. Jethro Tull
43. Moody Blues
44. Jimi Hendrix
45. Joan Baez

On a somewhat less happy note, it may be of interest to note that of these performers, at least five (Jimi Hendrix, Jim Morrison of the Doors, Keith Moon of the Who, Paul Kossoff of Free and Terry Kath of Chicago) are now deceased.

Jethro Tull

5. WITH A LITTLE HELP FROM MY FRIENDS

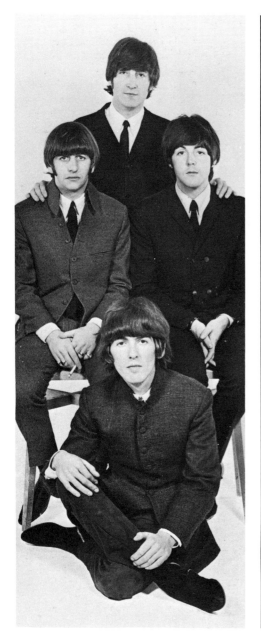

THE BEATLES ON NON-BEATLES RECORDS

Artist	Title	Beatle(s)
David Bowie	Young Americans	John Lennon
Elephant's Memory	Elephant's Memory	John Lennon
Yoko Ono	Fly	John Lennon, Ringo Starr
Yoko Ono	Yoko Ono/Plastic Ono Band	John Lennon, Ringo Starr
Yoko Ono	Feeling The Space	John Lennon
Yoko Ono	Approximately Infinite Universe	John Lennon
Alpha Band	Spark In The Dark	Ringo Starr
Attitudes	Good News	Ringo Starr
The Band	The Last Waltz	Ringo Starr
Lonnie Donegan	Puttin' On The Style	Ringo Starr
Cream	Goodbye	George Harrison
B. B. King	In London	Ringo Starr
Ian MacLagan	Troublemaker	Ringo Starr
Manhattan Transfer	Coming Out	Ringo Starr
Keith Moon	Two Sides Of The Moon	Ringo Starr
Carly Simon	Playing Possum	Ringo Starr
Lon and Derrek Van Eaton	Brother	Ringo Starr
Alvin Lee	Road To Freedom	George Harrison
Billy Preston	I Wrote A Simple Song	George Harrison
Leon Russell	Leon Russell	George Harrison, Ringo Starr
Tom Scott	New York Connection	George Harrison
Splinter	Harder To Live	George Harrison
Jackie Lomax	Is This What You Want?	Paul McCartney, Ringo Starr George Harrison
Denny Laine	Holly Days	Paul McCartney
Denny Laine	Japanese Tears	Paul McCartney
Steve Miller	Brave New World	Paul McCartney
Carly Simon	No Secrets	Paul McCartney

THE ROLLING STONES ON NON-ROLLING STONE LPS

Artist	Title	Rolling Stone(s)
Dr John	The Sun, Moon And Herbs	Mick Jagger
Carly Simon	No Secrets	Mick Jagger
Original Soundtrack	Performance	Mick Jagger
Original Soundtrack	Ned Kelly	Mick Jagger
Leslie West	The Great Fatsby	Mick Jagger

Ian MacLagan	Troublemaker	Keith Richard, Ron Wood
Howlin' Wolf	London Sessions	Charlie Watts, Bill Wyman
Howlin' Wolf	London Revisited	Charlie Watts, Bill Wyman
Alexis Korner	Bootleg Him	Charlie Watts
Alexis Korner	Get Off My Cloud	Keith Richard
Rocket 88	Rocket 88	Charlie Watts
Leon Russell	Leon Russell	Charlie Watts, Bill Wyman
Ben Sidran	Feel Your Groove	Charlie Watts
Pete Townshend/Ronnie Lane	Rough Mix	Charlie Watts
John Hammond	I Can Tell	Bill Wyman
Long John Baldry	It Ain't Easy	Ron Wood
The Band	The Last Waltz	Ron Wood
Jeff Beck	Truth	Ron Wood
Jeff Beck	Beck-Ola	Ron Wood
Jeff Beck	The Best Of Jeff Beck	Ron Wood
Jeff Beck	The Most Of Jeff Beck	Ron Wood
Eric Clapton	Rainbow Concert	Ron Wood
Rick Danko	Rick Danko	Ron Wood
Lonnie Donegan	Puttin' On The Style	Ron Wood
Faces	First Step	Ron Wood
Faces	Long Player	Ron Wood
Faces	A Nod's As Good As A Wink	Ron Wood
Faces	Ooh La La	
Faces	Coast To Coast	Ron Wood
Kinky Friedman	Lasso From El Paso	Ron Wood
George Harrison	Dark Horse	Ron Wood
Alvin Lee	Road To Freedom	Ron Wood
Rufus	Ask Rufus	Ron Wood
Rod Stewart	An Old Raincoat Won't Ever Let You Down	Ron Wood
Rod Stewart	Gasoline Alley	Ron Wood
Rod Stewart	Every Picture Tells A Story	Ron Wood
Original Soundtrack	Tommy	Ron Wood
Peter Tosh	Bush Doctor	Mick Jagger, Keith Richard

BEACH BOYS AS GUESTS ON OTHER ARTISTS' LPS

Note: This only covers the original five, as Bruce Johnston has appeared on more 'outside' LPs than I've had hot dinners.

Year	Title and Artist	Beach Boys featured
1963	Jan and Dean Take Linda Surfin' – Jan and Dean	All of them

BOB DYLAN ON OTHER PEOPLE'S RECORDS

1. Rock Of Ages – The Band
2. The Last Waltz – The Band
3. Barry Goldberg – Barry Goldberg
4. Al's Big Deal – Al Kooper
5. Roger McGuinn – Roger McGuinn
6. Doug Sahm And Band – Doug Sahm
7. Somebody Else's Troubles/The Essential Steve Goodman – Steve Goodman
8. Midnight Special – Harry Belafonte
9. Carolyn Hester – Carolyn Hester
10. The Blues Project – Geoff Muldaur
11. A Tribute To Woody Guthrie, Part One – Various Artists
12. The Concert For Bangla Desh – Various Artists
13. Richard Farina And Eric Von Schmidt – Richard Farina and Eric Von Schmidt
14. Holy Soul Jelly Roll – Allen Ginsberg
15. Songs For The New Depression – Bette Midler
16. No Reason To Cry – Eric Clapton
17. Death Of A Ladies Man – Leonard Cohen

Eric Clapton

1963	Surf City – Jan and Dean	Brian Wilson
1964	Dead Man's Curve/New Girl In School – Jan and Dean	Brian Wilson
1964	More Teenage Triangle – Paul Peterson, James Darren and Shelly Farbres	Carl Wilson
1968	Look Inside . . . – The Asylum Choir	Brian and Carl Wilson, Mike Love and Al Jardine
1970	Flame – Flame	All of them
1971	Warm Waters – Charles Lloyd	Mike Love, Carl Wilson and Al Jardine
1972	American Spring – American Spring Waves – Charles Lloyd	Carl Wilson
	Hat Trick – America	Carl Wilson
	Cass Elliot – Cass Elliot	Carl Wilson
1973	Amazing – Kathy Dalton	Carl Wilson
1974	Dazzle 'Em With Your Footwork – Martin and Finlay	Carl and Dennis Wilson, and Al Jardine
	Blue Moves – Elton John	Brian Wilson
	Chicago VII – Chicago	Carl Wilson
1975	New Lovers And Old Friends – Johnny Rivers	Carl Wilson
	Plug Me Into Something – Henry Gross	Brian Wilson
	The Higher They Climb – David Cassidy	Mike Love and Carl Wilson
	New Arrangement – Jackie de Shannon	Carl Wilson
1976	King Harvest – King Harvest	Carl Wilson
	Angelo – Angelo	Carl Wilson
1977	Warren Zevon – Warren Zevon	Carl and Dennis Wilson
	Chicago XI – Chicago	Brian Wilson
1978	Beached – Ricci Martin	Carl Wilson
1979	Boats Against The Current – Eric Carmen	Brian and Carl Wilson
	Lake II – Lake	
	Celebration – Celebration	

(Compiled by Andrew G. Doe.)

DAVID BOWIE ON OTHER PEOPLE'S RECORDS

1. Over The Wall We Go – Oscar
2. Oh Baby – Dib Cochran and the Earwigs
3. Oh, You Pretty Thing – Peter Noone
4. Right On Mother – Peter Noone
5. Hang On To Yourself – Arnold Corns
6. Moonage Daydream – Arnold Corns
7. All The Young Dudes – Mott the Hoople
8. Walk On The Wild Side – Lou Reed
9. The Man Who Sold The World – Lulu
10. Now We Are Six (LP) – Steeleye Span
11. The Idiot (LP) Iggy Pop
12. Lust For Life (LP) – Iggy Pop
13. Slaughter On 10th Avenue (LP) – Mick Ronson

David Bowie

EMMYLOU'S ANGELS, HOT BANDS AND FRIENDS

Between 1975 and 1981, Emmylou Harris released nine original albums and one compilation.
These are the albums:

1975 Pieces Of The Sky
1976 Elite Hotel
1977 Luxury Liner
1978 Quarter Moon In A Ten Cent Town
1978 Profile/Best Of Emmylou Harris
1979 Blue Kentucky Girl
1979 Light Of The Stable
1980 Roses In The Snow
1981 Evangeline
1981 Cimarron

These are the seventy-three musicians who lent their talents to the recording of the ninety-two songs contained therein.

Brian Ahern – Acoustic guitar/Electric guitar/12 string guitar/High strung guitar/Archtop guitar/Adamas guitar/Gut string guitar/Electric rhythm guitar/Bass guitar/6 string bass/Ernie Ball bass/Acoustic bass/6 string banjo/Percussion/Tambourine/Producer of all ten albums.
Nancy Ahern – Duet vocal
Joe Allen – Electric bass guitar
Bruce Archer – Acoustic guitar
Mike Auldridge – Dobro
Duke Bardwell – Bass guitar
Byron Berline – Fiddle/Mandolin
Hal Blaine – Drums
Mike Bowden – Bass guitar
Bryan Bowers – Autoharp
David Briggs – Piano
Dianne Brooks – Supporting vocals
Tony Brown – Clavinet/Piano/Electric piano
Barry 'Byrd' Burton – Acoustic guitar
James Burton – Electric guitar/Gut string guitar/Dobro
Johnny Cash – Harmony vocal
Charles Cochran – Electric piano
Donivan Cowart – Harmony vocal
Rodney Crowell – Electric guitar/Acoustic guitar/Rhythm guitar/High strung guitar/Supporting vocal
Mark Cuff – Drums
Rick Cunha – Acoustic guitar/High strung guitar
Rick Danko – Fiddle/Supporting vocal
Lincoln Davis Jr. – Accordion
Nick De Caro – String arrangements
Hank De Vito – Pedal steel guitar
Jerry Douglas – Dobro
Jonathan Edwards – Supporting vocal
Don Everly – Duet vocal
Steve Fishell – Dobro/Acoustic Hawaiian guitar/Percussion/Pedal steel guitar
Amos Garrett – Electric guitar
Wayne Goodwin – Fiddle/Mandolin
Emory Gordy – Bass guitar/Ernie Ball bass
Richard Greene – Fiddle
Tom Guidera – Bass guitar
Glen D. Hardin – Piano/Electric piano/String arrangements
Sharon Hicks – Harmony vocal
Garth Hudson – Accordion/Baritone saxophone
Waylon Jennings – Harmony vocal

Waylon Jennings

Don Johnson – Piano/Electric piano/Harmony vocal
Ben Keith – Pedal steel guitar
Paul Kennerly – Acoustic guitar
Dave Kirby – Acoustic guitar
Lynn Langham – Synthesizer
Nicolette Larson – Harmony vocal
Bernie Leadon – Banjo/Acoustic guitar/Dobro/Bass guitar/Supporting vocal
Albert Lee – Electric guitar/Acoustic guitar/Mandolin/Piano/Supporting vocal
Dave Lewis – Drums
Larrie Londin – Drums
Kenny Malone – Drums/Conga
Willie Nelson – Harmony vocal/Gut string guitar
Dolly Parton – Harmony vocal/Supporting vocal
Bill Payne – Piano/Electric piano
Herb Pedersen – Supporting vocal/Harmony vocal/Banjo/Acoustic guitar/ 12 string guitar
Danny Pendleton – Pedal steel guitar
Ray Pohlman – Bass guitar
Mickey Raphael – Harmonica/Bass harmonica
Mac Rebbenack – Piano
Frank Reckard – Electric guitar/Acoustic guitar/Gut string guitar
Tony Rice – Lead acoustic guitar/Acoustic guitar/Harmony vocal
Linda Ronstadt – Duet vocal/Harmony vocal/Supporting vocal
Craig Safan – String arrangement
Ricky Skaggs – Fiddle/Viola/Mandolin/Violin/Banjo/Acoustic guitar/Lead acoustic guitar/5 String fiddle/Lead vocal/Duet vocal/Harmony vocal
Buddy Spicher – Viola
Fayssoux Starling – Duet vocal/Harmony vocal/Supporting vocal
John Starling – Supporting vocal/Acoustic guitar
Barry Tashian – Harmony vocal/Acoustic guitar/Rhythm electric guitar
Tanya Tucker – Duet vocal
Ron Tutt – Drums
John Ware – Drums/Percussion
Cheryl Warren – Harmony vocal
Buck White – Piano
Don Williams – Duet vocal
Neil Young – Harmony vocal

List compiled by Peter O'Brien, editor of '*Omaha Rainbow*

ALBUMS ON WHICH SLY DUNBAR AND ROBBIE SHAKESPEARE HAVE PLAYED

1. Visions Of . . . — Dennis Brown
2. Two 7's Clash — Culture
3. Harder Than The Rest — Culture
4. Keep Rocking And Swinging — Big Joe
5. Gone Clear — Manu Dibango
6. Rasta Communication — Keith Hudson
7. Haile I Hymn — I Jahman
8. Forward To Zion — The Abyssinians
9. Arise — The Abyssinians
10. Sly, Wicked And Slick — Sly Dunbar
11. Sings The Wailers — Bunny Wailer
12. Equal Rights — Peter Tosh
13. Wild Suspense — Wailing Souls
14. Mystic Man — Peter Tosh
15. Black Moses — Jah Lloyd
16. Long Life — Prince Far I
17. Bible — Prince Hammer
18. In Fine Style — Ranking Trevor
19. Man From Wareika — Rico
20. Lord Upminster — Ian Dury
21. Sly And Robbie Present Taxi — Jimmy Riley, Tamlins, Junior Delgado, Dennis Brown, Wailing Souls, Black Uhuru, General Echo, Gregory Isaacs, Viceroys
22. Showcase — Black Uhuru
23. Sinsemilla — Black Uhuru

NICKY HOPKINS – KEYBOARD PLAYER TO THE STARS

Nicky Hopkins has probably played on more albums by famous acts than any other keyboard player, although, curiously, he has made very few records under his own name. A complete list of his credits would amount to nothing less than a *Who's Who* of the decade from 1965. The following list should illustrate that point, although only Hopkins himself would be able to complete it.

Artist	*Title*
Badfinger	Airwaves
Jeff Beck	Truth
Jeff Beck	Beck-Ola
Duster Bennett	Fingertips
Climax Blues Band	Flying The Flag
Joe Cocker	I Can Stand A Little Rain
Joe Cocker	Jamaica Say You Will
The Dingoes	Five Times The Sun
Lonnie Donegan	Puttin' On The Style
Various Artists	Flash Fearless vs. The Zorg Women
Peter Frampton	Something's Happening
Art Garfunkel	Breakaway
Lowell George	Thanks, I'll Eat It Here
George Harrison	Dark Horse
Hollywood Stars	Hollywood Stars
Various Artists	Jamming With Edward
Jackie Lomax	Is This What You Want?
McGuinness Flint	Happy Birthday, Ruthie Baby
Steve Miller	Brave New World
Steve Miller	Your Saving Grace
Steve Miller	Number 5
Eddie Money	Life Is For The Taking
New Riders	Powerglide
Night	Night
Andy Williams	Solitaire
Graham Parker	The Up Escalator
Poet and One Man Band	Poet And One Man Band
Pamela Polland	Pamela Polland
The Pointer Sisters	Priority
Jim Price	Kids Nowadays Ain't Got No Shame
Quicksilver Messenger Service	Shady Grove
Quicksilver Messenger Service	Just For Love
Quicksilver Messenger Service	What About Me?
Quicksilver Messenger Service	Solid Silver
Rolling Stones	Their Satanic Majesties Request
Rolling Stones	Beggar's Banquet
Rolling Stones	Exile On Main Street
Rolling Stones	It's Only Rock'n'Roll
Rolling Stones	Black And Blue
Carly Simon	No Secrets
Ringo Starr	Ringo

Artist	Title
Leigh Stephens	Red Weather
Rod Stewart	Blondes Have More Fun
Screaming Lord Sutch	Lord Sutch And Heavy Friends
Sweet Thursday	Sweet Thursday
Terry and the Pirates	Too Close For Comfort
Jennifer Warnes	I Can Remember
The Who	My Generation
The Who	The Who By Numbers

Herbie Flowers

MR BASS MAN

Herbie Flowers is perhaps best-known to the public as a member of Sky and as composer of Clive Dunn's solitary hit, 'Grandad'. He's also Paul McCartney's favourite bassist and a much in-demand session musician. In the latter capacity he has played on over 500 hits and, by his own admission, 'a hell of a lot more misses'. His simple, workmanlike style occasionally comes to the fore; the classic bass lines on Lou Reed's 'Walk On The Wild Side' and David Essex's 'Rock On' are both his. He's also a thoroughly nice man, unwilling to confirm his presence publicly on a number of hits for fear of embarrassing the credited musicians. Forced into a corner, he came up with a list of 50 records on which he admits playing, but makes light of his considerable talents, insisting 'but I'm only the bass player'.

1. Diamonds Are Forever – Shirley Bassey (1972)
2. Something Tells Me Something's Going To Happen Tonight – Cilla Black (1971)
3. Melting Pot – Blue Mink (1969)
4. Banner Man – Blue Mink (1971)
5. Space Oddity – David Bowie (1969)
6. Rebel, Rebel – David Bowie (1974)
7. Knock On Wood – David Bowie (1974)
8. Deck Of Cards – Max Bygraves (1973)
9. Whole Lotta Love – CCS (1970)
10. Super Nature – Cerrone (1978)
11. Side Show – Chanter Sisters (1976)
12. Softly Whispering I Love You – Congregation (1971)
13. Free Me – Roger Daltrey (1980)
14. I Want You To Be My Baby – Billie Davis (1968)
15. The Legend Of Xanadu – Dave Dee, Dozy, Beaky, Mick and Tich (1968)
16. Scotland Forever – Sidney Devine (1978)
17. Grandad – Clive Dunn (1970)
18. Rock On – David Essex (1973)
19. Imperial Wizard – David Essex (1979)
20. Let's Go To San Francisco – Flowerpot Men (1967)
21. You've Got Your Troubles – Fortunes (1965)
22. Tears On The Telephone – Claude Francois (1976)
23. All Those Years Ago – George Harrison (1981)
24. Forever Autumn – Justin Hayward (1975)
25. Congratulations – Cliff Richard (1968)
26. The Last Waltz – Engelbert Humperdinck (1967)
27. Your Song – Elton John (1971)
28. Delilah – Tom Jones (1968)
29. Superman – London Symphony Orchestra (1979)
30. Bringing On Back The Good Times – Love Affair (1969)
31. Rodrigo's Guitar Concerto De Aranjuez – Manuel and the music of The Mountains (1976)
32. Coconut – Nilsson (1972)
33. Mirrors – Sally Oldfield (1978)
34. Oh, You Pretty Thing – Peter Noone (1971)
35. Nothing Rhymed – Gilbert O'Sullivan (1970)
36. Sleepy Shores – Johnny Pearson (1971)
37. Welcome Home – Peters and Lee (1973)
38. Blue Angel – Gene Pitney (1974)

39. Walk On The Wild Side – Lou Reed (1973)
40. Jack In The Box – Clodagh Rodgers (1971)
41. Eloise – Barry Ryan (1968)
42. Thank U Very Much – Scaffold (1967)
43. Monsieur Dupont – Sandie Shaw (1969)
44. Toccata – Sky (1980)
45. Don't Let It Die – Hurricane Smith (1971)
46. I Was Kaiser Bill's Batman – Whistling Jack Smith (1967)
47. I Close My Eyes And Count To Ten – Dusty Springfield (1968)
48. The Soul Of My Suit – T. Rex (1977)
49. I'm Gonna Get Me A Gun – Cat Stevens (1967)
50. My Way – Dorothy Squires (1970)

THE GOLD RECORDS OF HAL BLAINE

Hal Blaine started playing drums at the age of eight and turned professional six years later. Now in his early fifties, Blaine was undeniably the leading session drummer on the West Coast of America during the 1960s. Since first venturing into the studios in 1958, Blaine has figured on over 25,000 recordings including almost 200 million sellers and seven Grammy winners, six of them consecutively. He's recorded four solo albums and a couple of highly collectable singles. The following list is a random selection of million sellers featuring the drumming of Hal Blaine.

1. A Little Bit Me, A Little Bit You – Monkees (1969)
2. All I Know – Art Garfunkel (1974)
3. Annie's Song – John Denver (1974)
4. Another Saturday Night – Sam Cooke (1960)
5. A Taste Of Honey – Herb Alpert and the Tijuana Brass (1965)
6. Aquarius/Let The Sunshine In/ – Fifth Dimension (1969)
7. Then He Kissed Me – Crystals (1964)

Hal Blaine

8. Baby, I Need Your Lovin' – Johnny Rivers (1967)
9. Barbara Ann – Beach Boys (1966)
10. Be My Baby – Ronettes (1963)
11. Bridge Over Troubled Water – Simon and Garfunkel (1970)
12. California Girls – Beach Boys (1965)
13. California Dreamin' – the Mamas and the Papas (1966)
14. Can't Help Fallin' In Love – Elvis Presley (1962)
15. Cara Mia – Jay and the Americans (1964)
16. Close To You – Carpenters (1971)
17. Count Me In – Gary Lewis and the Playboys (1965)
18. Cracklin' Rosie – Neil Diamond (1970)
19. Come Back When You Grow Up – Bobby Vee (1967)

20. Da Doo Ron Ron – Crystals (1963)
21. Dancing In The Streets – Martha and the Vandellas (1964)
22. Dedicated To The One I Love – Mamas and the Papas (1967)
23. Dizzy – Tommy Roe (1969)
24. Don't Pull Your Love – Hamilton, Joe Frank and Reynolds (1971)
25. Dead Man's Curve – Jan and Dean (1963)
26. Everybody Loves A Clown – Gary Lewis and the Playboys (1966)
27. Everybody Loves Somebody – Dean Martin (1964)
28. Eve Of Destruction – Barry McGuire (1965)
29. Fly Away – John Denver (1976)
30. For All We Know – Carpenters (1971)
31. Good Vibrations – Beach Boys (1966)
32. Galveston – Glen Campbell (1969)
33. Guantanamera – Sandpipers (1966)
34. Half Breed – Cher (1973)
35. Heartbeat (It's A Lovebeat) – DeFranco Family (1973)
36. Help Me Rhonda – Beach Boys (1965)
37. He's A Rebel – Crystals (1962)
38. Hey Jude – Jose Feliciano (1970)
39. Hey Little Cobra – Rip Chords (1964)
40. Holly Holy – Neil Diamond (1971)
41. Homeward Bound – Simon and Garfunkel (1966)
42. Hurting Each Other – Carpenters (1972)
43. I Get Around – Beach Boys (1964)
44. I Got You Babe – Sonny and Cher (1965)
45. If I Were A Carpenter – Bobby Darin (1966)
46. Indian Reservation – Paul Revere and the Raiders (1971)
47. I Saw Her Again – Mamas and the Papas (1966)
48. I Think I Love You – Partridge Family (1970)
49. I'm Sorry – John Denver (1975)
50. It's Now Or Never – Elvis Presley (1960)
51. Jambalaya (On The Bayou) – Carpenters (1974)
52. Jam Up, Jelly Tight – Tommy Roe (1969)

53. Leave Me Alone (Ruby Red Dress) – Helen Reddy (1973)
54. Love Story – Andy Williams (1972)
55. Love Story – Henry Mancini (1972)
56. Love Will Keep Us Together – Captain and Tennille (1975)
57. MacArthur Park – Richard Harris (1968)
58. Midnight Confessions – Grassroots (1966)
59. Monday, Monday – Mamas and the Papas (1966)
60. Mr Tambourine Man – Byrds (1965)
61. Mrs Robinson – Simon and Garfunkel (1968)
62. My Love – Petula Clark (1966)
63. Never My Love – Association (1967)
64. One Less Bell To Answer – Fifth Dimension (1971)
65. Rainy Days And Mondays – Carpenters (1971)
66. Return To Me – Dean Martin (1958)
67. Return To Sender – Elvis Presley (1962)
68. Rhythm Of The Rain – Cascades (1963)
69. Ringo – Lorne Greene (1964)
70. Save Your Heart For Me – Gary Lewis and the Playboys (1965)
71. Save The Last Dance For Me – DeFranco Family (1974)
72. San Francisco ('Be Sure To Wear Flowers In Your Hair') – Scott McKenzie (1967)
73. Sloop John B. – Beach Boys (1966)
74. Softly As I Leave You – Frank Sinatra (1964)
75. Sooner Or Later – Grassroots (1967)
76. Song Sung Blue – Neil Diamond (1972)
77. Somethin' Stupid – Frank and Nancy Sinatra (1967)
78. Strangers In The Night – Frank Sinatra (1966)
79. Sugartown – Nancy Sinatra (1967)
80. Superstar – Carpenters (1971)
81. Surf City – Jan and Dean (1963)
82. Surfin' USA – Beach Boys (1963)
83. Sweet Caroline – Neil Diamond (1969)
84. Temptation Eyes – Grassroots (1967)
85. The Way We Were – Barbra Streisand (1974)
86. These Boots Are Made For Walking – Nancy Sinatra (1966)
87. The Boxer – Simon and Garfunkel (1969)
88. The Happening – Supremes (1967)
89. The Lonely Bull – Herb Alpert and the Tijuana Brass (1962)
90. This Is My Song – Petula Clark (1967)
91. Turn Around, Look At Me – Vogues (1968)
92. This Diamond Ring – Gary Lewis and the Playboys (1965)
93. Top Of The World – Carpenters (1973)
94. Ventura Highway – America (1974)
95. Young Girl – Union Gap featuring Gary Puckett (1968)
96. Windy – Association (1967)
97. Yesterday Once More – Carpenters (1973)
98. Up Up And Away – Fifth Dimension (1967)
99. Where The Boys Are – Connie Francis (1961)
100. Wedding Bell Blues – Fifth Dimension (1969)

JAMES BURTON – SESSION MAN

James Burton is the most in-demand session guitar player in the world, having established a gleaming reputation working with Dale Hawkins, Rick(y) Nelson and Elvis Presley. While he has played on literally hundreds of LPs, James has never found time enough to document with any precision exactly which he has played on, and the list which follows is an attempt to give some idea of the extent of this ace player's influence. Nelson and Presley records have been excluded – James is on all Nelson LPs up to about 1969, and most Presley LPs subsequent to that date.

Artist	Title
Johnny Cash	John R. Cash
Rodney Crowell	Ain't Living Long Like This
Hoyt Axton	My Griffin Is Gone
Hoyt Axton	Life Machine
Hoyt Axton	Southbound
Hoyt Axton	Fearless
Hoyt Axton	Road Songs
Hoyt Axton	Free Sailin'
Hoyt Axton	A Rusty Old Halo
Buffalo Springfield	Again
Jonathan Edwards	Rockin' Chair
Jonathan Edwards	Sailboat
Arlo Guthrie	Running Down The Road
Phil Everly	Star Spangled Springer
Everly Brothers	Beat And Soul
Delaney and Bonnie	Genesis
John Denver	I Want To Live
John Denver	JD
John Denver	Autograph
John Denver and the Muppets	A Christmas Together
John Phillips	Wolfking of LA
Emmylou Harris	Pieces Of The Sky
Emmylou Harris	Elite Hotel
Emmylou Harris	Luxury Liner

Artist	Title
Emmylou Harris	Quarter Moon In A Ten Cent Town
Emmylou Harris	Blue Kentucky Girl
Emmylou Harris	Light Of The Stable
Emmylou Harris	Roses In The Snow
Emmylou Harris	Evangeline
John Hartford	John Hartford
Dale Hawkins	Dale Hawkins
Dale Hawkins	LA Memphis and Tyler, Texas
Ronnie Hawkins	The Hawk
Lee Hazelwood	Love And Other Crimes
James Hendricks	Songs Of James Hendricks
John Hurley	Sings About People
Jan and Dean	Save For A Rainy Day
Longbranch/Pennywhistle	Longbranch/Pennywhistle
Nicolette Larson	Nicolette
Dan McCorrison	Dan McCorrison
Michael Nesmith	The Wichita Train Whistle Sings
Michael Nesmith	Nevada Fighter
Randy Newman	Randy Newman
Gram Parsons	GP
Gram Parsons	Grievous Angel
Phil Ochs	Greatest Hits
Mary Kay Place	Aimin' To Please
Gary Puckett	Incredible
Johnny Rivers	Realization
Johnny Rivers	Slim Slo Slider
Johnny Rivers	Home Grown
Johnny Rivers	Wild Night
Silverado	Silverado
The Shacklefords	The Shacklefords
Mark Spoelstra	Mark Spoelstra
John Stewart	Sunstorm
Mickey Gilley	Urban Cowboy (soundtrack)
Sammy Walker	Sammy Walker
Jesse Winchester	Nothin' But A Breeze
Judy Collins	Who Knows Where The Time Goes
The Hagers	The Hagers
Jerry Lee Lewis	Jerry Lee Lewis
Joni Mitchell	For The Roses
J. J. Cale	Shades
P. F. Sloan	Raised On Records
Tongue And Groove	Tongue And Groove
Mac Davis	Burning Thing
Gram Parsons	Sleepless Nights

HITS WITH LEAD VOCALS BY TONY BURROWS

1. Let's Go To San Francisco – Flowerpot Men (1967)
2. Love Grows (Where My Rosemary Goes) – Edison Lighthouse (1970)
3. My Baby Loves Lovin' – White Plains (1970)
4. United We Stand – Brotherhood of Man (1970)
5. Gimme Dat Ding – Pipkins (1970)
6. I've Got You On My Mind – White Plains (1970)
7. Where Are You Going To, My Love – Brotherhood of Man (1970)
8. It's Up To You, Petula – Edison Lighthouse (1971)
9. Beach Baby – First Class (1974)

Born 14 April 1942, Tony Burrows was one of the top session singers of the late sixties/ early seventies and holds the all time record for most appearances on a single edition of *Top Of The Pops*. This historic feat was performed on 26 January 1970 when 'Love Grows', 'My Baby Loves Lovin'' and 'United We Stand' were all included in the show.

ALBUMS FEATURING ERIC CLAPTON AS A SESSION MAN

1. We're Only In It For The Money – Mothers of Invention
2. Fiends And Angels – Martha Velez
3. Lost In Austin – Marc Benno
4. Jesse Davis – Jesse Davis
5. Get Ready – King Curtis
6. Leon Russell – Leon Russell
7. The Sun, The Moon And The Herbs – Dr John
8. Rough Mix – Pete Townshend and Ronnie Lane
9. London Sessions – Howlin' Wolf
10. All Things Must Pass – George Harrison
11. White Mansions – Various Artists
12. Lady Soul – Aretha Franklin
13. See Me – Ronnie Lane

Eric Clapton

14. Is This What You Want? – Jackie Lomax
15. The Beatles (double white album) – The Beatles
16. Stephen Stills and Stephen Stills 2 – Stephen Stills
17. Play The Blues – Buddy Guy and Junior Wells
18. Rick Danko – Rick Danko
19. Rotogravure – Ringo Starr
20. Burglar – Freddie King

Ry Cooder

TWENTY BEST SOLOS BY JAMES BURTON
(In no particular order)

Track	Album/Artist
1. Stop Sneakin' Round	Album 7 (Rick Nelson)
2. Till I Can Gain Control Again	Elite Hotel (Emmylou Harris)
3. Down Home	For You (Rick Nelson)
4. Mighty Good	Rick Nelson (single)
5. I've Been Thinking	Songs by Ricky (Rick Nelson)
6. Bucket's Got A Hole In It	Rick Nelson (single)
7. Hello Mary Lou	Rick Nelson (single)
8. Blood From A Stone	Songs By Ricky (Rick Nelson)
9. I've Got A Woman	The Very Thought Of You (Rick Nelson)
10. My Babe	Ricky Nelson
11. Ooh! Las Vegas	Grievous Angel (Gram Parsons)
12. You Never Know What You're Missing	Songs By Ricky (Rick Nelson)
13. Every Time You Leave	Blue Kentucky Girl (Emmylou Harris)
14. Just A Little Too Much	Rick Nelson (single)
15. Milk Cow Blues	Rick Nelson (single)
16. That's All Right	Life Machine (Hoyt Axton)
17. Rockin' My Life Away	Jerry Lee Lewis (Jerry Lee Lewis)
18. You Tear Me Up	Ricky Nelson
19. Salty Dog	Country Fever (Ricky Nelson)
20. Mississippi	Wolf King Of LA (John Phillips)

List submitted by Rocky Prior, who is James Burton's biggest fan. By day, he is disguised as a bank manager.

RY COODER AS A SESSION MAN

In the 1980s, Ry Cooder has finally been recognized as possibly the most innovative guitarist of the recent rock era, but in previous years he was probably better known for his sterling contributions to the records of others than for his excellent, but generally under-rated, solo albums. The list below details some of the places where his work can be found, other than on his own indispensable records.

Artist	Title
Original Soundtrack	Blue Collar
Rod Taylor	Rod Taylor
David Blue	Stories
Clarence White	Why You Been Gone So Long
Taj Mahal	Taj Mahal
Buffy Sainte Marie	She Used To Want To Be A Ballerina
Brenda Patterson	Brenda Patterson
Phil Ochs	Greatest Hits
Randy Newman	12 Songs
Randy Newman	Sail Away
Randy Newman	Good Old Boys

Phil Everly
Leon Russell

Randy Newman	Little Criminals
Terry Melcher	Terry Melcher
Little Feat	Little Feat
Longbranch/Pennywhistle	Longbranch/Pennywhistle
Ron Nagle	Bad Rice
Van Morrison	Into The Music
Arlo Guthrie	Arlo Guthrie
Arlo Guthrie	Last Of The Brooklyn Cowboys
Arlo Guthrie	Running Down The Road
Gentle Soul	Gentle Soul
Don Everly	Don Everly
Everly Brothers	Stories We Could Tell
Marc Benno	Marc Benno
Rodney Crowell	Ain't Living Long Like This
Johnny Cash	John R. Cash
Captain Beefheart	Safe As Milk
Nicky Hopkins	Jamming With Edward
Original Soundtrack	Performance
Rita Coolidge	Rita Coolidge
Maria Muldaur	Maria Muldaur
Rolling Stones	Sticky Fingers
Crazy Horse	Crazy Horse
Doobie Brothers	Stampede
Claudia Lennear	Phew
John Sebastian	The Tarzana Kid
The Gabby Pahinui Hawaiian Band	The Gabby Pahinui Hawaiian Band

LEON RUSSELL AS A SESSION MUSICIAN

During the early years of the 1970s, Leon Russell distinguished himself by becoming almost an obligatory guest on albums by (mostly) famous rock stars. In fact, his career in the studio had begun many years before, when he was often used by Phil Spector as one of the components of his celebrated 'Wall Of Sound'. Below are listed some of Russell's many credits on albums which do not bear his name as an artist.

Artist	Title
Delaney and Bonnie and Friends	Accept No Substitute
Eric Clapton	Eric Clapton
Gene Clark	Gene Clark And The Gosdin Brothers
Joe Cocker	Joe Cocker
Joe Cocker	Mad Dogs And Englishmen
Rita Coolidge	Rita Coolidge
Ron Davies	Silent Song Throughout The Land
Jesse Ed Davis	Jesse Ed Davis
Jesse Ed Davis	Ululu
Various Artists	The Concert For Bangla Desh
B. B. King	Indianola Mississippi Seeds
Freddie King	Getting Ready
Freddie King	Texas Cannonball
Freddie King	Woman Across The Water

Dave Mason	Alone Together
Bob B. Soxx and the Blue Jeans	Zip-A-Dee-Doo-Dah
Bob B. Soxx and the Blue Jeans	Wall Of Sound Volume 2
Dwight Twilley	Sincerely
Bill Wyman	Monkey Grip
Asylum Choir	Look Inside The Asylum Choir
Asylum Choir	Asylum Choir II
Daughters Of Albion	Daughters Of Albion
The Crystals	Wall Of Sound Volume 3
The Crystals	He's A Rebel
The Crystals	Twist Uptown
The Crystals	Greatest Hits
The Ronettes	The Fabulous Ronettes
The Ronettes	Wall Of Sound Volume 1
The Ronettes	The Greatest Hits Volume 2
Darlene Love	Masters
Various Artists	A Christmas Gift For You (Phil Spector's Christmas LP)
B. B. King	The Best Of B. B. King

ALBUMS FEATURING JOHN SEBASTIAN AS A SESSION PLAYER

John Sebastian is best known as the leader and main songwriter of the much missed Lovin' Spoonful, but he is also in demand as a session musician, chiefly on harmonica, an instrument on which his father was also expert.

Artist	*Album Title*
Aztec Two Step	Aztec Two Step
Valerie Carter	Just A Stone's Throw Away
Judy Collins	Fifth Album
Rita Coolidge	The Lady's Not For Sale
Crosby, Stills, Nash and Young	Déjà Vu
The Doors	Morrison Hotel (as G. Puglese)
Even Dozen Jug Band	Even Dozen Jug Band (as John Benson)
Steven Fromholz	A Rumour In My Time
Tim Hardin	1
Keith Moon	Two Sides Of The Moon
Laura Nyro	Nested
Ohio Knox	Ohio Knox
Bonnie Raitt	Home Plate
J. D. Souther	You're Only Lonely
Stephen Stills	Stephen Stills

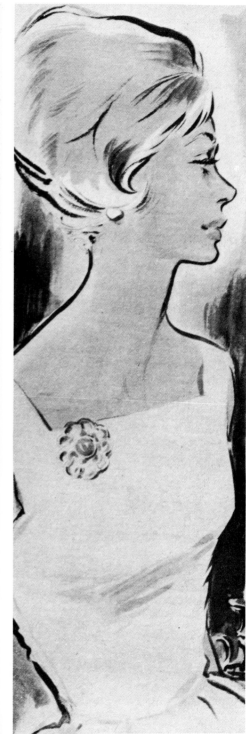

HIT RECORDS FEATURING UNCREDITED LEAD VOCALISTS

1. Barbara Ann – Beach Boys
Guest vocalist was Dean Torrance of Jan and Dean.

2. Street Life – Crusaders
Featuring the unmistakable Randy Crawford.

3. Just The Two Of Us – Grover Washington Jr
The loaned larynx here belongs to Bill Withers who also guested on 'Soul Shadows' by the Crusaders (not a hit).

4. Parisienne Walkways – Gary Moore
Moore was at the time a member of Thin Lizzy and coaxed group leader Phil Lynott to lend a hand.

5. In A Broken Dream – Python Lee Jackson
There are several conflicting stories as to why he did it, and how much he was paid but there's no mistaking the sound of Rod Stewart.

6. Stuff Like That – Quincy Jones
Talented arranger, composer and producer he may be, but Quincy Jones is no great shakes as a singer. Luckily he knows it, and had the sense to let talented husband/wife team Nickolas Ashford and Valerie Simpson handle vocal chores on this midcharting 1978 effort.

7. (You're) Having My Baby – Paul Anka
With considerable assistance from Odia Coates.

8. Come Outside – Mike Sarne
Are You Being Served star Wendy Richard provides the foil for Mike Sarne on this 1962 novelty.

9. Swinging On A Star – Big Dee Irwin
A duet with Little Eva.

10. Fooled Around And Fell In Love – Elvin Bishop
Featured vocalist was Mickey Thomas, then a member of Bishop's band and now one of Jefferson Starship's leading lights.

MARC BOLAN: SESSIONMAN

In addition to appearing on the hit singles listed below, Bolan also worked on less successful projects with Donovan, Tony Visconti, Gloria Jones, Steve Harley and Marsha Hunt.

	Hst. Chart Position	
	UK	US
1. Back Off Boogaloo – Ringo Starr (1972)	2	9
2. Elected – Alice Cooper (1972)	4	26
3. Hello, Hurray – Alice Cooper (1973)	6	35
4. Nutbush City Limits – Ike and Tina Turner (1973)	4	22
5. Showdown – Electric Light Orchestra (1973)	12	53
6. Rebel, Rebel – David Bowie (1974)	5	64
7. Ma-Ma-Ma-Belle – Electric Light Orchestra (1974)	22	–

Mark Bolan

LOWELL GEORGE AS A SESSION GUITARIST

The great Lowell George was a remarkable guitar player, and the gap left by his unfortunate death has never been filled. The group which he led from obscurity to stardom, Little Feat, occupied much of Lowell's time during the 1970s, but he also found space to play on other records, including those listed below.

Artist	Title
Mike Auldridge	Blues And Bluegrass
Jackson Browne	The Pretender
Valerie Carter	Just A Stone's Throw Away
Kathy Dalton	Amazing
Kathy Dalton	Boogie Bands And One Night Stands

Yvonne Elliman	Night Flight
John Hall	John Hall
Chico Hamilton	Chico The Master
Linda Lewis	Not A Little Girl Anymore
Kate and Anna McGarrigle	Kate And Anna McGarrigle
Maria Muldaur	Waitress In A Donut Shop
Robert Palmer	Sneakin' Sally Through The Alley
Robert Palmer	Pressure Drop
Van Dyke Parks	Discover America
Bonnie Raitt	Takin' My Time
Linda Ronstadt	Prisoner In Disguise
John Sebastian	The Tarzana Kid
Carly Simon	No Secrets
Carly Simon	Another Passage
J. D. Souther	Black Rose
Mick Taylor	Mick Taylor
Jimmy Webb	El Mirage
Frank Zappa	Hot Rats
Mothers of Invention	Weasels Ripped My Flesh
Mothers of Invention	Burnt Weeny Sandwich

LINDA RONSTADT – SESSION SINGER

Linda Ronstadt became a superstar during the second half of the 1970s, but for many years she could often be found singing on records starring her friends from Los Angeles, among them being those listed below, several of which were recorded after she achieved worldwide fame.

Artist	*Title*
American Flyer	Spirit Of A Woman
Mike Auldridge	Blues And Bluegrass
Hoyt Axton	Life Machine
Hoyt Axton	Road Songs
Various Artists	Escalator Over The Hill
Karla Bonoff	Karla Bonoff
David Bromberg	Midnight On The Water
Various Artists	Music From Free Creek
Andrew Gold	What's Wrong With This Picture?
Andrew Gold	Andrew Gold
Emmylou Harris	Pieces Of The Sky
Emmylou Harris	Elite Hotel
Emmylou Harris	Light Of The Stable
Nicolette Larson	Nicolette
Maria Muldaur	Waitress In A Doughnut Shop
Maria Muldaur	Sweet Harmony
Tracy Nelson	Tracy Nelson
Nitty Gritty Dirt Band	American Dream
Danny O'Keefe	So Long Harry Truman
Orleans	Walking And Dreaming
Gram Parsons	Grievous Angel

Linda Ronstadt

47

Herb Pedersen	South West
Herb Pedersen	Sandman
Seldom Scene	The Seldom Scene Album
Carly Simon	Another Passage
J. D. Souther	Black Rose
B. W. Stevenson	Calabasas
John Stewart	Dream Babies Go Hollywood
James Taylor	One Man Dog
James Taylor	J.T.
Kate Taylor	Sister Kate
Wendy Waldman	The Main Refrain
Michael Dinner	The Great Pretender
Neil Young	Harvest
Warren Zevon	Excitable Boy
Warren Zevon	Bad Luck Streak In Dancing School

JIMMY PAGE – SESSIONMAN

Jimmy Page is best known as a member of Led Zeppelin but served his apprenticeship in the sixties as a respected and much in-demand session guitarist. The hit singles he is known to have played on include the following:

	Highest Chart Position	
	UK	US
1. Diamonds – Jet Harris and Tony Meehan (1963)	1	–
2. My Baby Left Me – Dave Berry (1964)	37	–
3. Candy Man – Brian Poole and the Tremeloes (1964)	6	–
4. Together – P. J. Proby (1964)	8	–
5. All Day And All Of The Night – Kinks (1964)	2	7
6. Baby Please Don't Go – Them (1965)	10	6
7. Silhouettes – Herman's Hermits (1965)	3	7
8. I Can't Explain – Who (1965)	8	93
9. Here Comes The Night – Them (1965)	2	9
10. Wonderful World – Herman's Hermits (1965)	7	10
11. You Were On My Mind – Christian St Peters (1966)	2	36
12. Gloria – Them (1966)	–	71
13. Out Of Time – Chris Farlowe (1966)	1	–
14. Sunshine Superman – Donovan (1966)	3	1
15. With A Little Help From My Friends – Joe Cocker (1968)	1	68

Page also played on album sessions for a wide variety of artists including the Everly Brothers, Rolling Stones, Jeff Beck, Brenda Lee, Screaming Lord Sutch, Pretty Things, Dubliners, Twice As Much and Burt Bacharach.

The above list was compiled with the assistance of Howard Mylett, recognized authority on Led Zeppelin and author of the books *Led Zeppelin* (Panther) and *In The Light* (Savoy-Proteus).

Brian Poole and the Tremeloes

6. TRICKS, TRACKS & THEMES

ROCK'N'ROLL ANTHEMS

1. It Will Stand – The Showmen
2. Do You Believe in Magic? – Lovin' Spoonful
3. Rock'n'Roll Dreams Come Thru – Jim Steinman
4. Sex And Drugs And Rock'n'Roll – Ian Dury
5. Rock, Rock, Rock – Jimmy Cavallo and the House Rockers
6. Rock'n'Roll – Lou Reed
7. Rock'n'Roll Music – Chuck Berry
8. Hang Up My Rock'n'Roll Shoes – Chuck Willis
9. I Love Rock'n'Roll – Joan Jett and the Blackhearts
10. Rock And Roll Never Forgets – Bob Seger and the Silver Bullet Band
11. It's Only Rock'n'Roll – The Rolling Stones

MISTER HITS

1. Mr Bass Man – Johnny Cymbal
2. Mr Big Stuff – Joan Knight
3. Mr Blue – David Macbeth, the Fleetwoods, Mike Preston
4. Mr Blue Sky – Electric Light Orchestra
5. Mr Bojangles – Jerry Jeff Walker/Nitty Gritty Dirt Band
6. Mr Business Man – Ray Stevens
7. Mr Crowley – Ozzy Osbourne
8. Mr Guder – The Carpenters
9. Mr Guitar – Bert Weedon
10. Mr Porter – Mickie Most
11. Mr President – D, B, M, &T
12. Mr Soft – Steve Harley
13. Mr Lonely – Bobby Vinton
14. Mr Second Class – Spencer Davis
15. Mr Dieingly Sad – The Critters

16. Mr Tambourine Man – The Byrds
17. Mr Spaceman – The Byrds
18. Mr Zero – Keith Relf
19. Mr Pitiful – Otis Redding
20. Please Mr Postman – The Marvelettes

MY ROCKIN' DAYS (OF THE WEEK)

Sunday Will Never Be The Same (Spanky and Our Gang)
Monday Monday (Mamas and Papas)/Blue Monday (Fats Domino)
Everything's Tuesday (Chairman Of The Board)/Ruby Tuesday (Rolling Stones)
Wednesday Week (Undertones)
Think About Thursday (Eddie Vincent and Establishment)
Friday On My Mind (Easybeats)
Saturday Night At The Movies (Drifters)

NUMERICAL HITS

One Fine Day – The Chiffons
Two Out Of Three Ain't Bad – Meat Loaf

Three Steps To Heaven – Eddie Cochran
Four Strong Winds – Neil Young
Five Minutes – The Stranglers
Six Teens – The Sweet
Seven Seas of Rhye – Queen
Eight Miles High – The Byrds
Nine Times Out Of Ten – Cliff Richard
Big Ten – Judge Dread

TAILOR'S TOP 21

1. Hats Off To Larry – Del Shannon
2. Homburg – Procol Harum
3. Raincoat In The River –
4. Blue Collar Man – Captain Beefheart
5. Green Shirt – Elvis Costello
6. Tie A Yellow Ribbon – Dawn
7. Tie Me Kangaroo Down Sport – Rolf Harris
8. Bras On 45 – Ivor Biggun
9. Coat Of Many Colours – Dolly Parton
10. This Pullover – Jess Conrad
11. Leap Up And Down, Wave Your Knickers In The Air – St Cecelia
12. Ants In My Pants – James Brown
13. Red Dress – Alvin Stardust
14. Baggy Trousers – Madness
15. Short Shorts – Royal Teens
16. Itsy Bitsie Teeny Weeny Yellow Polka Dot Bikini – Brian Hyland
17. Bobby Sox To Stockings – Frankie Avalon
18. Sock It To 'Em J.B. – Rex Garvin and the Mighty Cravers
19. Sock It To Me – Mitch Ryder
20. These Boots Are Made For Walking – Nancy Sinatra
21. Red Shoes – Elvis Costello

And to carry them home? 'Another Suitcase In Another Hall' – Barbara Dickson

49

INITIAL HIT TITLES

1. A.B.C. (Jackson 5)
2. B.Y.O.F. (Fantastic Four)
3. D.I.S.C.O. (Ottawan)
4. D.I.V.O.R.C.E. (Tammy Wynette; Billy Connolly)
5. D.J. (David Bowie)
6. DK–50–80 (Otway and Barrett)
7. FBI (The Shadows)
8. FM (No Static At All) (Steely Dan)
9. I.O.I.O. (The BeeGees)
10. L.O.V.E. (Al Green)
11. OK? (Rock Follies)
12. SOS (Abba)
13. TSOP (MFSB)
14. T.R.O.U.B.L.E. (Elvis Presley)
15. TV (Flying Lizards)
16. TVC15 (David Bowie)
17. Y.M.C.A. (The Village People)
18. W.O.L.D. (Harry Chapin)

List compiled by Keith Lambourne, an over enthusiastic record buyer with a patient wife. (Hello, Tish!)

(HITS WITH) BRACKETS (IN THEIR TITLES)

1. (Marie's The Name Of) His Latest Flame – Elvis Presley
2. Fa Fa Fa Fa Fa (Sad Song) – Otis Redding
3. Make Me Smile (Come Up And See Me) – Steve Harley and Cockney Rebel
4. (I'm Always Touched By Your) Presence, Dear – Blondie
5. When I Grow Up (To Be A Man) – Beach Boys
6. Ernie (The Fastest Milkman In The West) – Benny Hill
7. Movin' Out (Anthony's Song) – Billy Joel
8. What Does It Take (To Win Your Love) – Junior Walker and the All Stars
9. Stop Me (If You've Heard It All Before) – Billy Ocean
10. San Francisco (Be Sure To Wear Flowers In Your Hair) – Scott McKenzie
11. Remember (Walkin' In The Sand) – Shangri-Las
12. Hello This Is Joannie (The Telephone Answering Machine Song) – Paul Evans
13. Give Me Love (Give Me Peace On Earth) – George Harrison
14. 59th Street Bridge Song (Feeling Groovy) – Harpers Bizarre/Simon and Garfunkel
15. Judy In Disguise (With Glasses) – John Fred and his Playboy Band
16. Hands Up (Give Me Your Heart) – Ottawan
17. Love Action (I Believe In Love) – Human League
18. Calling Occupants Of Interplanetary Craft (The Recognized Anthem Of World Contact Day) – The Carpenters
19. Fool (If You Think It's Over) – Chris Rea
20. (Get A) Grip (On Yourself) – Stranglers
21. I (You) Can Dance All By My (Your) Self – Dalton and Dubarri
22. (I Can't Get No) Satisfaction – Rolling Stones
23. (Your Love Keeps Lifting Me) Higher And Higher – Jackie Wilson
24. Opus 17 (Don't You Worry 'Bout Me) – Four Seasons
25. Mirror, Mirror (Mon Amour) – Dollar

REPETITIOUS HIT TITLES

Qualification – the title of a hit record which is made up of a word repeated two or more times, or two words repeated two or more times.

1. Bang Bang – Cher
2. Bang Bang – B.A. Robertson
3. Bang Bang – Squeeze
4. Clean Clean – Buggles
5. Dance Dance Dance – Beach Boys
6. Dance Dance Dance (Yowsah Yowsah Yowsah) – Chic
7. Fa-Fa-Fa-Fa-Fa – Otis Redding
8. Gimme Gimme Gimme – Abba
9. Girls Girls Girls – Fourmost
10. Girls Girls Girls – Kandidate
11. Girls Girls Girls – Steve Lawrence
12. Girls Girls Girls – Sailor
13. Give Give Give – Tommy Steele
14. Gone Gone Gone – Everly Brothers
15. Gone Gone Gone – Johnny Mathis
16. Helule Helule – Tremeloes
17. Hi Hi Hi – Wings
18. I Do I Do I Do I Do I Do – Abba
19. Jam Jam Jam – People's Choice
20. Jeannie Jeannie Jeannie – Eddie Cochran
21. Looks Looks Looks – Sparks
22. Louie Louie – Motorhead/Kingsmen
23. Love Love Love – Bobby Hebb
24. Money Money Money – Abba
25. Ne Ne Na Na Na Na Nu Nu – Bad Manners/Dickie Doo and the Dont's
26. Never Never Never – Shirley Bassey
27. Ring Ring – Abba
28. Shoot Shoot – UFO
29. Stop Stop Stop – Hollies
30. Sugar Sugar – Archies/Sakkarin/Wilson Pickett
31. Tomorrow Tomorrow – Bee Gees
32. Turn Turn Turn – Byrds
33. You You You – Alvin Stardust
34. Yummy Yummy Yummy – Ohio Express
35. Um Um Um Um Um Um – Major Lance/Wayne Fontana and the Mindbenders

Wayne Fontana and the Mindbenders

The Hollies

MOST REPETITIVE LYRICS

1. *Non-consecutive*

Trying to establish which hit record has the most repetitive lyrics proved to be something of a headache for the authors. Whilst making no claims that the following are the most lyrically repetitive songs to make the chart, we humbly offer them as outstanding examples of the genre:

● Bill Withers takes 58 seconds to get around to singing 'Lovely Day' on his outstanding 1978 hit of the same name. But in the remaining 3 minutes and 16 seconds he repeats the title 105 times (see also longest held note on a hit record).

● In one of his greatest hits 'Um Um Um Um Um Um', Major Lance sings the title phrase four times at the end of each of the first two verses, and six times at the end of the third verse. Thus, during a song which lasts a mere two minutes and seventeen seconds, Major (the title is, of course, honorary) sings the word 'Um' no less than 84 times. As a footnote, the title of this track has probably been incorrectly announced by more disc jockeys than any other, without singing the song.

● Last year, tacky British family ensemble the Dooleys made significant inroads into the chart with a bouncy little number entitled 'And I Wish'. In just 3 minutes and 41 seconds the songtitle crops up no less than 51 times. For good measure the Dooleys throw in 'And I Hope' 18 times, and 'And I Dream' 19 times. 'And I' is thus sung a total of 88 times. The authors of the song will remain anonymous to protect their reputations as lyricists of the first order.

● In 1968, American group the Human Beinz scaled the US charts with 'Nobody But Me', which employs the word 'No' over 100 times and 'Nobody' 46 times in a smidgeon over two minutes.

2. *Consecutive*

● The record with the most consecutively repeated phrase is Bill Withers' 'Ain't No Sunshine' wherein Withers sings 'I know' 26 times in a row.

● In the junior league, fifteen-year-old Stacy Lattisaw managed 'Go 'head' 16 times in a row in her 1980 smash 'Jump To The Beat'

20 EPIC LONG TRACKS

1. Sister Ray – Velvet Underground
2. Bat Out Of Hell – Meat Loaf
3. Marquee Moon – Television
4. Goin' Home – Rolling Stones
5. Sad Eyed Lady Of The Lowlands – Bob Dylan
6. When The Music's Over – The Doors
7. Free Bird – Lynyrd Skynyrd
8. Listen To The Lion – Van Morrison
9. MacArthur Park – Richard Harris
10. Layla – Derek and the Dominoes
11. The End – The Doors
12. Suite: Judy Blue Eyes – Crosby, Stills and Nash
13. A Quick One (While He's Away) – The Who
14. Macho City – Steve Miller
15. California Saga – The Beach Boys
16. In The Light – Led Zeppelin
17. Season Of The Witch – Al Kooper and Stephen Stills
18. Bohemian Rhapsody – Queen
19. Light My Fire – The Doors
20. Yours Is No Disgrace – Yes

This is a very subjective list. Many long tracks would tax the patience of the proverbial saints. However, those listed above were selected for their enduring ability to entertain rather than become soporific.

Queen

LONGEST WORD USED IN A HIT SONG

From repetitive lyrics to longest word used in a hit song – and here we have to call a no-contest as the leader is so far ahead of anything else. The longest word is a 116 letter Maori placename used in Quantum Jump's British hit 'The Lone Ranger'. It is: Taumata-whaka tangihangako ayayauotama teaturipuk akapikimau ngahoronuky pokaiwhenua kitanatahymat akooatan anookawami ckitoura. It means 'A hill whereon was played a flute of Tamatea, circumnavigator of lands for his lady love'.

As to why Quantum Jump should incorporate a Maori word into a song about the Lone Ranger, group leader Rupert Hine explains: 'There were two reasons for using that word. **First, we didn't have anything at the start to grab the listener's attention** . . . And then I came across the word, apparently the longest in the world and decided that, as nobody knows where the Lone Ranger is supposed to come from, we could put forward the theory that it was there.'

RECORDS WITH VERY LONG TITLES

1. Sir B. McKenzie's Daughter's Lament For The 77th Mounted Lancers' Retreat From The Straits Of Lock Knombe In The Year Of Our Lord 1727, On The Occasion Of The Announcement Of Her Marriage To The Laird Of Kinleakie – Fairport Convention
2. Ever See A Diver Kiss His Wife While The Bubbles Bounce About Above The Water – Shirley Ellis
3. I Wanna Find A Woman That'll Hold My Big Toe Till I Have To Go – Captain Beefheart
4. I've Been Carrying A Torch For You For So Long It's Burnt A Great Big Hole In My Heart – Nino Tempo and April Stevens
5. Claude Pellieu And J. J. Lebel Discuss The Early Verlaine Bread Crust Fragments – Fugs
6. Jeremiah Peabody's Poly-Unsaturated Quick Dissolving Fast Acting Pleasant Tasting Green And Purple Pills – Ray Stevens
7. Could The Christians Wait Five Minutes? The Lions Are Having A Draw – Man
8. You Wouldn't Know A Real Live True Love If It Walked Right Up And Kissed You On The Cheek And Said Hello Baby – Odyssey
9. Green With Envy, Purple With Passion, White With Anger, Scarlet With Fever, What Were You Doin' In His Arms Last Night Blues – Julie Rayne
10. Medley: Intro Venus/Sugar Sugar/No Reply/I'll Be Back/Drive My Car/Do You Want To Know A Secret/We Can Work It Out/I Should Have Known Better/Nowhere Man/You're Going To Lose That Girl/Stars On 45 – Star Sound

THE BEAT GOES ON – AND ON AND ON AND ON . . .

Disco 12-inchers are almost expected to last 10 minutes or more. Maximum Penetration's eponymous 1980 12-incher ran for 37 minutes and several PRT 12-inch releases in the UK have contained more than 40 minutes music. Most notable amongst these is Lipps Inc's 'Funky Town' which featured boringly long tracks by three other Casablanca acts on the flipside.

The length of 12-inchers is, however, usually balanced by the succinct nature of their little brother; the 7-inch single. But just occasionally lengthy 7-inch singles are released. Somewhat less often they chart. The following is a complete list of those of more than seven minutes duration which have made the UK singles chart.

Grand Funk Railroad

1. Inside Looking Out – Grand Funk Railroad .... 9 Min 27 Sec
A 33⅓ rpm release which charted for a single week in 1971.

2. Free Bird – Lynyrd Skynyrd .... 9 Min 00 Sec
A hit three times, proof of its long-standing status as a heavy-metal classic.

3. Biko – Peter Gabriel .... 8 Min 56 Sec
Another 33⅓ rpm single. Charisma wanted to edit it, but Gabriel rightly argued that to shorten it would be to lessen its impact as a political song for the sake of commerciality. Gabriel won the argument but the record garnered little airplay. Few programmers were willing to subject their listeners to such a lengthy and unrelenting protest song. It peaked at No. 38

4. O Superman – Laurie Anderson .... 8 Min 21 Sec
Readers of British music papers voted this their least favourite hit of 1981. It's easy to see why. The longest single ever to make the top ten.

5. Love Like A Man – Ten Years After .... 8 Min 08 Sec
Live 33⅓ rpm rendition of the Alvin Lee classic. The record is a double A-side with the 3 Min 14 Sec studio version of 'Love Like A Man' on the other side.

6. MacArthur Park – Richard Harris .... 7 Min 19 Sec
Jimmy Webb-penned epic which earned Harris a place in the top ten in 1966 and returned to the chart in 1972

7. Hey Jude – Beatles .... 7 Min 15 Sec
The longest number one single ever, bar none.

America is far less receptive to long singles than Britain and only three US hitmakers have broken the seven minute barrier.

1. American City Suite – Cashman & West .... 7 Min 35 Sec
2. MacArthur Park – Richard Harris .... 7 Min 19 Sec
3. Hey Jude – Beatles .... 7 Min 15 Sec

LONGEST HELD NOTE ON A HIT RECORD

18 seconds Lovely Day – Bill Withers (1978)
On his 1978 hit 'Lovely Day', Bill Withers took a deep breath and hung on to a note for eight seconds. Not bad – but he was only limbering up. Twice later in the same record, Bill's unwavering vocals held a note for eighteen seconds. Bill performed the feat without a safety net or a tape loop. The record reached No. 30 in America and a more worthy No. 7 in Britain.

16 seconds Dim All The Lights – Donna Summer (1979)
One of Giorgio Moroder's less inspired vehicles for the limitless talents of Donna Summer. 'Dim All The Lights' includes a powerful – nay, jarring – sixteen second burst from Donna. See if you can spot it. The disc could go no higher than No. 29 in Britain but reached No. 2 in America.

15½ seconds My Cup Runneth Over – Ed Ames (1967)
Ames held the record for eleven years until overhauled by Bill Withers. A No. 8 in America which bombed out in the UK.

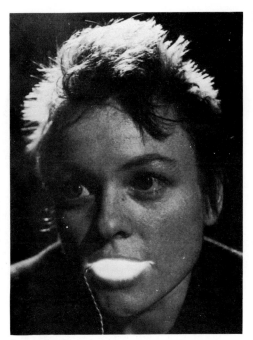
Laurie Anderson

Barbra Streisand

14 seconds No More Tears (Enough Is Enough) – Barbra Streisand (1979)
Streisand's unique collaboration with Donna Summer gave both girls plenty of room for vocal gymnastics. More of a duel than a duet. Many of Streisand's recordings prior to this featured notes sustained for ten, maybe twelve, seconds. On this she goes for the big one – a fourteen second note which bridges the slow and quick portions of the song. Streisand can not really be said to hold a note – she hovers in its immediate vicinity. Nevertheless, she's one of the great stylists of our time. 'No More Tears' topped the American chart for two weeks. In Britain it reached No. 3

57 VARIETIES OF
SILLY PSYCHEDELIC SONG

During the late 1960s, the psychedelic era provoked an alarming plethora of imaginative but meaningless song titles. This is a representative selection, many of which were inspired by the ingestion of various hallucinogenic substances. Or at least that's what their authors would like us to believe!

1. Ah Feel Like Ahcid – Captain Beefheart
2. Away Bounce My Bubbles – Country Joe and the Fish
3. Children Could Help Us Find The Way – Sunshine Company
4. Children Of The Sun – Dino Valente
5. Colored Balls Falling – Love.
6. Crystal Blue Persuasion – Tommy James and the Shondells
7. Effervescing Elephant – Syd Barrett
8. Faster Than The Speed Of Life – Steppenwolf
9. Flowers And Beads – Iron Butterfly
10. Flying On The Ground Is Wrong – Jefferson Airplane
11. From A Parachute – Third Rail
12. Fruit And Icebergs – Blue Cheer
13. Genetic Memory – Ralph Metzner
14. Get Me To The World On Time – Electric Prunes
15. Gilded Lamp Of Cosmos – Ultimate Spinach
16. Glimpses Of The Next World's World – Autosalvage
17. Golden Road To Unlimited Devotion – Grateful Dead
18. Granny Takes A Trip – Purple Gang
19. Have You Seen The Saucers? – Jefferson Airplane
20. How Lew Sin Ate – Dr West's Medicine Show and Jug Band
21. I Can Fly – The Herd
22. I Can Hear The Grass Grow – The Move
23. I Can Take You To The Sun – The Misunderstood
24. I Can't See Your Face In My Mind – The Doors
25. I'm Dying, Or Am I? – Eric Burdon and the Animals
26. In My Mind Lives A Forest – Rainy Daze
27. I Think I'm Going Weird – Art
28. I've Got Levitation – 13th Floor Elevators
29. Journey To The Centre Of Your Mind – Amboy Dukes
30. LSD – Pretty Things
31. Looking Through The Mirror – The Smoke
32. March Of The Flower Children – The Seeds
33. Mind Flowers – Ultimate Spinach
34. Mind Gardens – The Byrds
35. My Friend Jack Eats Sugar Lumps – The Smoke
36. My Mind Capsized – Holy Modal Rounders
37. Orange And Red Beams – Eric Burdon and the Animals
38. People Let's Freak Out – Belfast Gypsies
39. Pulsating Dream – Kaleidoscope
40. Rainy Day Mushroom Pillow – Strawberry Alarm Clock
41. Real Life Peppermint Dream – Tomorrow
42. Rose Petals, Incense And Kitten – The Association
43. Set Your Controls For The Heart Of The Sun – Pink Floyd
44. Shadows Breaking Over My Head – Left Banke
45. She's Too Much For My Mirror – Captain Beefheart
46. Sit With The Guru – Strawberry Alarm Clock
47. Spontaneous Apple Creation – Arthur Brown
48. Standing On The Moon – Lothar and the Hand People
49. Subliminal Sonic Laxative – Blue Magoos
50. Technicolor Dream – Alan Bown
51. The Beauty Of Time Is That It's Snowing – Steve Miller Band
52. Two Thousand Light Years From Home – Rolling Stones
53. Tripping – Pretty Things
54. When My Mind Is Not Live – Status Quo
55. Why Did I Get So High? – Peanut Butter Conspiracy
56. Why Is A Carrot More Orange Than An Orange? – Amboy Dukes
57. Wispy Paisley Skies – Fraternity of Man

NUGGETS

'Nuggets', subtitled 'Original Artyfacts (sic) From The First Psychedelic Era 1965–1968', is a double album generally regarded as the original blueprint for punk rock. The track listing of the album, which was compiled by Lenny Kaye, later guitarist and right-hand man to Patti Smith, follows . . .

Side One
1. I Had Too Much To Dream Last Night – The Electric Prunes
2. Dirty Water – The Standells
3. Night Time – The Strangeloves
4. Lies – The Knickerbockers
5. Respect – The Vagrants
6. A Public Execution – Mouse
7. No Time Like The Right Time – The Blues Project

Side Two
1. Oh Yeah – The Shadows of Knight
2. Pushin' Too Hard – The Seeds
3. Moulty – The Barbarians
4. Don't Look Back – The Remains
5. Invitation To Cry – The Magicians
6. Liar Liar – The Castaways
7. You're Gonna Miss Me – Thirteenth Floor Elevators

Side Three
1. Psychotic Reaction – Count Five
2. Hey Joe – The Leaves
3. Just Like Romeo And Juliet – Michael and the Messengers
4. Sugar And Spice – The Cryan Shames
5. Baby Please Don't Go – The Amboy Dukes
6. Tobacco Road – The Blues Magoos

Side Four
1. Let's Talk About Girls – The Chocolate Watch Band
2. Sit Down I Think I Love You – The Mojo Men
3. Run Run Run – The Third Rail
4. My World Fell Down – Sagittarius
5. Open My Eyes – The Nazz

6. Farmer John – The Premiers
7. It's-A-Happening – The Magic Mushrooms

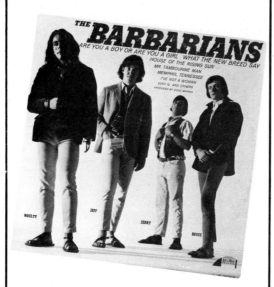

It may be of additional interest to note that among the latter day celebrities who emerged from these groups are:

1. Richard Gottehrer (The Strangeloves), now a record producer for Blondie among others.
2. Leslie West (né Weinstein) (The Vagrants), later a guitar hero with Mountain.
3. Al Kooper (The Blues Project), later formed Blood, Sweat and Tears, and is now a record producer who includes Lynyrd Skynyrd, the Tubes and David Essex among his credits.
4. Barry Tashian (The Remains) now plays with Emmylou Harris.
5. Gary Bonner (The Magicians) co-wrote 'Happy Together' and 'She'd Rather Be With Me', both big hits for the Turtles.
6. Roky Erickson (Thirteenth Floor Elevators) is now a solo artist with a devoted cult following.
7. Jim Pons (The Leaves), later joined the Turtles and the Mothers of Invention.
8. Ted Nugent (The Amboy Dukes) became a legend in his own mind, and that of numerous others as leader of his own group.
9. Bruce Johnston (Sagittarius) became a Beach Boy.
10. Todd Rundgren (The Nazz) became a wizard and a true star, a noted record producer, solo star and leader of his own group, Utopia.

10 ESSENTIAL BRITISH PUNK ROCK ALBUMS

(Original albums from the punk rock movement which most accurately convey the spirit of punk)

1. Never Mind The Bollocks, It's The Sex Pistols
2. Rattus Norvegicus – The Stranglers
3. In The City – The Jam
4. Third World War
5. The Black Album – The Damned
6. Give 'Em Enough Rope – The Clash
7. London Calling – The Clash
8. No More Heroes – The Stranglers
9. Tell Us the Truth – Sham 69
10. The Hollywood Brats

10 NON-ESSENTIAL BRITISH PUNK ALBUMS

(A series of albums which were either made by bandwagon jumpers or by bands who tried unsuccessfully to follow up their first album with a hastily recorded second LP.)

1. Slam – The Suburban Studs
2. Sid Sings – Sid Vicious
3. Crossing The Red Sea – The Adverts
4. This Is the Modern World – The Jam
5. Hersham Boys – Sham 69
6. Music For Pleasure – The Damned
7. Pure Mania – The Vibrators
8. V2 – The Vibrators
9. Everything by the Cockney Rejects
10. Everything by the Angelic Upstarts

Johnny Rotten

50 ESSENTIAL PUNK/NEW WAVE SINGLES OF THE SEVENTIES

1. Anarchy In The UK – Sex Pistols
2. Pretty Vacant – Sex Pistols
3. White Riot – The Clash
4. Gary Gilmore's Eyes – The Adverts
5. London's Burning – The Clash
6. Neat! Neat! Neat! – The Damned
7. In The City – The Jam
8. David Watts – The Jam
9. Down In The Tube Station At Midnight – The Jam
10. (Get A) Grip (On Yourself) – The Stranglers
11. Peaches – The Stranglers
12. Something Better Change – The Stranglers
13. No More Heroes – The Stranglers
14. Suspect Device – Stiff Little Fingers
15. Cranked Up Really High – Slaughter and the Dogs
16. Blank Generation – Richard Hell and the Voidoids
17. X Offender – Blondie
18. Little Johnny Jewel – Television
19. Marquee Moon – Television
20. Psycho Killer – Talking Heads
21. Chinese Rocks – The Heartbreakers
22. Spanish Stroll – Mink De Ville
23. Big A, Little A – Crass
24. Sheena Is A Punk Rocker – Ramones
25. Dirty Pictures – Radio Stars

Sham 69

26. You Can't Put Your Arms Round A Memory – Johnny Thunders
27. Do Anything You Wanna Do – Eddie and the Hot Rods
28. Is That All There Is – Cristina
29. Because The Night – Patti Smith Group
30. Holiday In Cambodia – Dead Kennedys
31. Prove It – Television
32. God Save The Queen – Sex Pistols
33. California Uber Alles – Dead Kennedys
34. In A Rut – The Ruts
35. Babylon's Burning – The Ruts
36. Rich Kids – Rich Kids
37. One Chord Wonders – The Adverts
38. Sex And Drugs And Rock'n'Roll – Ian Dury and the Blockheads
39. Inside Out – The Stiffs
40. I Don't Wanna – Sham 69
41. Sheep Farming In Barnet (EP) – Toyah
42. Get Over You – The Undertones
43. Sonic Reducer – Dead Boys
44. I'm On Fire – Dwight Twilley
45. Germ-Free Adolescence – X-Ray Spex
46. My Best Friend's Girl – The Cars
47. Dream Baby Dream – Suicide
48. Louisa On A Horse – John Otway
49. Bank Robber – The Clash
50. Denis – Blondie

COMEDY ALBUMS WHICH ARE FUNNY MORE THAN ONCE

1. A Child's Garden Of Grass ('A Pre-Legalisation Comedy')
2. At Last The 1948 Show (John Cleese, Tim Brooke-Taylor, Graham Chapman, Marty Feldman)
3. Chris Rush – First Rush
4. Inside Shelley Berman/Outside Shelley Berman/The Edge Of Shelley Berman
5. Woody Allen Volumes I and II
6. Mel Brooks and Carl Reiner 'The 2000 Year Old Man'.
7. Bob Newhart 'The Button Down Mind Of . . .'

8. David Frye 'I Am The President'.
9. Gerard Hoffnung 'Hoffnung'.
10. I'm Sorry, I'll Read That Again (Cleese, Brook-Taylor, Graeme Garden, Bill Oddie)
11. Fawlty Towers (John Cleese, Prunella Scales)
12. The Frost Report (David Frost, Cleese, Ronnie Barker, Ronnie Corbett)
13. Monty Python's Flying Circus (1st album)
14. Anything by Jasper Carrott

COMEDY ALBUMS WHICH ARE FUNNY LESS THAN TWICE

1. The Wit And Wisdom Of Ronald Reagan
2. The Uncle Dirty Primer
3. Having Fun With Elvis (Presley) On Stage
4. Toledo Window Box – George Carlin
5. The Second Coming – Vaughn Meader
6. The Crazy World Of Marty Feldman
7. The Third Woody Allen Album
8. David Steinberg – Disguised As A Normal Person
9. Murray Roman – You Can't Beat People Up And Have Them Say 'I Love You'
10. Anything by Blaster Bates
11. Peter Cook and Dudley Moore – Anything released since the 1960s
12. Peter Sellers – Sellers Market
13. Anything by the Barron Knights
14. National Lampoon – That's Not Funny, That's Sick
15. Anything by Bernard Wrigley
16. David Frye – Radio Free Nixon
17. Take Offs And Put Ons – George Carlin
18. The Sick Humour Of Lenny Bruce
19. Not The Nine O'Clock News
20. A Blind Man's Movie – Murray Roman
21. The Great White North – Bob and Doug MacKenzie

FOOTBALL HITS BY NON-TEAM ACTS

	Hst. Pos UK
1. Ally's Tartan Army – Andy Cameron (1978)	6
2. Nice One Cyril – Cockerel Chorus (1973)	14
3. We'll Be With You – Potters (1972)	34
4. Chelsea – Stamford Bridge (1970)	47

HITS BY FOOTBALL TEAMS/PLAYERS

Title/Artist/Date	Highest pos. (UK)
1. Back Home – England World Cup Squad (1970)	1
2. This Time (We'll Get It Right)/England, We'll Fly The Flag – England World Cup Squad (1982)	2
3. Olé Ola (Muler Brazileira) Rod Stewart and the Scotland World Cup Squad (1978)	4
4. We Have A Dream – Scotland World Cup Squad (1982)	5
5. Ossie's Dream (Spurs Are On Their Way To Wembley) – Tottenham Hotspur FA Cup Final Squad (1980–81)	5
6. Blue Is The Colour – Chelsea FC (1972)	5
7. Leeds United – Leeds United FC (1972)	10
8. We Can Do It – Liverpool FC (1977)	15
9. Good Old Arsenal – Arsenal FC (1971)	16
10. Tottenham, Tottenham – Tottenham Hotspur FA Cup Final Squad (1981–82)	19
11. Easy Easy – Scotland World Cup Squad (1974)	20
12. We've Got The Whole World In Our Hands – Nottingham Forest FC and Paper Lace (1978)	24
13. I'm Forever Blowing Bubbles – West Ham United FC (1975)	31
14. Head Over Heels In Love – Kevin Keegan (1979)	31
15. Manchester United – Manchester United FC (1976)	50

7. RADIO, TV & FILM

MOST INFLUENTIAL AMERICAN DJs

1. Alan Freed
2. Murray the K
3. Bruce Morrow (Cousin Brucie)
4. Tom Donohue
5. Wolfman Jack
6. Dr Demento
7. Kid Leo
8. Scott Muni
9. Steve Dahl
10. B. Mitchell Reed

Wolfman Jack

STUART COLMAN'S FIFTY FAVE INSTRUMENTALS
(in no particular order)

1. Behave Yourself – Booker T and the MGs
2. Knocked Out – Ernie Fields Orchestra
3. Image (Parts 1 and 2) – Hank Levine
4. Nervous Boogie – Paul Gayten
5. Blue Feeling – Chuck Berry
6. Ramrod – Duane Eddy
7. The Claw – Jerry Reed
8. Soul Motion – Don and Dewey
9. Teen Beat – Sandy Nelson
10. Memphis Soul Stew – King Curtis
11. Red River Rock – Johnny and the Hurricanes
12. Main Title Theme – Jet Harris
13. Hoppin' Mad – Plas Johnson
14. Hard Work – John Handy
15. FBI – The Shadows
16. You Can't Sit Down – Phil Upchurch
17. Goofin' Around – Bill Haley and the Comets
18. Mandrake – Mandrake
19. Black Bill – Dave Edmunds
20. Quite A Party – The Fireballs
21. Surfin' Steel – Chuck Berry
22. Oh Yeah – The Dakotas
23. Pink Panther Theme – Henry Mancini
24. Honky Tonk – Bill Doggett
25. Nothin' But The Soul – Junior Walker and the All Stars
26. Boo Boo Stick Beat – Chet Atkins
27. The Sandpaper Ballet – Leroy Anderson
28. Teasin' – Eric Clapton and Delaney Bramlett
29. Peter Gunn – Duane Eddy
30. Slim Jenkin's Place – Booker T and the MGs
31. Jam Up – Tommy Ridgeley
32. What's All That About – The Zephyrs
33. Funk 48 – The James Gang
34. Strictly For The Birds – Dudley Moore
35. Canvas – Brian Bennett
36. Stick Shift – The Duals
37. Funky Donkey – Pretty Purdie
38. Rumble – Link Wray
39. The Silver Meter – John Patton
40. Windy And Warm – Chet Atkins
41. 77 Sunset Strip – Don Ralke
42. Baby Elephant Walk – Henry Mancini
43. Grab This Thing – The Mar Keys
44. Sleep Walk – Santo and Johnny
45. MG Blues – Jimmy McGriff
46. Nola – Les Paul
47. Jeff's Boogie – Jeff Beck
48. Prayer Meetin' – Willie Mitchell
49. No Trespassing – The Ventures
50. Spinning Rock Boogie – Hank C. Burnette

Stuart Colman hosts 'Echoes,' a BBC Radio London programme substantially devoted to great records of the past with particular emphasis on the first rock'n'roll era.

Dr. Demento

Frank Sinatra

PAUL GAMBACCINI'S TOP FIFTY ALL TIME FAVOURITES

Paul Gambaccini, an American who lives in London, has written for *Rolling Stone*, and has appeared as host of a BBC Radio One American chart programme for several years. He has also written several published books, including co-authoring the highly successful *Guinness Book of British Hit Singles*. Records are listed alphabetically, not by merit.

1.	All The Way	Frank Sinatra
2.	American Pie	Don McLean
3.	At The Hop	Danny and the Juniors
4.	Baker Street	Gerry Rafferty
5.	Band Of Gold	Freda Payne
6.	Born To Run	Bruce Springsteen
7.	Can I Get A Witness	Marvin Gaye
8.	City Of New Orleans	Arlo Guthrie
9.	Cry Baby	Garnett Mimms and the Enchanters
10.	Don't Make Me Over	Dionne Warwick
11.	Eleanor Rigby	The Beatles
12.	The French Song	Lucille Starr
13.	Gimme Some Lovin'	Spencer Davis Group
14.	Gone	Ferlin Husky
15.	He's A Rebel	The Crystals
16.	Hey Jude	The Beatles
17.	(I Can't Get No) Satisfaction	The Rolling Stones
18.	I Can't Help Myself	The Four Tops
19.	I Heard It Through The Grapevine	Gladys Knight and the Pips
20.	I Wonder Why	Dion and the Belmonts
21.	I'm Gonna Be Strong	Gene Pitney
22.	(I Know) I'm Losing You	The Temptations
23.	I've Been Loving You Too Long	Otis Redding
24.	Like A Rolling Stone	Bob Dylan
25.	Light My Fire	The Doors
26.	MacArthur Park	Richard Harris
27.	Mala Femmena	Jimmy Roselli
28.	Manhattan Spiritual	Reg Owen
29.	Mr Bojangles	Jerry Jeff Walker
30.	Non, Je Ne Regrette Rien	Edith Piaf
31.	Penny Lane	The Beatles
32.	Rat Trap	Boomtown Rats
33.	The Second Time Around	Shalamar
34.	September Song	Walter Huston
35.	So Rare	Jimmy Dorsey
36.	Sorry (I Ran All the Way Home)	The Impalas
37.	Sound Of Silence	Simon and Garfunkel
38.	Sultans Of Swing	Dire Straits
39.	Tammy	Debbie Reynolds
40.	Teardrops	Lee Andrews and the Hearts
41.	This Is My Prayer	Theola Kilgore
42.	Tired of Being Alone	Al Green
43.	Tonight	Ferrante and Teicher

44.	Tracks Of My Tears	Smokey Robinson and the Miracles
45.	Uptight	Stevie Wonder
46.	Urge For Going	Tom Rush
47.	What Becomes Of The Brokenhearted	Jimmy Ruffin
48.	Where Did Our Love Go	The Supremes
49.	Yesterday	The Beatles
50.	You've Lost That Lovin' Feeling	The Righteous Brothers

John Peel

JOHN PEEL'S FESTIVE FIFTY

John Peel's Festive Fifty is compiled at the end of each year from nominations provided by his listeners. They are then broadcast on BBC Radio One.

1978	1979	1980	1981			
–	–	2	1	Atmosphere	Joy Division
1	1	1	2	Anarchy In The UK	Sex Pistols
–	–	3	3	Love Will Tear Us Apart	Joy Division
–	–	–	4	Ceremony	New Order
–	–	20	5	New Dawn Fades	Joy Division
10	2	7	6	Teenage Kicks	Undertones
–	–	14	7	Decades	Joy Division
–	–	18	8	A Forest	Cure
–	–	6	9	Holiday In Cambodia	Dead Kennedys
7	3	5	10	White Man In Hammersmith Palais	Clash
–	–	64	11	Dead Souls	Joy Division
13	10	8	12	New Rose	Damned
24	4	4	13	Down In The Tube-Station	Jam
–	–	10	14	Transmission	Joy Division
–	–	–	15	Dead Pop-Stars	Altered Images
11	6	9	16	Alternative Ulster	Stiff Little Fingers
18	14	12	17	Holidays In The Sun	Sex Pistols
2	5	15	18	Complete Control	Clash
–	–	–	19	Release The Bats	Birthday Party
–	12	17	20	Get Over You	Undertones
–	–	–	21	Ghost Town	Specials
–	–	–	22	The 'Sweetest Girl'	Scritti Politti
–	–	13	23	Going Underground	Jam
–	15	16	24	Johnny Was	Stiff Little Fingers
–	–	–	25	Legion	Theatre of Hate
9	9	11	26	Public Image	Public Image Ltd
–	–	35	27	Requiem	Killing Joke
–	–	–	28	Follow The Leaders	Killing Joke
–	–	–	29	No Fascist Groove Thang	Heaven 17
–	–	38	30	Fiery Jack	Fall
–	11	19	31	In A Rut	Ruts
4	8	24	32	Suspect Device	Stiff Little Fingers
–	–	26	33	How I Wrote 'Elastic man'	Fall
–	–	–	34	O Superman	Laurie Anderson
43	42	37	35	Jigsaw Feeling	Siouxsie and the Banshees
–	–	–	36	Remembrance Day	B-Movie
–	–	–	37	Israel	Siouxsie and the Banshees

3	13	25	38	God Save The Queen	Sex Pistols
–	–	–	39	Papa's Got A Brand New Pigbag	Pigbag
–	35	45	40	Icon	Siouxsie and the Banshees
17	20	28	41	Another Girl, Another Planet	Only Ones
–	33	31	42	California Uber Alles	Dead Kennedys
–	–	41	43	Twenty-Four Hours	Joy Division
–	–	–	44	Isolation	Joy Division
–	–	36	45	Psyche	Killing Joke
–	–	–	46	Over The Wall	Echo and the Bunnymen
–	–	–	47	Lie, Dream Of A Casino Soul	Fall
–	–	–	48	Procession	New Order
41	38	44	49	Switch	Siouxsie and the Banshees
–	–	–	50	Happy Birthday	Altered Images

ANDY PEEBLES' 10 MOTOWN FAVOURITES

1. Ain't That Peculiar? – Marvin Gaye
2. Girl, Why Do You Wanna' Make Me Blue? – The Temptations
3. Good Lovin' Is Just A Dime Away – The Originals
4. Baby, I Need Your Lovin' – The Four Tops
5. Alfie – Eivets Rednow
6. Get Ready For The Get Down – Willie Hutch
7. These Things Will Keep Me Lovin' You – The Velvettes
8. What's Going On – Marvin Gaye
9. One Out Of Every Six – Thelma Houston
10. Hey Girl – The Temptations

Andy Peebles is a Radio One Disc Jockey, whose fame became world wide after his long taped interview with John Lennon and Yoko Ono, which took place only hours before Lennon's murder. The results were broadcast internationally and also published in book form as *The Lennon Tapes* (BBC Publications).

ANDY PEEBLES 10 FAVOURITES FROM SOUL TRAIN (PICCADILLY RADIO 1974–78)

1. Kiss My Love Goodbye – Bettye Swann
2. 'Cause I Love You – Larry Williams
3. Fish Ain't Bitin' – Lamont Dozier
4. Don't Ask My Neighbour – The Emotions
5. Bad Luck – Harold Melvin and the Blue Notes
6. Reason To Survive – The Rance Allen Group
7. Once You Get Started – Rufus
8. Give The Little Man A Great Big Hand – William DeVaughn
9. Both Ends Against The Middle – Jackie Moore
10. Good Things Don't Last Forever – Ecstasy, Passion and Pain

Before becoming a member of BBC Radio One's disc jockey team, Andy Peebles achieved local fame with his very popular 'Soul Train' radio show on Piccadilly Radio in Manchester.

The Four Tops

TEMPTATIONS

MIKE READ'S FAVOURITE 50 TRACKS

1. Survival – Yes
2. Grantchester Meadows – Pink Floyd
3. Tuesday Afternoon – Moody Blues
4. Since I Lost My Baby – The Action
5. Waterloo Sunset – The Kinks
6. The Sun Ain't Gonna' Shine Anymore – The Walker Brothers
7. Montague Terrace (In Blue) – Scott Walker
8. Hot Rod USA – Rip Chords
9. I Found A Girl – Jan and Dean
10. Woman – John Lennon
11. Across The Universe – The Beatles
12. It's Now Or Never – Elvis Presley
13. Apache – The Shadows
14. Since I Don't Have You – The Skylines
15. It's Over – Roy Orbison
16. Hushabye – The Mystics
17. Girl Don't Tell Me – The Beach Boys
18. The Next Time – Cliff Richard
19. Paper Plane – Status Quo
20. Wedding Bells (This Old Gang Of Mine) – Gene Vincent
21. Down In The Park – Tubeway Army
22. Eton Rifles – The Jam
23. Ca Plane Pour Moi – Plastic Bertrand
24. All The Young Dudes – Mott the Hoople
25. Play With Fire/The Last Time – Rolling Stones
26. A Day In The Life – The Beatles
27. My Friend Jack – Smoke
28. I'd Rather Be Out With The Boys – Toggery Five
29. Like I've Never Been Gone – Billy Fury
30. It's Almost Tomorrow – Dreamweavers
31. My Girl The Month Of May – Dion
32. Lights Out – Jerry Byrne
33. Think Of Me – Eddie Cochran
34. Listen To Me – Buddy Holly
35. Positively 4th Street – Bob Dylan
36. Let It Be Me – Everly Brothers
37. Ain't Too Proud To Beg – Temptations
38. For No One – The Beatles
39. Paper Sun – Traffic
40. How Sweet It Is – Junior Walker and the All Stars
41. Dambusters – The Central Band of the Royal Air Force
42. Oliver's Army – Elvis Costello
43. Blitzkrieg Bop – The Ramones
44. Anyway, Anyhow, Anywhere – The Who
45. Sky Pilot – Eric Burdon
46. It's All Too Much – Steve Hillage
47. Dual Carriageway Pain – Taste
48. Close Another Door – The Bee Gees
49. Try A Little Tenderness – Percy Sledge
50. Castles in the Air – Don McLean

Eddie Cochran

BBC DJ and TV presenter Mike Read adds, 'The broader one's taste in music, the more difficult it is to compile a list of favourites. I suppose I could have added at least a dozen classic Beatle tracks, half a dozen Jam tracks, more early Floyd, more soul and Motown, some of Bowie's classics, but you've got to stop somewhere.'

Gene Vincent

CRUISIN'

GRT Records released a series of LPs which reflected the style of one of the most popular radio stations in America for each year from 1955–67, each one featuring a notable disc jockey from the appropriate station introducing some of the year's hits.

1955	KSAN, San Francisco	'Jumpin'' George Oxford
1956	WKMH, Detroit	Robin Seymour
1957	WIBG, Philadelphia	Joe Niagara
1958	WIL, St Louis	Jack Carney
1959	KGFJ, Los Angeles	Hunter Hancock
1960	WKBW, Buffalo	Dick Biondi
1961	WMEX, Boston	Arnie 'Woo Woo' Ginsburg
1962	KLIF, Dallas	Russ 'Weird Beard' Knight
1963	WMCA, New York	B. Mitchell Reed
1964	WHK, Cleveland	Johnny Holliday
1965	KHJ, Los Angeles	Robert W. Morgan
1966	KJR, Seattle	Pat O'Day
1967	WQXI, Atlanta	Dr Don Rose

ALL TIME TOP 30 COMPILED BY DRAKE-CHENAULT

Drake-Chenault is an American company specializing in syndicated radio shows. Listeners to one such show, *The Weekly Top Thirty*, were invited to select their three favourite tracks. From over 20,000 respondents in America, Canada, New Zealand and Australia came the following *All Time Top Thirty* which was aired on 4 July 1980.

1. Stairway To Heaven – Led Zeppelin
2. Mandy – Barry Manilow
3. Call Me – Blondie
4. Hey Jude – Beatles
5. Another Brick In The Wall (Part II) – Pink Floyd
6. The Way We Were – Barbra Streisand
7. Stayin' Alive – Bee Gees
8. Babe – Styx
9. Bridge Over Troubled Water – Simon and Garfunkel
10. Three Times A Lady – Commodores
11. How Deep Is Your Love – Bee Gees
12. Yesterday – Beatles
13. Hotel California – Eagles
14. I Write The Songs – Barry Manilow
15. You Light Up My Life – Debby Boone
16. Just The Way You Are – Billy Joel
17. Still – Commodores
18. American Pie – Don McLean
19. If – Bread
20. Love Theme From *A Star Is Born* ('Evergreen') – Barbra Streisand
21. Dreams – Fleetwood Mac
22. Colour My World – Chicago
23. Night Fever – Bee Gees
24. On The Radio – Donna Summer
25. Could It Be Magic – Barry Manilow
26. I Honestly Love You – Olivia Newton-John
27. Reunited – Peaches and Herb
28. Do Ya' Think I'm Sexy – Rod Stewart
29. You Don't Bring Me Flowers – Barbra (Streisand) and Neil (Diamond)
30. I Will Survive – Gloria Gaynor

IRELAND'S ALL TIME TOP 30

Radio Telefis Eirann producer Robbie Irwin and presenter Marty Whelan compiled the following list of records from over 5,000 listeners' votes during the summer of 1980.

1. Bohemian Rhapsody – Queen
2. Baker Street – Gerry Rafferty
3. Nights In White Satin – Moody Blues
4. A Whiter Shade Of Pale – Procol Harum
5. Hotel California – Eagles
6. I'm Not In Love – 10CC
7. Honey – Bobby Goldsboro
8. Bridge Over Troubled Water – Simon and Garfunkel
9. I Don't Like Mondays – Boomtown Rats
10. Satisfaction – Rolling Stones
11. Two Out Of Three Ain't Bad – Meat Loaf
12. The House Of The Rising Sun – Animals
13. Rat Trap – Boomtown Rats
14. Lyin' Eyes – Eagles
15. Mull Of Kintyre – Wings
16. Stairway To Heaven – Led Zeppelin
17. Sailing – Rod Stewart
18. Hey Jude – Beatles
19. Bright Eyes – Art Garfunkel
20. Bat Out Of Hell – Meat Loaf
21. We Don't Talk Any More – Cliff Richard
22. American Pie – Don McLean

The Bee Gees

23. If You Leave Me Now – Chicago
24. Yesterday – Beatles
25. Layla – Derek and the Dominoes
26. Freebird – Lynyrd Skynyrd
27. Where Do You Go To My Lovely – Peter Sarstedt
28. At Seventeen – Janis Ian
29. Without You – Nilsson
30. Are You Lonesome Tonight – Elvis Presley

RADIO ONE'S FIRST PROGRAMME

BBC Radio One was launched at 7 am on Saturday 30 September 1967. The first programme was *The Tony Blackburn Show*, described in BBC minutes as 'A daily disc delivery' and produced by Johnny Beerling. Legend has it that the first record played on the new station was the Move's 'Flowers In The Rain' – not so! That honour fell to John Dankworth's 'Beefeaters' – Blackburn's theme in those far off days when Radio One shows had themes. After thirty seconds 'Beefeaters' gave way to 'Flowers In The Rain', the first record to be played *in full* on Radio One. The records featured on the ninety minute show were:

1. Beefeaters – John Dankworth
2. Flowers In The Rain – Move
3. Massachusetts – Bee Gees
4. Even The Bad Times Are Good – Tremeloes

Eric Burdon

5. Fakin' It – Simon and Garfunkel
6. The Day I Met Marie – Cliff Richard
7. You Can't Hurry Love – Supremes
8. The Last Waltz – Engelbert Humperdinck
9. Baby Now That I've Found You – Foundations
10. Good Times – Eric Burdon and the Animals
11. A Banda (Chico Bur Ve De Hollanda) – Herb Alpert and the Tijuana Brass
12. I Feel Love Comin' On – Felice Taylor
13. How Can I Be Sure – Young Rascals
14. Major To Minor – Settlers
15. Homburg – Procol Harum
16. You Keep Running Away – Four Tops
17. Let's Go To San Francisco – Flowerpot Men
18. Handy Man – Jimmy Jones
19. You Know What I Mean – Turtles
20. The House That Jack Built – Alan Price Set
21. Excerpt From A Teenage Opera – Keith West
22. Reflections – Diana Ross and the Supremes
23. King Midas In Reverse – Hollies
24. Ode To Billy Joe – Bobbie Gentry
25. Then He Kissed Me – Crystals
26. Anything Goes – Harpers Bizarre
27. The Letter – Box Tops
28. Beefeaters – John Dankworth

THE BEATLES AT THE BEEB

At the start of their career, the Beatles, much like most other up and coming British bands, recorded 'sessions' for the BBC – a session has the dual advantage of not attracting 'needle time' payments by the BBC (a body purportedly representing the various record companies collects often substantial fees from the Corporation for records played on the air) and allowing an act to recreate a part of their repertoire under BBC auspices. Sessions are used extensively, although few have become so vital in historical terms as those by the

Beatles. The following list of tracks recorded by the Fab Four is taken from a bootleg titled 'The Beatles Broadcasts', whose sleeve contains this interesting note: 'Even though these particular tracks survived BBC company house cleanings for nearly two decades, there has been some deterioration in sound due to chemical changes on the tapes themselves. Using the highest quality equipment available, every effort has been made to restore them to their original condition.' (Incidentally, the authors have no idea where copies of any bootlegs mentioned in this book can be obtained, and correspondence on this subject will *not* be welcome...)

1. Opening Theme; Pop Go The Beatles
2. Long Tall Sally
3. Carol
4. Soldier Of Love (Lay Down Your Arms)
5. Lend Me Your Comb
6. Clarabella
7. Memphis
8. I Got A Woman
9. Sure To Fall
10. Do You Want To Know A Secret?
11. Hippy Hippy Shake
12. Till There Was You
13. Matchbox
14. I'm A Loser
15. She's A Woman
16. I Feel Fine
17. Everybody's Trying To Be My Baby
18. I'll Follow The Sun

CAPITAL RADIO'S HALL OF FAME 1953–78

The 50 best records of the past 25 years according to the votes of London's Capital Radio listeners.

1. I'm Not In Love – 10CC
2. Bridge Over Troubled Water – Simon and Garfunkel
3. Nights In White Satin – The Moody Blues
4. A Whiter Shade Of Pale – Procol Harum

Don Maclean

The Eagles

Procul Harum

5. Bohemian Rhapsody – Queen
6. Layla – Derek and the Dominoes
7. Hey Jude – The Beatles
8. Maggie May – Rod Stewart
9. Jailhouse Rock – Elvis Presley
10. Stairway To Heaven – Led Zeppelin
11. Without You – Nilsson
12. House Of The Rising Sun – The Animals
13. All Right Now – Free
14. Brown Sugar – The Rolling Stones
15. Albatross – Fleetwood Mac
16. Good Vibrations – The Beach Boys
17. Lay Lady Lay – Bob Dylan
18. If You Leave Me Now – Chicago
19. Satisfaction – The Rolling Stones

20. Hotel California – The Eagles
21. Your Song – Elton John
22. Sailing – Rod Stewart
23. American Pie – Don McLean
24. River Deep, Mountain High – Ike and Tina Turner
25. Rock Around The Clock – Bill Haley
26. Like A Rolling Stone – Bob Dylan
27. Yesterday – The Beatles
28. Let It Be – The Beatles
29. The Sound Of Silence – Simon and Garfunkel
30. Penny Lane/Strawberry Fields Forever – The Beatles
31. You've Lost That Lovin' Feelin' – The Righteous Brothers

The Righteous Brothers

32. Vincent – Don Maclean
33. Space Oddity – David Bowie
34. Night Fever – The Bee Gees
35. I Heard It Through The Grapevine – Marvin Gaye
36. The Air That I Breathe – The Hollies
37. The First Time Ever I Saw Your Face – Roberta Flack
38. The Long And Winding Road – The Beatles
39. Imagine – John Lennon
40. Samba Pa Ti – Santana
41. How Deep Is Your Love – The Bee Gees
42. Blueberry Hill – Fats Domino
43. In The Ghetto – Elvis Presley
44. My Generation – The Who
45. Get Back – The Beatles

The Beatles

46. Heartbreak Hotel – Elvis Presley
47. Easy – The Commodores
48. Dock Of The Bay – Otis Redding
49. My Sweet Lord – George Harrison
50. Life On Mars – David Bowie

NEW YORK'S TOP 50

Compiled from listeners' polls of WCBS–FM

1. In The Still Of The Night – Five Satins (1956)
2. Earth Angel – Penguins (1955)
3. Tonight Tonight – Mello Kings (1957)
4. My Way – Elvis Presley (1977)
5. Can't Help Falling In Love – Elvis Presley (1962)
6. Since I Don't Have You – Skyliners (1959)
7. Mack The Knife – Bobby Darin (1959)
8. Love Me Tender – Elvis Presley (1956)
9. Rock Around The Clock – Bill Haley and His Comets (1955)
10. Sixteen Candles – Crests (1959)
11. Hey Jude – Beatles (1968)
12. Rag Doll – Four Seasons (1964)
13. The Things I Love – Fidelitys (1958)
14. Cara Mia – Jay and the Americans (1965)
15. The Wonder Of You – Elvis Presley (1970)
16. Imagine – John Lennon (1971)
17. Sherry – Four Seasons (1962)
18. Great Pretender – Platters (1956)
19. You Belong To Me – Duprees (1962)
20. Jailhouse Rock – Elvis Presley (1957)
21. My Way – Frank Sinatra (1969)
22. Little Star – Elegants (1958)
23. Yesterday – Beatles (1965)
24. Runaround Sue – Dion (1961)
25. Are You Lonesome Tonight – Elvis Presley (1960)
26. A Teenager In Love – Dion and the Belmonts (1959)
27. New York, New York – Frank Sinatra (1980)
28. Satisfaction – Rolling Stones (1965)
29. Don't Be Cruel – Elvis Presley (1956)
30. Worst That Could Happen – Brooklyn Bridge (1969)
31. Come Go With Me – Del Vikings (1957)
32. My Prayer – Platters (1956)
33. Why Do Fools Fall In Love – Frankie Lymon and the Teenagers (1956)
34. Dawn (Go Away) – Four Seasons (1964)
35. Blueberry Hill – Fats Domino (1956)
36. Tears On My Pillow – Little Anthony and the Imperials (1958)
37. Suspicious Minds – Elvis Presley (1969)
38. Deserie – Charts (1957)
39. Could This Be Magic – Dubs (1957)
40. American Pie – Don McLean (1972)
41. The Wanderer – Dion (1962)
42. Silhouettes – Rays (1962)
43. I Want To Hold Your Hand – Beatles (1964)
44. Light My Fire – Doors (1967)
45. Endless Love – Diana Ross and Lionel Richie (1981)
46. Image Of A Girl – Safaris (1960)
47. Bridge Over Troubled Water – Simon and Garfunkel (1970)
48. Stardust – Billy Ward and the Dominos (1957)
49. One Summer Night – Danleers (1958)
50. Whispering Bells – Del Vikings (1957)

Jim Morrison

TELEVISION THEMES WRITTEN BY TONY HATCH

Tony Hatch was one of Britain's most successful producers in the 1960s, producing numerous chart acts, notably Petula Clark, for whom he also wrote, and the Searchers. In recent years he has concentrated on publishing and is now living in Australia with his wife Jackie Trent. Throughout his career he has supplemented his earnings by composing television programme theme tunes.

1. *Crossroads*
2. *Emmerdale Farm*
3. *Man Alive*
4. *Sportsnight*
5. *Hadleigh*
6. *Backs To The Land*
7. *Love Story*
8. *Out Of This World*
9. *Mr And Mrs*

THE FIRST *TOP OF THE POPS* . . .

was transmitted at 6.35 pm on Wednesday 1 January 1964, live from Manchester. The opening credits were accompanied by a seventeen second drumroll from top session drummer Bobby Midgley. The programme was hosted by Jimmy Savile and Denise Sampey spun the discs. Alan Freeman made a guest appearance trailing the following week's show.

Appearing in the studio miming to their records were:

Dusty Springfield ('I Only Want To Be With You')

The Rolling Stones ('I Wanna Be Your Man')
The Dave Clark Five ('Glad All Over')
The Hollies ('Stay')
The Swinging Blue Jeans ('Hippy Hippy Shake')

Appearing in specially filmed sequences were:
Cliff Richard and the Shadows ('Don't Talk To Him')
Freddie and the Dreamers ('You Were Made For Me')

The studio audience were shown dancing to Gene Pitney's '24 Hours From Tulsa' and 'She Loves You' by the Beatles who were also heard performing 'I Wanna Hold Your Hand' over '219 feet of standard BBC Beatles footage'!

20 ROCK-ORIENTED MOVIES (OF VARYING QUALITY) WHICH OUGHT TO BE SEEN

The Blackboard Jungle (1955) – The first movie to feature rock-as-we-know-it. Bill Haley plays 'Rock Around The Clock' behind the main titles and new teacher Glenn Ford gets titled 'Daddy-O' and 'Teach' by his juvenile roughnecks. Wonderful stuff.

Rock Around The Clock (1956) – Flung together with indecent haste by quick-buck flickmaker Sam Katzman to cash in on Haley's popularity. The first real rock'n'roll movie and one that caused riots wherever it was screened. Pure crapola really.

The Girl Can't Help It (1956) – Colour, a director of some quality, a script boasting intentional humour – and performances from Little Richard, Fats Domino, Gene Vincent and Eddie Cochran. Whoopee!

Jailhouse Rock (1957) – Not that hot – though it's still one of Elvis's best. Which indicates what a right old load of garbage he was normally lumbered with!

Jimmy Savile on 'Top of the Pops'

Jazz On A Summer's Day (1960) – The Newport Jazz Festival of 1958 – with Chuck Berry duckwalking his way to glory. The first concert movie – and still one of the best.

Beach Party (1963) – Back to inanity again as hirsute Prof. Robert Cummings studies the mating habits of sickening surfers. Could such an offering spawn a whole series of imitators providing employment for everyone from Brian Wilson through to Stevie Wonder and Little Richard? Surprisingly – yes.

Scorpio Rising (1963) – Twenty-five mins filled with biker-inspired images set against an innovative background of rock records. An underground classic never intended to darken the door at the Granada, Tooting (RIP).

A Hard Day's Night (1964) – The best film about a band ever made? Possibly. And the best band that ever was? Probably. The Beatles plus director Dick Lester – like England and Alf Ramsey in '66.

Help! (1965) – More Beatles, more Dick Lester – this time with additional colour. Lotsa Goon-inspired humour and songs like 'Ticket To Ride', 'Help', 'You're Gonna Lose That Girl' and 'You've Got To Hide Your Love Away'. Can you imagine anyone complaining?

Don't Look Back (1965) – *Cinéma-verité* glimpse of Bob Dylan's 1965 UK tour and the most revealing Zim-cine of them all. Dylan later had it withdrawn to clear the way for *Renaldo And Clara*. Twit.

Performance (1968) – Complex treatment (thank you, Harold Pinter) of an on-the-run-gangster tale which provided Mick Jagger with the opportunity to make the grade as a thespian. Bowie should be so lucky!

Easy Rider (1969) – America in the late sixties as seen through the dust-filled eyes of a brace of dope-dealing, gleam-machine sit-astriders. Scores of others followed in the wake of director-actor Dennis Hop-

per's tyre-tracks – but no-one else caught the feel of the period to such perfection.

Woodstock (1970) – Music amid the mud. Starring every rock star in the universe and 400,000 punters. Replete with stereo sound and split screen techniques. *The* concert movie, in fact.

Shaft (1971) – Not really that much of a deal – just a super-dude all-actioner of considerable mayhem content. But it established a genre and featured a great score by Isaac Hayes – though a certain Tom McIntosh later claimed that he had penned most of it.

The Harder They Come (1972) – The film that caused Jamaican box-office tills to move into overdrive. Rudies, rip-offs, reggae and Jimmy Cliff.

American Graffiti (1973) – The world of hamburger heavens, cruisin' and Saturday night hops, peopled by small town America and the kids of '62. Lashings of humour and a non-stop musical backdrop of oldies but goodies. Another of the great unbeatables.

The Last Waltz (1978) – The Band and assorted superstars in a better-class concert flick that poses the question – why hasn't Robbie Robertson yet made it as a movie idol?

Jubilee (1978) – Punk strikes lucky – caught soon after birth by Derek Jarman and not some seventies' equivalent of Sam Katzman. The then unknowns featured include Adam Ant, Toyah and Siouxsie and the Banshees. Not a bad talent-spotting job!

Quadrophenia (1979) – The Who's mighty meaty concept job given the kiss of life by director Franc Roddam. It's fault-filled in minor ways but generally well ahead of the game.

Babylon (1980) – Brixton, the world of suss and sound-system men. An ultimately frightening movie that benefits from a fit-tight score, courtesy of Dennis Bovell.

List donated by Fred Dellar, journeyman rock journalist and writer of several substantial books on country music, as well as the highly recommended *NME Guide To Rock Cinema* (Hamlyn, 1981).

SONGS FEATURED IN 'THE GIRL CAN'T HELP IT'

1. The Girl Can't Help It – Little Richard
2. Ready Teddy – Little Richard
3. She's Got It – Little Richard
4. Cool It Baby – Eddie Fontaine
5. A Cinnamon Sinner (Selling Lollipop Lies) – The Chuckles
6. Spread The Gospel, Spread The Word – Abby Lincoln
7. Be Bop-A-Lula – Gene Vincent
8. Twenty Flight Rock – Eddie Cochran
9. You're My Idea Of Love – Johnny Olenn
10. I Ain't Gonna Cry No More – Johnny Olenn
11. Rockin' Is My Business – The Treniers
12. Cry Me A River – Julie London
13. Blue Monday – Fats Domino
14. You'll Never Never Know – The Platters
15. Rock Around The Rockpile – Ray Anthony
16. Rock Around The Rockpile –

Edmond O'Brien
17. Every Time It Happens – Jayne Mansfield

The Girl Can't Help It was the finest rock'n'roll film of the 1950s, and arguably of all time. Made in 1956, it was the first, and possibly only rock'n'roll movie actually to possess a story line less flimsy than a spider's web. This list was prepared via the good offices of that unlikely duo, Lee Kristofferson and Paul McCartney, who have probably never met, although both are British recording artists.

BEACH BOYS SONGS USED FOR COMMERCIALS

1. Barbara Ann – used for Club candy bar (UK)
2. California Girls – used for Clairol shampoo (UK)
3. Fun, Fun, Fun – used for Kodak film (US)
4. Good Vibrations – used for Sunkist soda (US)
5. This Whole World – used for TWA (US)
6. Wouldn't It Be Nice? – used for Persil washing powder (UK)

(List by Andrew Doe.)

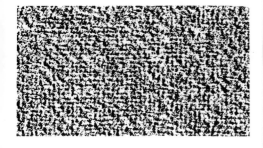

GREAT GRAFFITI

In 1973, the excellent film *American Graffiti* was released, containing a well chosen selection of oldies which provided a nostalgic backdrop to a day in the life of half a dozen American teenagers. Listed below

TV COMMERCIALS WHICH BECAME UK HIT SINGLES

Hst. Pos.	Artist	Title	Product
40	Peter Blake	Lipsmackin' Rock'n'Rollin'	Pepsi Cola
1	New Seekers	I'd Like To Teach The World To Sing	Coca Cola
37	Lyn Paul	It Oughta Sell A Million	Coca Cola
3	David Dundas	Jeans On	Brutus Jeans
35	Kenny Williams	(You're) Fabulous Babe	'Babe' perfume
30	Danny Williams	Dancin' Easy	Martini
21	White Plains	Step Into A Dream	Butlins
52	Ronnie Bond	It's Written On Your Body	Levi Jeans
13	Chas and Dave	Rabbit	Courage Beer
52	Chas and Dave	Strummin'	Courage Beer
20	Chas and Dave	Gertcha	Courage Beer
55	Chas and Dave	The Sideboard Song	Courage Beer
62	Cirrus	Rollin' On	Yorkie Bar

COUNTRY-STYLE COMMERCIALS

C&W stars featured on American television advertisements.

1. Eddie Rabbitt (Miller Beer)
2. Rex Allen Jr (Ford Farm Tractors)
3. Lynn Anderson (Nabisco Country Crackers)
4. Jim Ed Brown (Dollar General Stores)
5. Ed Bruce (Big Duke Chewing Tobacco)
6. Janie Fricke (Budweiser Beer)
7. Crystal Gayle (Avon)
8. Mickey Gilley (Schlitz Beer and Gilley's Western Wear)
9. Tom T. Hall (Purina Puppy Chow and Tyson Foods)
10. Roger Miller (General Foods Mellow Roast Coffee)
11. Charley Pride (Chicken Franks)
12. Jerry Reed (Laredo Boots, Mercury Outboard Motors and Truckstops of America)
13. Charlie Rich (Dr Pepper)
14. T. G. Sheppard (Shure Instruments)
15. The Statler Brothers (Kraft Miracle Margarine)
16. Mel Tillis (What-A-Burger)
17. Freddy Fender (McDonald's Hamburgers. This ad is in Spanish, and is aimed at the large Spanish-American population living in Texas.)

are the contents of the soundtrack double album.

Side One
Rock Around The Clock – Bill Haley and the Comets
Sixteen Candles – The Crests

Runaway – Del Shannon
Why Do Fools Fall In Love – Frankie Lymon and the Teenagers
That'll Be The Day – The Crickets (credited on sleeve only to Buddy Holly)
Fanny Mae – Buster Brown

At The Hop – Flash Cadillac and the Continental Kids
She's So Fine – Flash Cadillac and the Continental Kids
The Stroll – The Diamonds
See You In September – The Tempos

Side Two
Surfin' Safari – The Beach Boys
He's The Great Impostor – The Fleetwoods
Almost Grown – Chuck Berry
Smoke Gets In Your Eyes – The Platters
Little Darlin' – The Diamonds
Peppermint Twist – Joey Dee and the Starliters

Barbara Anne – The Regents
Book Of Love – The Monotones
Maybe Baby – The Crickets (credited on sleeve only to Buddy Holly)
Ya Ya – Lee Dorsey
The Great Pretender – The Platters

Side Three
Ain't That A Shame – Fats Domino
Johnny B. Goode – Chuck Berry
I Only Have Eyes For You – The Flamingos
Get A Job – The Silhouettes
To The Aisle – The Five Satins
Do You Wanna Dance – Bobby Freeman
Party Doll – Buddy Knox
Come Go With Me – The Del-Vikings
You're Sixteen – Johnny Burnette
Love Potion No. 9 – The Clovers

Side Four
Since I Don't Have You – The Skyliners
Chantilly Lace – The Big Bopper
Teen Angel – Mark Dinning
Crying In The Chapel – Sonny Til and the Orioles
A Thousand Miles Away – The Heartbeats
Heart And Soul – The Cleftones
Green Onions – Booker T and the MGs
Only You – The Platters
Goodnight Sweetheart – The Spaniels
All Summer Long – The Beach Boys

COMEDIANS WHO MADE HITS

1. Lance Percival
2. Guy Marks
3. Jerry Lewis
4. Ken Dodd
5. Stan Laurel and Oliver Hardy
6. John Inman
7. Benny Hill
8. Rolf Harris
9. The Goons
10. Norman Wisdom
11. Norman Vaughan
12. Allan Sherman
13. George Formby
14. Dick Emery
15. Charlie Drake
16. Bernard Cribbins
17. Tommy Cooper
18. Bernard Bresslaw
19. Wilfred Brambell and Harry H. Corbett
20. Hylda Baker and Arthur Mullard
21. Jasper Carrott
22. Peter Sellers

Peter Sellers

23. Harry Secombe
24. Michael Medwin, Alfie Bass, Bernard Bresslaw and Leslie Fyson
25. Russ Abbott
26. Steve Martin
27. Blues Brothers (John Belushi and Dan Akroyd)

10 POP STARS WHO CAUGHT THE ACTING BUG

1. Olivia Newton-John: Made her film debut in 1978 with John Travolta in *Grease*. She then tried her hand at a Hollywood-style musical with Gene Kelly in *Xanadu*, probably the most panned film of 1980. One reviewer described her as 'the most wooden actress I've seen'.

2. Bette Midler: Her performance in her first film, *The Rose*, in which she more or less played herself, garnered an Oscar nomination. Reviewers, however, said her over-acting was gross.

3. John Denver: The man who's done more to promote wire-framed glasses than anyone else, first appeared with Dennis Weaver in an episode of *McCloud*, where he was spotted by a Hollywood producer who co-starred him with George Burns in 1977's *Oh God*. The movie was successful, but Denver put in a poor performance.

4. Dolly Parton: Her first film role was *9 to 5* in which she co-starred with Jane Fonda and Lily Tomlin. This was followed up by another successful move, *The Best Little Whorehouse in Texas*, in which her co-star was macho man Burt Reynolds.

5. Diana Ross: The ex-lead singer of the Supremes was actually nominated for an Oscar for her film debut in *Lady Sings the Blues*. She later successfully played a model in *Mahogany* but her film with Michael Jackson, an update of *The Wizard of Oz* entitled *The Wiz*, bombed completely.

6. David Essex: A singing drummer named David Cook, who took his new name from the English county in which he lived, David Essex was unsuccessful in chart terms during his early years. However, after appearing to great acclaim in the British stage version of *Godspell*, and starring in the film *That'll Be the Day*, Essex became a major British teenybop idol with ten hits between 1973 and 1976, a period which also saw him starring in a cinematic sequel to *That'll Be the Day*, entitled *Stardust*. Subsequently, as his teenage following grew older, Essex became an established actor, appearing both on the screen, in *Silver Dream Racer*, and in the London cast of *Evita*.

7. Sting: Gordon Sumner, songwriter/singer/bass player of the Police, and better known as Sting, was an obvious choice for the move to the silver screen, since he is in possession of the Face of the Eighties.

After a major role in the film of Pete Townshend's *Quadrophenia* and a cameo appearance in the acclaimed *Radio On*, he also appeared in a supporting role in the TV fantasy *Artemis 81* by David Hare, as well as starring in *Brimstone and Treacle*.

8. John Lennon: Although Lennon obviously appeared in all the Beatles' movies, he also appeared as a straight actor in the supporting role of Private Gripwood in the 1967 Dick Lester film *How I Won the War*, starring Michael Crawford and Lee Montague.

9. Adam Faith: After a highly successful singing career, Adam Faith moved into films in the sixties, appearing in *Beat Girl* and *What a Whopper*, which showcased his vocal abilities, but also in *Never Let Go*, which starred Peter Sellers, and *Mix Me a Person*, in which Faith played a condemned prisoner. After appearing in the title role of the highly successful TV series, *Budgie*, he appeared in the David Essex film *Stardust*, in a dramatic role.

10. Ringo Starr: Like Lennon, Ringo made his acting debut in the Beatles' movie, *A Hard Day's Night*. His performance in the film, particularly in a poignant riverside scene with a small boy, won critical acclaim. In 1968, he took a cameo role in *Candy*, and followed this with a starring role in *The Magic Christian*. His most convincing performance came in *That'll Be the Day* where he provided the perfect foil for David Essex. His movie roles since then have been few and distinctly second rate.

List by Steve Wright, BBC Radio 1 DJ.

SINGING MOVIE STARS WHO SHOULD STICK TO ACTING

1. Clint Eastwood: The man who normally doesn't talk much anyway recorded 'Bar-room Buddies' with his pal Merle Haggard as part of the 1980 picture *Bronco Billy*. It even reached the Top Ten of the American Country charts.

Clint Eastwood

2. Lee Marvin: Thought of as the original hell raiser, he played a loveable tramp in the film *Paint Your Wagon* in which he sang 'I Was Born Under A Wandering Star', a record which consisted of a lavish chorus and string backing, with Lee mumbling through the song. Believe it or not, it made No. 1 in the UK chart.

3. Cissy Spacek: It's rumoured that she sat down every night for three months just studying the vocal style of Loretta Lynn, the country singer. Cissy eventually cut the soundtrack of the movie *Coalminer's Daughter*.

4. Richard Harris: An Irish actor of significant renown, whose credits included starring parts in *This Sporting Life*, *Guns of Navarone* and *Mutiny on the Bounty*, Harris was recruited in a 'singing' role in the film version of *Camelot*. Subsequently he 'talked' his way through Jim Webb's epic 1968 million selling 'MacArthur Park'. Harris also made a couple of albums on the strength of his huge hit, but most recently, we are pleased to report, he appears to confine his singing to the stage and the bath.

5. Hayley Mills: 'All the thrills an' Hayley Mills' proclaimed the posters for one of the many Hayley Mills films during the swinging sixties. In 1961, there appeared to be some doubt about the infant prodigy's choice of career after her raucous version of 'Let's Get Together' made the UK and US Top 20s. Fortunately, she opted for acting . . .

List also by Steve Wright, King of Trivia.

8. INDIVIDUAL EFFORTS

BEATLES FOR SALE: PART ONE: THEIR EMI SINGLES RANKED IN SALES ORDER

1. I Want To Hold Your Hand
2. She Loves You
3. Can't Buy Me Love
4. We Can Work It Out/Day Tripper
5. I Feel Fine
6. Help!
7. Hey Jude
8. Hello Goodbye
9. A Hard Day's Night
10. Get Back
11. From Me To You
12. Strawberry Fields Forever/Penny Lane
13. Ticket To Ride
14. Yellow Submarine/Eleanor Rigby
15. All You Need Is Love
16. Paperback Writer
17. Ballad Of John And Yoko
18. Lady Madonna
19. Let It Be
20. Please Please Me
21. Something
22. Yesterday
23. Beatles Movie Medley
24. Back In The USSR
25. Love Me Do
26. Sgt. Pepper's Lonely Hearts Club Band – With A Little Help From My Friends

Compiled exclusively for *The Rock Lists Album* by EMI Records (UK) Ltd.

BEATLES FOR SALE: PART TWO: THEIR EMI ALBUMS RANKED IN SALES ORDER

1. Abbey Road
2. The Beatles 1962–66
3. The Beatles 1967–70
4. Sgt. Pepper's Lonely Hearts Club Band
5. A Collection of Beatles Oldies
6. Beatles (White Album)
7. Let It Be
8. Help!
9. Revolver
10. A Hard Day's Night
11. Rubber Soul
12. The Beatles At The Hollywood Bowl
13. Love Songs
14. Beatles For Sale
15. Please Please Me
16. With The Beatles
17. Rock And Roll
18. Beatles Ballads
19. Magical Mystery Tour
20. Rarities
21. Yellow Submarine
22. Reel Music
23. Hey Jude

Compiled exclusively for *The Rock Lists Album* by EMI Records (UK) Ltd.

BEATLES FOR SALE: PART THREE: THEIR EMI EPS RANKED IN SALES ORDER

1. Magical Mystery Tour
2. Twist And Shout
3. Beatles Hits
4. All My Loving
5. Long Tall Sally
6. Number Ones
7. A Hard Day's Night
8. Million Sellers
9. Beatles For Sale 1
10. Beatles For Sale 2
11. Yesterday
12. Nowhere Man

Compiled exclusively for *The Rock Lists Album* by EMI Records (UK) Ltd.

MADNESS ALL-TIME TOP NINE SINGLES

Based on actual UK sales figures (Through 1981)

1. Baggy Trousers (1980)
2. Embarrassment (1980)
3. My Girl (1980)
4. One Step Beyond (1979)
5. The Return Of The Los Palmas 7 (1981)
6. Shut Up (1981)
7. Grey Day (1981)
8. The Prince (1979)
9. Work Rest And Play (EP) (1980)

THIN LIZZY ALL-TIME TOP TEN SINGLES

Based on actual UK sales figures (Through 1981)

1. Whisky In The Jar (1973)
2. The Boys Are Back In Town (1976)
3. Waiting For An Alibi (1979)
4. Killer On The Loose (1980)
5. Don't Believe A Word (1977)
6. Dancin' In The Moonlight (It's Caught Me In The Spotlight) (1977)
7. Do Anything You Want To (1979)
8. Killers Live (EP) (1981)
9. Rosalie (1978)
10. Chinatown (1980)

ADAM AND THE ANTS ALL-TIME TOP EIGHT (Through 1981)

1. Stand And Deliver (1981)
2. Prince Charming (1981)
3. Antmusic (1980)
4. Kings Of The Wild Frontier (1980)
5. Young Parisiennes (1979)
6. Dog Eat Dog (1980)
7. Cartrouble (1979)
8. Zerox (1979)

BLONDIE ALL-TIME TOP TEN SINGLES (Through 1981)

Based on actual UK sales figures

1. Heart Of Glass (1979)
2. Sunday Girl (1979)
3. The Tide Is High (1980)
4. Denis (Denee) (1978)
5. Atomic (1980)
6. Dreaming (1979)
7. Rapture (1981)
8. Call Me (1980)
9. Hanging On The Telephone (1978)
10. Picture This (1978)

THE UK HITS OF THE JAM RANKED IN SALES ORDER

1. Going Underground/The Dreams Of Children
2. Start
3. Town Called Malice/Precious
4. The Eton Rifles
5. Funeral Pyre
6. Absolute Beginners
7. Strange Town
8. Down In The Tube Station At Midnight
9. All Around The World
10. When You're Young
11. David Watts/'A' Bomb In Wardour Street
12. That's Entertainment
13. News Of The World
14. The Modern World
15. In The City

THE UK HITS OF THE POLICE RANKED IN SALES ORDER

1. Don't Stand So Close To Me
2. Message In A Bottle
3. Walking On The Moon
4. De Do Do Do, De Da Da Da
5. Every Little Thing She Does Is Magic
6. Invisible Sun
7. Can't Stand Losing You
8. So Lonely
9. Roxanne
10. Fall Out
11. Six Pack

Total UK sales of Police singles through the end of 1981 exceeded 4,500,000.

PAUL McCARTNEY'S BEST-SELLING POST-BEATLES SINGLES (UK)

1. Mull Of Kintyre
2. Ebony And Ivory
3. Silly Love Songs
4. Goodnight Tonight
5. Let 'Em In
6. With A Little Luck
7. Hi Hi Hi/C Moon
8. Band On The Run
9. Jet
10. Live And Let Die

CLIFF RICHARD ALL-TIME TOP TEN SINGLES

Based on actual UK sales figures

1. The Young Ones (1962)
2. Bachelor Boy/The Next Time (1962)
3. We Don't Talk Anymore (1979)
4. Living Doll (1959)
5. Summer Holiday (1963)
6. Travellin' Light (1959)
7. Congratulations (1968)
8. The Minute You're Gone (1965)
9. Wind Me Up (Let Me Go) (1965)
10. Don't Talk To Him (1963)

Cliff Richard

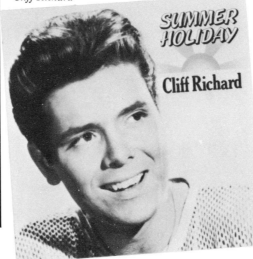

CLIFF RICHARD'S BRITISH FLOPS

With more than seventy hit singles to his credit, Cliff Richard is the definitive chart regular. But even Cliff has occasionally recorded a stiff. The following is a list of his flops – the records which didn't even make the charts for a single week.

1. This Was My Special Day (January 1965)
2. A Brand New Song (November 1972)
3. It's Only Me You've Left Behind (March 1975)
4. Honky Tonk Angel (September 1975)
5. Yes He Lives (January 1978)
6. Please Remember Me (July 1978)
7. Can't Take The Hurt Anymore (November 1978)

NB: 'This Was My Special Day' was a song from the pantomine *Aladdin* in which Cliff starred. The record was sold mainly at the theatre staging the production but was available on order from record dealers. Columbia did not publicize it and consequently many Cliff fans were unaware of its existence.

RECORD OF THE YEAR 1981

Bette Davis Eyes – Kim Carnes
Written by Donna Weiss and Jackie De Shannon
Produced by Val Garay
Keyboards by Steve Goldstein
Bass by Brian Garafalo
Drums by Craig Kramph
Electric Guitars by Craig Hull, Josh Leo and Waddy Wachtel
Percussion by M. L. Benoit
Engineered by Niko Bolas
Arranged by Bill Cuomo
Recorded at Record One, Los Angeles 15–20 December 1980 and 6–12 January 1981

Within weeks of its release last summer, Kim Carnes' version of 'Bette Davis Eyes' stormed to the top of the American singles chart and stayed there for nine weeks. It went on to become a hit in every major market in the world and was easily the best-selling single of 1981. Why a six-year-old song should suddenly become such a hot property is worth investigating.

'Bette Davis Eyes' first appeared on Jackie De Shannon's 1975 LP 'New Arrangement'. Few who heard it then could have imagined it to be a potential multi-million seller. De Shannon gave the song a light-hearted 1920s bar-room style treatment. It received little airplay and was never considered a potential single.

Jackie co-wrote the song with Donna Weiss. In 1980, knowing that Kim Carnes was selecting material for a forthcoming album, Donna recommended 'Bette Davis Eyes'. Carnes liked the song and decided to include it on the album, 'Mistaken Identity'.

Bill Cuomo was commissioned to write the arrangements for the LP. And what he came up with for 'Bette Davis Eyes' was quite revolutionary. Cuomo had married the essential melodic ingredients of American AOR music to a British new wave/futurist type arrangement. The result was a stunning success giving Kim Carnes the biggest hit of her career and guaranteeing a long queue for the services of Bill Cuomo.

BETTE DAVIS EYES by Kim Carnes

Country	Highest Chart Position
Argentina	1
Australia	1
Austria	1
Belgium	1
Bolivia	1
Brazil	1
Canada	1
Chile	1
Finland	1
France	1
Germany	1
Guatemala	1
Israel	1
Italy	1
Norway	1
Panama	1
Peru	1
Portugal	1
South Africa	1
Spain	1
United States Of America	1
Hong Kong	2
New Zealand	2
Denmark	4
Sweden	4
Ireland	5
United Kingdom	10

UK MILLION SELLING SINGLES

The governing body of the British record industry, the BPI, has been compiling record companies' sales since 1961. The following is a complete list of singles to have been awarded a platinum disc for sales exceeding one million copies. Before American readers scoff at the small number (28) of records to achieve this landmark they should consider that a comparable sales figure for the United States is over four million.

Year	Title – Artist
1961	Stranger On The Shore – Acker Bilk
1962	I Remember You – Frank Ifield
1963	I Want To Hold Your Hand – Beatles
1963	She Loves You – Beatles
1964	Can't Buy Me Love – Beatles
1964	I Feel Fine – Beatles

Slade

1965	Tears – Ken Dodd
1965	We Can Work It Out – Beatles
1965	The Carnival Is Over – Seekers
1966	Green, Green Grass Of Home – Tom Jones
1967	Last Waltz – Engelbert Humperdinck
1967	Release Me – Engelbert Humperdinck
1973	I Love You, Love Me Love – Gary Glitter
1975	Bohemian Rhapsody – Queen
1976	Save All Your Kisses For Me – Brotherhood of Man
1977	Don't Give Up On Us – David Soul
1978	Mull Of Kintyre/Girls School – Wings
1978	Eye Level/Distant Hills – Simon Park Orchestra
1978	Rivers Of Babylon/Brown Girl In The Ring – Boney M
1978	You're The One That I Want – John Travolta and Olivia Newton-John
1978	Summer Nights – John Travolta and Olivia Newton-John
1978	Mary's Boy Child – Oh, My Lord (Medley) – Boney M
1979	YMCA – Village People
1979	Heart Of Glass – Blondie
1979	Bright Eyes – Art Garfunkel
1980	Another Brick In The Wall (Part II) – Pink Floyd
1980	Merry Xmas Everybody – Slade
1981	Imagine – John Lennon
1982	Don't You Want Me – Human League

NB: Years shown are those on which the millionth sale was achieved and are not necessarily those in which the records were issued.

Prior to 1960 million-sellers were something of a rarity, and the following records are probably the only ones to pass the magical seven figure mark.

1955	Rock Around The Clock – Bill Haley and His Comets (Brunswick)
1957	Diana – Paul Anka (Columbia)

Bill Haley

1957 Mary's Boy Child – Harry Belafonte
(RCA)
1959 What Do You Want To Make Those
Eyes At Me For – Emile Ford and
the Checkmates (Pye)

Bing Crosby's 'White Christmas' (first released in 1942) has never been certified as a million-seller but has sold over 500,000 copies since 1967 indicating cumulative sales of at least a million in the UK.

Bing Crosby

AMERICA'S MOST CHARTED RECORD

Bing Crosby's 'White Christmas' is the best-selling single of all-time. The most recent estimate puts its worldwide sales at over fifty million. This most seasonal of songs was recorded on 29 May 1942. It was released in September of 1942 and entered the chart on 2 October. Three weeks later it was Number One, a position it didn't relinquish for eleven weeks. It recharted for all but two of the next twenty Christmases appearing on the chart more times (72) in more chart runs (19) than any other single.

Date entered chart	Highest position	Weeks on chart
2 Oct 1942	1	15
23 Dec 1943	9	1
21 Dec 1944	6	2
6 Dec 1945	9	4
13 Dec 1946	2	4
28 Nov 1947	3	5
3 Dec 1948	6	6
9 Dec 1949	7	4
22 Dec 1950	16	2
14 Dec 1951	16	3
15 Dec 1954	21	3
7 Dec 1955	18	3
19 Dec 1956	65	1
7 Dec 1957	34	6
28 Dec 1958	66	2
3 Jan 1960	59	1
18 Dec 1960	26	3
17 Dec 1961	12	4
15 Dec 1962	38	3
	1	72

BRITAIN'S MOST CHARTED RECORD

Frank Sinatra's version of 'My Way' is far from being Britain's best-selling single of all-time. In fact, it only ranks as the 60th top tune of the sixties. Yet it's one of the most consistently popular songs of the modern era, so popular that it has spent a total of 122 weeks on the British chart in a total of 9 chart runs.

Date entered chart	Highest position	Weeks on chart
2 April 1969	5	42
31 January 1970	49	1
28 February 1970	30	5
11 April 1970	33	9
27 June 1970	28	21
28 November 1970	18	16
27 March 1971	22	19
4 September 1971	39	8
1 January 1972	50	1
	5	122

Fats Domino

Hank Snow

THE FIRST WORLDWIDE GOLD ROCK'N'ROLL RECORDS

Before 1954 (When *Rock Around The Clock* was released)

Artist	*Title*	*Year*
Fats Domino	The Fat Man	1948
Roy Brown	Hard Luck Blues	1950
Ivory Joe Hunter	I Almost Lost My Mind	1950
Joe Liggins	Pink Champagne	1950
Joe Liggins	Honeydripper	1950
Moon Mullican	I'll Sail My Ship Alone	1950
Hank Snow	I'm Movin' On	1950
Percy Mayfield	Please Send Me Someone To Love	1951
Joe Turner	Chains Of Love	1951
Ruth Brown	Five, Ten, Fifteen Hours	1952
Fats Domino	Goin' Home	1952
Lloyd Price	Lawdy Miss Clawdy	1952
Hank Williams	Jambalaya (On The Bayou)	1952
Hank Williams	Your Cheatin' Heart	1952
Hank Williams	Honky Tonk Blues	1952
Ruth Brown	Mama, He Treats Your Daughter Mean	1953
Fats Domino	Going To The River	1953
Fats Domino	You Said You Loved Me	1953
Fats Domino	Please Don't Leave Me	1953
Fats Domino	I Lived My Life	1953
The Drifters	Money Honey	1953
The Orioles	Crying In The Chapel	1953
Joe Turner	Honey Hush	1953
Hank Ballard	Work With Me, Annie	1954
Hank Ballard	Sexy Ways	1954
Hank Ballard	Annie Had a Baby	1954
The Crew Cuts	Sh-Boom	1954
Fats Domino	Love Me	1954
Fats Domino	Don't Leave Me This Way	1954
Guitar Slim	Things I Used To Do	1954
Bill Haley	Shake Rattle And Roll	1954
Bill Haley	Rock Around The Clock	1954
The Penguins	Earth Angel	1954
Link Wray	Rumble	1954

BEATLES SOLO ALBUMS

John Lennon

1. Unfinished Music No 1 – Two Virgins (with Yoko Ono) (1968)
2. Unfinished Music No 2 – Life With The Lions (with Yoko Ono) (1969)
3. The Wedding Album – (with Yoko Ono) (1969)
4. Plastic Ono Band/Live Peace In Toronto (1969)
5. John Lennon/Plastic Ono Band (1970)
6. Imagine (1971)
7. Some Time In New York City (1972)
8. Mind Games (1973)
9. Walls And Bridges (1974)
10. Rock'n'Roll (1975)
11. Shaved Fish (Collectable Lennon) (1975)
12. Double Fantasy (with Yoko Ono) 1980)

Paul McCartney

1. McCartney (1970)
2. Ram (1971)
3. McCartney II (1980)
4. The McCartney Interview (1981)
5. Tug Of War (1982)

George Harrison

1. Wonderwall Music (1968)
2. Electronic Sounds (1969)
3. All Things Must Pass (1970)
4. The Concert For Bangla Desh (1972)
5. Living In The Material World (1973)
6. Dark Horse (1974)
7. Extra Texture (1975)
8. Thirty Three and $\frac{1}{3}$ (1976)
9. A Personal Dialogue With George Harrison At 33⅓ (1976)
10. The Best Of George Harrison (1976)
11. George Harrison (1979)
12. Somewhere In England (1981)

Ringo Starr

1. Sentimental Journey (1970)
2. Beaucoups Of Blues (1970)
3. Ringo (1973)
4. Good Night Vienna (1974)

5. Blast From Your Past (1975)
6. Ringo's Rotogravure (1976)
7. Ringo The Fourth (1977)
8. Bad Boy (1978)
9. Stop And Smell The Roses (1981)

SOLO ALBUMS BY MEMBERS OF THE WHO

Pete Townshend
1. Who Came First (1972)
2. Rough Mix (with Ronnie Lane) (1977)
3. Empty Glass (1980)
4. Chinese Eyes (1982)

Roger Daltrey
1. Daltrey (1973)
2. Ride A Rock Horse (1975)
3. One Of The Boys (1977)
4. McVicar (Original Soundtrack) (1980)
5. Best Bits (1982)

John Entwistle
1. The Ox (1970)
2. Smash Your Head Against The Wall (1971)
3. Whistle Rhymes (1972)
4. Rigor Mortis Sets In (1973)
5. Mad Dog (1975)
6. Too Late The Hero (1981)

Keith Moon
1. Two Sides Of The Moon (1975)

MILLION SELLING BRITISH SINGLES PRIOR TO 1960

Artist	Title	Year
Bert Shepard	Laughing Song	1910
Joe Hayman	Cohen On The Telephone	1914
Ernest Lough	Oh For The Wings Of A Dove	1927
Edmundo Ros	Wedding Samba	1949
Anton Karas	'Harry Lime' Theme	1950
Mantovani	Charmaine	1951
Mantovani	Wyoming	1951
Winifred Atwell	Black And White Rag	1952
Vera Lynn	Auf Wiederseh'n Sweetheart	1952
Vera Lynn	Yours	1952
Mantovani	Greensleeves	1952
Winifred Atwell	Let's Have A Party	1953
Eddie Calvert	Oh Mein Papa	1953
Frank Chacksfield	'Limelight' Theme	1953
Frank Chacksfield	Ebb Tide	1953
Mantovani	Song From 'Moulin Rouge'	1953
Mantovani	Swedish Rhapsody	1953
Winifred Atwell	Let's Have Another Party	1953
Mantovani	Lonely Ballerina	1954
Lonnie Donegan	Rock Island Line	1955
Cyril Stapleton	Blue Star	1955
Russ Hamilton	We Will Make Love	1957
Nancy Whiskey	Freight Train	1957
Laurie London	He's Got The Whole World In His Hands	1958
Chris Barber	Petite Fleur	1959
Russ Conway	Side Saddle	1959
Lonnie Donegan	Does Your Chewing Gum Lose It's Flavour	1959
Emile Ford	What Do You Want To Make Those Eyes At Me For	1959
Cliff Richard	Living Doll	1959
Cyril Stapleton	Children's Marching Song – Nick Nack Paddy Whack	1959

FIRST 10 MILLION SELLING BRITISH LPS

Artist	Title	Year
Mantovani	Xmas Carols	1953
Mantovani	Strauss Waltzes	1953
Mantovani	Plays The Immortal Classics	1954
Mantovani	Song Hits From Theatreland	1955
Mantovani	Film Encores	1957
Mantovani	Gems Forever	1958
Mantovani	'Exodus' And Other Great Themes	1960
Mantovani	Italia Mia	1961
Beatles	Please Please Me/Introducing The Beatles	1963
Beatles	With The Beatles/Meet The Beatles	1963

SOLO LPS BY MEMBERS OF FLEETWOOD MAC

Lindsay Buckingham
1. Law and Order (1982)

Lindsay Buckingham and Stevie Nicks
1. Buckingham/Nicks (1973)

Mick Fleetwood
1. The Visitor (1981)

Peter Green
1. The End Of The Game (1970)
2. In The Skies (1979)
3. Little Dreamer (1980)
4. Whatcha Gonna Do (1981)

Danny Kirwan
1. Second Chapter (1978)

Christine McVie
1. The Christine Perfect Album (1970)

Stevie Nicks
1. Bella Donna (1981)

Jeremy Spencer
1. Jeremy Spencer (1970)
1. Jeremy Spencer And The Children of God (1972)

Bob Welch
1. French Kiss (1977)
2. Three Hearts (1979)
3. The Other One (1980)
4. Bob Welch (1981)

ROXY MUSIC SOLO ALBUMS

Bryan Ferry
1. These Foolish Things (1973)
2. Another Time, Another Place (1974)
3. Let's Stick Together (1976)
4. In Your Mind (1977)
5. The Bride Stripped Bare (1978)

Andy Mackay
1. In Search Of Eddie Riff (1974)
2. Resolving Contradictions (1978)

Phil Manzanera
1. Diamond Head (1974)
2. Main Stream (with Quiet Sun) (1975)
3. 801 Live (1976)
4. Listen Now (with 801) (1976)
5. K-Scope (1978)
6. Primitive Guitars (1982)

Eno
1. No Pussyfooting (with Robert Fripp) (1973)
2. Here Come The Warm Jets (1973)
3. June 1, 1974 (with Kevin Ayers, John Cale and Nico) (1974)
4. Taking Tiger Mountain By Strategy (1974)
5. Another Green World (1975)
6. Discreet Music (1975)
7. Evening Star (with Robert Fripp) (1976)
8. Before And After Science (1977)
9. Music For Airports (1978)
10. Music For Films (1978)
11. The Plateaux Of Mirror (with Harold Budd) (1980)
12. Possible Musics (with Jon Hassell) (1980)
13. My Life In The Bush Of Ghosts (with David Byrne) (1981)
14. On Land (1982)

Roxy Music

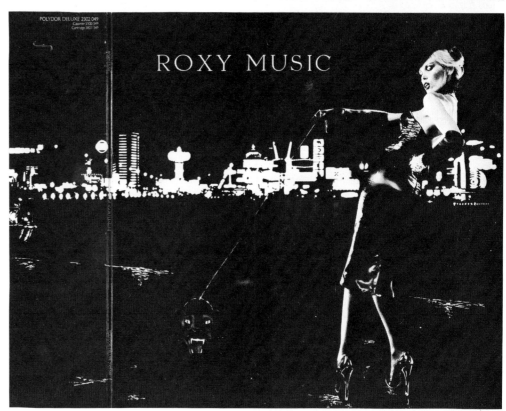

CROSBY, STILLS, NASH AND YOUNG ALBUMS

David Crosby
1. If I Could Only Remember My Name (1971)

David Crosby and Graham Nash
1. Graham Nash/David Crosby (1972)
2. Wind On The Water (1975)
3. Whistling Down The Wire (1976)
4. Live (1977)
5. The Best Of David Crosby And Graham Nash (1978)

David Crosby, Stephen Stills and Graham Nash
1. Crosby, Stills And Nash (1969)
2. CSN (1977)
3. Replay (1980)
4. Daylight Again (1982)

David Crosby, Stephen Stills, Graham Nash and Neil Young
1. Déjà Vu (1970)
2. Four Way Street (1972)
3. So Far (1974)

Crosby, Stills, Nash and Young

Stephen Stills
1. Stephen Stills (1970)
2. Stephen Stills 2 (1971)
3. Manassas (1972)
4. Down The Road (1973)
5. Stills (1975)
6. Live (1975)
7. Still Stills – The Best Of Stephen Stills (1976)
8. Illegal Stills (1976)
9. Thoroughfare Gap (1978)

Stephen Stills and Neil Young
1. Long May You Run (1976)

Graham Nash
1. Songs For Beginners (1971)
2. Wild Tales (1974)
3. Earth And Sky (1980)

Neil Young
1. Neil Young (1969)
2. Everybody Knows This Is Nowhere (1969)
3. After The Gold Rush (1970)
4. Harvest (1972)
5. Time Fades Away (1973)
6. Journey Through The Past (1972)
7. On The Beach (1974)
8. Tonight's The Night (1975)
9. Zuma (1976)
10. American Stars And Bars (1977)
11. Decade (1977)
12. Comes A Time (1978)
13. Rust Never Sleeps (1979)
14. Live Rust (1979)
15. Hawks And Doves (1980)
16. Re·Ac·Tor (1981)

VELVET UNDERGROUND SOLO ALBUMS

Without any doubt at all, the ex-member of the Velvet Underground with the highest solo profile is Lou Reed. However, both John Cale and Nico have also released solo albums, as follows:

Lou Reed
1. Lou Reed (1972)
2. Transformer (1972)
3. Berlin (1973)
4. Rock'n'Roll Animal (1974)
5. Sally Can't Dance (1974)
6. Metal Machine Music (1975)
7. Coney Island Baby (1975)
8. Live (1975)
9. Rock and Roll Heart (1976)
10. Walk On The Wild Side (1977)
11. Vicious (1978)
12. Street Hassle (1978)
13. Live – Take No Prisoners (1978)
14. The Bells (1979)

15. Growing Up In Public (1980)
16. Rock and Roll Diary 1967–1980 (1980)
17. The Blue Mask (1982)

John Cale
1. Vintage Violence (1971)
2. Church Of Anthrax (with Terry Riley) (1971)
3. Academy In Peril (1972)
4. Paris 1919 (1973)
5. June 1, 1974 (with Eno, Nico and Kevin Ayers) (1974)

6. Fear (1974)
7. Slow Dazzle (1975)
8. Helen Of Troy (1975)
9. Guts (1977)
10. Sabotage/Live (1979)
11. Honi Soit (1981)

Nico
1. Chelsea Girl (1968)
2. The Marble Index (1968)
3. Desert Shore (1971)
4. June 1, 1974 (with Eno, John Cale and Kevin Ayers) (1974)
5. The End . . . (1974)
6. Drama Of Exile (1981)

JEFFERSON AIRPLANE/STARSHIP SOLO ALBUMS

Paul Kantner
1. Blows Against The Empire (1970)
2. Sunfighter (with Grace Slick) (1971)
3. Baron Von Tollbooth And The Chrome Nun (with Grace Slick and David Freiberg) (1973)

Grace Slick
1. Sunfighter (with Paul Kantner) (1971)
2. Baron Von Tollbooth And The Chrome Nun (with Paul Kantner and David Freiberg) (1973)
3. Manhole (1974)
4. Dreams (1980)
5. Welcome To The Wrecking Ball (1981)

Jorma Kaukonen
1. Quah (1975)
2. Jorma (1979)
3. Barbecue King (Jorma Kaukonen and Vital Parts) (1980)

Jack Casady
1. SVT (with SVT) (1979)
2. No Regrets (with SVT) (1981)

David Freiberg
1. Baron Von Tollbooth And The Chrome Nun (with Grace Slick and Paul Kantner) (1973)

Hot Tuna (Jorma Kaukonen and Jack Casady)
1. Hot Tuna (1970)
2. First Pull Up Then Pull Down (1971)
3. Burgers (1972)
4. The Phosphorescent Rat (1974)
5. America's Choice (1974)
6. Yellow Fever (1975)

7. Hoppkorv (1976)
8. Double Dose (1978)

Skip Spence
1. Oar (1968)

Joe E. Covington
1. Fat Fandango (1973)

Marty Balin
1. Bodacious (with Bodacious) (1974)
2. Balin (1980)

Papa John Creach
1. Papa John Creach (1971)
2. Filthy (with Zulu) (1972)
3. Playing My Fiddle For You (1974)
4. I'm The Fiddle Man (1975)
5. The Cat And The Fiddle (1977)

(List by John Platt.)

SOLO ALBUMS BY MEMBERS OF THE GRATEFUL DEAD

Jerry Garcia
1. Garcia (1971)
2. Hooteroll (with Howard Wales) (1971)
3. Heavy Turbulence (with Merl Saunders) (1972)
4. Fire Up (with Merl Saunders) (1973)
5. Live At The Keystone (with Merl Saunders) (1973)
6. Compliments Of Garcia (1974)
7. Reflections (1975)
8. Cats Under The Stars (Jerry Garcia Band) (1978)

Bob Weir
1. Ace (1972)
2. Heaven Help The Fool (1978)
3. Bobby And The Midnites (1981)

Mickey Hart
1. Rolling Thunder (1972)
2. Diga (Mickey Hart and the Diga Rhythm Band) (1976)
3. The Apocalypse Now Sessions (Mickey Hart and the Rhythm Devils) (1980)

Phil Lesh
1. Seastones (with Ned Lagin) (1975)

Robert Hunter
1. Tales Of The Great Rum Runners (1974)
2. Tiger Rose (1975)
3. Jack O'Roses (1980)

Keith and Donna Godchaux
1. Keith And Donna (1975)

List donated by John Platt, editor of *Comstock Lode.*

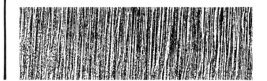

9.PEOPLE & PLACES

THIRD WORLD ROCK STARS

1. Bob Marley
2. Fela Anikupalo-Kuti
3. Peter Tosh
4. Bunny Wailer
5. Osibisa
6. Toots and the Maytals
7. Third World
8. Black Uhuru
9. Burundi Black
10. Biddu
11. King Sunny Ade

Bob Marley

SCOTTISH PUNK/NEW WAVE BANDS

1. Aztec Camera
2. Orange Juice
3. Scars
4. Another Pretty Face
5. The Exploited
6. Skids
7. Zones
8. Simple Minds
9. Altered Images
10. Josef K
11. The Revillos

IRISH PUNK/NEW WAVE BANDS

1. Rudi
2. The Undertones
3. Stiff Little Fingers
4. Xdreamysts
5. The Outcasts
6. Boomtown Rats
7. U2
8. Virgin Prunes
9. Moving Hearts
10. Protex

WELSH GROUPS

1. Man
2. Lone Star
3. Amen Corner
4. The Neutrons
5. The Flying Aces
6. Love Sculpture
7. Lucifer and the Corn Crackers
8. Memphis Bend
9. Bystanders
10. Wild Turkey
11. Eyes of Blue
12. Plum Crazy

CANADIAN SUPERSTARS

1. Gordon Lightfoot
2. Neil Young
3. Joni Mitchell
4. The Band
5. Bachman-Turner Overdrive
6. Anne Murray

Aldo Nova

7. Steppenwolf
8. R. Dean Taylor
9. Terry Jacks/The Poppy Family
10. Andy Kim (alias Baron Longfellow)
11. The Guess Who
12. Leonard Cohen
13. Loverboy
14. Aldo Nova
15. Rush
16. Bob and Doug MacKenzie

SWEDISH ACTS WHICH HAVE MADE THE UK SINGLES CHART

1. Alice Babs
2. Spotnicks
3. Abba
4. Harpo
5. Hank C. Burnette
6. Sylvia
7. Stardust

GREEK ACTS WHICH HAVE MADE THE UK SINGLES CHART

1. Vicky Leandros
2. Aphrodites Child
3. Makadopulos and his Greek Serenaders
4. Yannis Markopoulos
5. Demis Roussos
6. Vangelis

AMERICAN PIE

ALABAMA: Sweet Home Alabama – Lynyrd Skynyrd
ALASKA: North To Alaska – Johnny Horton
ARIZONA: Arizona Stomp – The East Texas Serenaders
ARKANSAS: Mary, Queen Of Arkansas – Bruce Springsteen
CALIFORNIA: California Bloodlines – John Stewart
COLORADO: Colorado – Flying Burrito Brothers

DELAWARE: Delaware Slide – George Thorogood and the Destroyers
FLORIDA: Western Florida – Bat McGrath
GEORGIA: Up From Georgia – James Talley
HAWAII: Hawaii – Beach Boys
IDAHO: Idaho Home – Ronee Blakley
ILLINOIS: Illinois – Everly Brothers
INDIANA: Indiana Wants Me – R. Dean Taylor
IOWA: Jenny (Iowa Sunrise) – Janis Ian
KANSAS: Kansas Legend – Frummox
KENTUCKY: Blue Kentucky Girl – Emmylou Harris
LOUISIANA: Leaving Louisiana In The Broad Daylight – Rodney Crowell
MARYLAND: There's A Girl In The Heart Of Maryland – Steve Goodman
MASSACHUSETTS: Massachusetts – Bee Gees
MICHIGAN: Michigan Water Blues – Rambling Jack Elliott
MISSISSIPPI: Mississippi – John Phillips
MISSOURI: Missouri Birds – John Stewart
MONTANA: Helena Montana – Terry Allen and the Panhandle Mystery Band
NEBRASKA: Nebraska Widow – John Stewart
NEVADA: Nevada Fighter – Michael Nesmith
NEW JERSEY: Little New Jersey Town – Sammy Walker
NEW MEXICO: Clovis, New Mexico – Hank Williams, Jr.
NEW YORK: The Only Living Boy In New York – Simon and Garfunkel
NORTH CAROLINA: Carolina In My Mind – James Taylor
OHIO: Ohio – Crosby, Stills, Nash and Young
OKLAHOMA: My Oklahoma – Steve Young
OREGON: The Waves Roll In On Oregon – Jim Post
PENNSYLVANIA: Pittsburgh, Pennsylvania – Guy Mitchell
RHODE ISLAND: Sweet Rhode Island Red – Norman Greenbaum

SOUTH CAROLINA: Carolina Soldier Boy – Sammy Walker
SOUTH DAKOTA: Rapid City, South Dakota – Kinky Friedman
TENNESSEE: Tennessee Is Not The State I'm In – Joe Ely
TEXAS: Texas I Miss You – Ian Tyson
UTAH: The Red Hill Of Utah – Marty Robbins
VERMONT: Moonlight In Vermont – Willie Nelson
VIRGINIA: I Was Born In East Virginia – Pete Seeger
WASHINGTON: My Washington Woman – Kenny Rogers and the First Edition
WEST VIRGINIA: Hills Of West Virginia – Phil Ochs
WYOMING: The Emperor Of Wyoming – Neil Young

(List compiled by Peter O'Brien of *Omaha Rainbow*.)

LONDON GEOGRAPHY IN SONG AND ALBUM TITLES

1. Sunny Goodge Street – Donovan
2. Baker Street – Gerry Rafferty
3. Waterloo Sunset – The Kinks
4. Finchley Central – The New Vaudeville Band
5. Portobello Road – Cat Stevens

6. Walking Down The Kings Road – Squire
7. Wombling Song (The Wombles of Wimbledon Common Are We) – Wombles
8. Shepherd's Bush Cowboy – Third World War
9. Guns Of Brixton – The Clash
10. 'A' Bomb In Wardour Street – The Jam
11. (I Don't Want To Go To) Chelsea – Elvis Costello
12. Abbey Road – The Beatles

NEW YORK GEOGRAPHY IN SONG AND ALBUM TITLES

1. 14th Street – Sylvain Sylvain
2. 59th Street Bridge Song (Feelin' Groovy) – Simon and Garfunkel
3. Central Park Arrest – Thunderthighs
4. 10th Avenue Freeze Out – Bruce Springsteen
5. Incident On 57th Street – Bruce Springsteen
6. Rockaway Beach – The Ramones
7. On Broadway – The Drifters
8. Funky Broadway – Wilson Pickett
9. Positively 4th Street – Bob Dylan
10. The Wall Street Shuffle – 10cc
11. Spanish Harlem – Ben E. King
12. Second Avenue – Art Garfunkel

LOS ANGELES GEOGRAPHY IN SONG AND ALBUM TITLES

1. Hollywood Nights – Bob Seger and the Silver Bullet Band
2. Train To Anaheim – David Blue
3. Ventura Highway – America
4. 77 Sunset Strip – Edward Byrnes
5. The Hollywood Waltz – The Eagles
6. The Anaheim, Azusa And Cucamonga Sewing Circle, Book Review And Timing Association – Jan and Dean

7. LA International Airport – Susan Raye
8. Zuma – Neil Young
9. Dead Man's Curve – Jan and Dean
10. MacArthur Park – Richard Harris
11. Coldwater Canyon – Dory Previn
12. Laurel Canyon – John Mayall

MERSEYBEAT GROUPS OF THE SIXTIES

1. The Beatles
2. The Searchers
3. Gerry and the Pacemakers
4. Billy J. Kramer and the Dakotas
5. Kingsize Taylor and the Dominoes
6. The Big Three
7. The Merseybeats
8. The Mojos
9. The Pete Best Four
10. Scaffold
11. The Swinging Blue Jeans
12. The Dennisons
13. Rory Storm and the Hurricanes
14. The Undertakers
15. Faron's Flamingos
16. Johnny Sandon and the Remo Four
17. Tommy Quickly and the Remo Four
18. Ian and the Zodiacs
19. The Escorts
20. Freddie Starr and the Midnighters

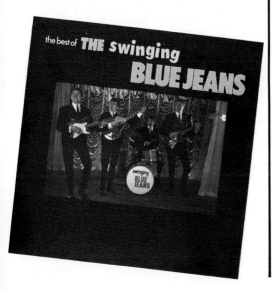

MERSEYBEAT GROUPS OF THE EIGHTIES

1. Echo and the Bunnymen
2. The Teardrop Explodes
3. Orchestral Manoeuvres in the Dark
4. Wah! (previously Wah! Heat)
5. Yachts
6. Dalek I
7. Pink Military
8. Original Mirrors
9. Planets
10. Lori and the Chameleons
11. Modern Eon
12. China Crisis

The Yachts

THE AMERICAN SIDE OF THE BRITISH INVASION

The so-called 'British Invasion' of 1964, when hipness was Britain-shaped, was in fact partially American, in that a number of the hits scored by British acts were cover versions of original American songs. The list below indicates just how reliant British acts were on American music.

Artist	Title	Highest US Chart Position
Beatles	Twist And Shout	2
Beatles	Matchbox	17
Animals	House Of The Rising Sun	1
Animals	I'm Crying	19
Animals	Don't Let Me Be Misunderstood	15
Animals	We've Gotta Get Out Of This Place	13
Dave Clark Five	Do You Love Me	11
Wayne Fontana	The Game Of Love	1
Herman's Hermits	I'm Into Something Good	13
Herman's Hermits	Silhouettes	5
Herman's Hermits	Wonderful World	4
Herman's Hermits	Just A Little Bit Better	7
Billy J. Kramer	Little Children	7
Manfred Mann	Do Wah Diddy Diddy	1
Manfred Mann	Sha La La	12
Mindbenders	A Groovy Kind Of Love	2
Moody Blues	Go Now	10
Nashville Teens	Tobacco Road	14
Peter and Gordon	I Go To Pieces	9
Peter and Gordon	True Love Ways	14
Rolling Stones	Time Is On My Side	6
Searchers	Needles And Pins	13
Searchers	Don't Throw Your Love Away	16
Searchers	Love Potion No 9	3
Dusty Springfield	Wishin' And Hopin'	6
Troggs	Wild Thing	1

WIGAN HITS

During the 1970s, the Wigan Casino, a dance palace in a most unlikely part of England, exercised an enormous influence on popular music as a result of its all night soul presentations. Many of the records played were long forgotten obscurities, while several others were specially recorded to cater for the Wigan dancers, and a number achieved sufficient national popularity to figure in the charts.

1. The Joker (The Wigan Joker) – The Allnight Band
2. Under My Thumb – Wayne Gibson
3. Crackin' Up – Tommy Hunt
4. Loving On The Losing Side – Tommy Hunt
5. Weak Spot – Evelyn Thomas
6. Footsee – Wigan's Chosen Few
7. Skiing In The Snow – Wigan's Ovation
8. Per-So- Nal-Ly – Wigan's Ovation
9. South African Man – Hamilton Bohannon
10. Disco Stomp – Hamilton Bohannon
11. Goodbye, Nothing To Say – The Javells featuring Nosmo King
12. I've Been Hurt – Guy Darrell
13. Reaching For The Best – The Exciters
14. A Touch Of Velvet, A Sting Of Brass – Ron Grainer Orchestra
15. I Go To Pieces (Every Time) – Gerri Grainger
16. Tainted Love – Gloria Jones
17. I Can Prove It – Tony Etoria
18. Ain't Nothin' But A House Party – Showstoppers
19. What – Judy Streett
20. Sign On The Dotted Line – Gene Latter

AN-AKRON-ISM

During the late 1970s, immediately following the emergence of Devo, a group who have confused everyone most successfully with their ludicrous but plausible 'de-evolution' propaganda, Stiff Records decided that if the city of Akron, Ohio, could produce such a remarkable group, then there must be other talent lurking in the 'Rubber Capital of The World'. In fact, although several of the acts involved in Stiff's *Akron Compilation* probably never really existed, several of the others have achieved some subsequent success, including, of course, Devo, who are actually rather a good rock'n'roll band (something which they will probably consider the ultimate insult).

1. Devo
2. Rachel Sweet
3. Jane Aire and the Belvederes
4. The Waitresses
5. Chi Pig
6. The Bizarros
7. Tin Huey
8. Rubber City Rebels
9. Idiot's Convention
10. Terraplane
11. Sniper

Plus an honourable mention for another lady who seems to have made a few major steps into the big league – Miss Chrissie Hynde.

ACTUAL SIZE

DEVO

EUROVISION SONG CONTEST 1982

The 27th annual Eurovision Song Contest was held in Harrogate, England on 24 April 1982. As always the standards of the songs entered ranged from the almost acceptable to the downright laughable. It was won by West Germany's 'Ein Bisschen Frieden' sung by 17 year old schoolgirl Nicole.

Worst of all was 'Nuku Pommiin', a meandering chunk of glamrock from Finland's Kojo, which failed to score a single point, as did the Norwegian entries in 1979 and 1981.

It's not easy to offend 216 jurors from 17 other countries, but Kojo, strutting around in extremely tight red trousers, did so with a display of historic incompetence. The only person surprised by his lack of success was Kojo himself who told the London *Standard* by way of explanation 'I didn't want to enter. I was talked into it'. He added 'The world can stuff itself' before making a dramatic and tearful exit.

FULL COMPETITION RESULT

1. Ein Bisschen Frieden – Nicole (West Germany)	167 points
2. Hora – Avi Toledano (Israel)	100 points
3. Amour. On T'Aime – Arlette Zola (Switzerland)	97 points
4. Si Tu Aimes Ma Musique – Stella (Belgium)	96 points

5. Mono I Agapi – Anne Vishy (Cyprus) — 85 points
6. Cours Apres Le Temps – Svetlana (Luxembourg) — 78 points
7. One Step Further – Bardo (United Kingdom) — 76 points
8. Dag Efter Dag – Chips (Sweden) — 67 points
9. Sonntag – Mess (Austria) — 57 points
10. El – Lucia (Spain) — 52 points
11. Here Today, Gone Tomorrow – Duskeys (Ireland) — 49 points
12. Adieu – Jahn Teigen and Anita Skorgan (Norway) — 40 points
13. Bem Bom – Doce (Portugal) — 32 points
14. Halo Halo – Aska (Yugoslavia) — 21 points
15. Hani – Neco (Turkey) — 20 points
16. Jig En Ik – Bill van Dijke (Netherlands) — 8 points
17. Video, Video – Brixx (Denmark) — 5 points
18. Nuku Pommiin – Kojo (Finland) — 0 points

SUMMARY OF WINNERS

Country	Wins	Years
FRANCE	4¼	1958, 1960, 1962, 1977, Shared with Spain, United Kingdom and Holland 1969
LUXEMBOURG	4	1961, 1965, 1972, 1973
HOLLAND	3¼	1957, 1959, 1975, Shared with France, Spain and United Kingdom 1969
UNITED KINGDOM	3¼	1967, 1976, 1981, Shared with France, Spain and Holland 1969
IRELAND	2	1970, 1980
ISRAEL	2	1978, 1979
SPAIN	1¼	1968, Shared with France, Holland and United Kingdom 1969
SWITZERLAND	1	1956
DENMARK	1	1963
ITALY	1	1964
AUSTRIA	1	1966
MONACO	1	1971
SWEDEN	1	1974
WEST GERMANY	1	1982

Nicole

1966

Udo Jurgens

Lulu

1969

UNITED KINGDOM EUROVISION ENTRIES 1957–1981

Year Song/Singer	Eurovision Position	Hst. Pos UK Singles Chart
1967 Puppet On A String – Sandie Shaw	1	1
1976 Save Your Kisses For Me – Brotherhood of Man	1	1
1981 Making Your Mind Up – Bucks Fizz	1	1
1969 Boom Bang-A-Bang – Lulu	1=	2
1968 Congratulations – Cliff Richard	2	1
1961 Are You Sure? – Allisons	2	2
1970 Knock Knock, Who's There? – Mary Hopkin	2	2
1972 Beg, Steal Or Borrow – New Seekers	2	2
1959 Sing, Little Birdie – Pearl Carr and Teddy Johnson	2	12

1975	Let Me Be The One – Shadows	2	12
1977	Rock Bottom – Lynsey De Paul and Mike Moran	2	19
1960	Looking High, High, High – Bryan Johnson	2	20
1965	I Belong – Kathy Kirby	2	36
1964	I Love The Little Things – Matt Monro	2	–
1973	Power To All Our Friends – Cliff Richard	3	4
1980	Love Enough For Two – Prima Donna	3	48
1971	Jack In The Box – Clodagh Rodgers	4	4
1963	Say Wonderful Things – Ronnie Carroll	4	6
1962	Ring A Ding Girl – Ronnie Carroll	4	46
1974	Long Live Love – Olivia Newton-John	4 =	11
1982	One Step Further – Bardo	7	2
1957	All – Patricia Bredin	7	–
1966	A Man Without Love – Kenneth McKellar	9	30
1978	Bad Old Days – Co-Co	10	13
1979	Mary Ann – Black Lace	12	42

N.B.: The United Kingdom did not enter the contest in 1956 or 1958.

Dana

Teach In

IRISH EUROVISION ENTRIES 1965–1981

Ireland first entered the Eurovision Song Contest in 1965 and has since carried off the Grand Prix twice, as detailed below. Both winning entries subsequently topped the British charts, in stark contrast to the Republic's fifteen other Eurovision efforts, none of which even came close.

Johnny Logan

Year	Song/Singer	Position
1965	Walking The Streets In The Rain – Butch Moore	6th
1966	Come Back To Stay – Dickie Rock	4th
1967	If I Could Choose – Sean Dunphy	2nd
1968	Chance Of A Lifetime – Pat McGeegan	4th
1969	The Wages Of Love – Muriel Day	4th
1970	All Kinds Of Everything – Dana	1st
1971	One Day Love – Angela Farrell	10th
1972	Ceol An Ghra – Sandie Jones	15th
1973	Do I Dream – Maxi	10th
1974	Cross Your Heart – Tina	7th
1975	That's What Friends Are For – Tommy and Jimmy Swarbrigg	9th
1976	When – Red Hurley	10th
1977	It's Nice To Be In Love – Swarbriggs + Two	9th
1978	Born To Sing – Colm Wilkinson	5th
1979	Happy Man – Cathal Dunne	5th
1980	What's Another Year – Johnny Logan	1st
1981	Horoscopes – Sheeba	5th
1982	Here Today, Gone Tomorrow – Duskeys	11th

10. COUNTRY COUSINS

MOST NUMBER ONES: US COUNTRY SINGLES CHART

1. Conway Twitty – 29

Conway Twitty

2. Merle Haggard – 27
3. Charley Pride – 26
4. Sonny James – 23
5. Buck Owens – 20
   Ronnie Milsap – 20
7. Tammy Wynette – 16
8. Eddy Arnold – 15
9. Dolly Parton – 14
   Marty Robbins – 14

Dolly Parton

THE 11 BEST (WORST) COUNTRY SONG TITLES

1. Drop Kick Me Jesus (Through The Goal Posts Of Life)
2. If I Said You Had A Beautiful Body (Would You Hold It Against Me)
3. I'm Playing The Jukebox To Remember What I'm Drinkin' To Forget
4. They Ain't Making Jews Like Jesus Anymore
5. I've Never Been To Bed With An Ugly Woman (But I've Sure Woken Up With A Few)
6. Don't Come Home A Drinkin' (With Lovin' On Your Mind)
7. You Can't Get Milk From A Cow Named Ben
8. Don't The Girls Get Prettier At Closing Time
9. May The Bird of Paradise Fly Up Your Nose
10. My Head Hurts, My Feet Stink, And I Don't Love Jesus
11. I'd Rather Have A Bottle In Front Of Me Than A Frontal Lobotomy

List compiled by Richard Wootton, *Melody Maker*'s Country Music correspondent and author of *Honky Tonkin' USA: A Rock'n'Roll Travel Guide*.

AMERICAN COUNTRY STATIONS

This list shows how country music radio has boomed in the US, particularly in the last few years. The total number of stations that programme country music, part or full time, now exceeds 3,000.

Year	No. full time stations
1961	81
1963	97
1965	208
1969	606
1971	525
1972	633
1973	764
1974	856
1975	1,116
1977	1,140
1978	1,150
1979	1,434
1980	1,534
1981	1,785
1982	2,033

ALL TIME TOP 20 COUNTRY TRACKS

1. Your Cheatin' Heart – Hank Williams
2. Blue Yodel (T For Texas) – Jimmie Rodgers

Jimmie Rodgers

3. Folsom Prison Blues – Johnny Cash
4. Walking The Floor Over You – Ernest Tubb

Ernest Tubb

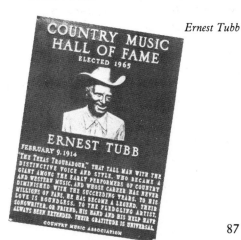

5. Movin' On – Hank Snow
6. If You've Got The Money (I've Got The Time) – Lefty Frizzell
7. Why Baby Why – George Jones
8. San Antonio Rose – Bob Wills and the Texas Playboys
9. He'll Have To Go – Jim Reeves
10. Lucille – Kenny Rogers
11. Blue Eyes Cryin' In The Rain – Willie Nelson

Willie Nelson

12. Jolene – Dolly Parton
13. Blue Moon Of Kentucky – Bill Monroe
14. Stand By Your Man – Tammy Wynette
15. Great Speckled Bird – Roy Acuff
16. Crazy Arms – Ray Price
17. Six Days On The Road – Dave Dudley
18. Blanket On The Ground – Billie Jo Spears
19. Good Hearted Woman – Waylon (Jennings) and Willie (Nelson)
20. Crystal Chandeliers – Charley Pride

(Selected by Adrian Scott.)

HANK WILLIAMS TOP 20

1. Your Cheatin' Heart
2. I'm So Lonesome I Could Cry
3. Hey Good Lookin'
4. Jambalaya (On The Bayou)
5. Long Gone Lonesome Blues
6. Take These Chains From My Heart
7. You Win Again
8. Ramblin' Man
9. Mind Your Own Business
10. Move It On Over
11. Honky Tonk Blues
12. I'll Never Get Out Of This World Alive
13. Cold Cold Heart
14. (I Heard That) Lonesome Whistle Blow
15. Lost Highway
16. I Can't Help It (If I'm Still In Love With You)
17. Crazy Heart
18. Nobody's Lonesome For Me
19. Settin' The Woods On Fire
20. Kaw-Liga

List by Adrian Scott who selects rock books to be sold in W. H. Smith and Son, the biggest bookstore chain in the UK.

A TRIBUTE TO HANK WILLIAMS
BY CHET ATKINS · RONNIE MILSAP · HANK SNOW
Eddy Arnold · Jim Ed Brown · Floyd Cramer · Skeeter Davis · Hank Locklin
Vernon Oxford · Porter Wagoner and others

JOHNNY CASH'S FIRST 25 COUNTRY HITS

1. Cry, Cry, Cry
2. Folsom Prison Blues/So Doggone Lonesome
3. I Walk The Line
4. There You Go/Train Of Love
5. Next In Line/Don't Make Me Go
6. Home Of The Blues/Give My Love To Rose
7. Ballad Of A Teenage Queen
8. Guess Things Happen That Way
9. The Ways Of A Woman In Love/You're The Nearest Thing To Heaven
10. It's Just About Time
11. Luther Played The Boogie/Thanks A Lot

Johnny Cash

12. Katy Too
13. Goodbye Little Darling
14. Straight As In Love/I Love You Because
15. Mean Eyed Cat
16. Oh Lonesome Me
17. What Do I Care?/All Over Again
18. Don't Take Your Guns To Town
19. Frankie's Man Johnny/You Dreamer You
20. I Got Stripes/Five Feet High And Rising
21. The Little Drummer Boy
22. Seasons Of My Heart/Smiling Bill McCall
23. Second Honeymoon

24. The Rebel Johnny Yuma
25. Tennessee Flat-Top Box

Note. Nos 1–16 were on Sun, Nos. 17–25 were on CBS, and the whole list only takes him up to 1961!

BEST COUNTRY DUETTISTS

1. George Jones and Tammy Wynette

George Jones and Tammy Wynette

2. Porter Wagoner and Dolly Parton
3. Gram Parsons and Emmylou Harris
4. Bill Danoff and Taffy Nivert
5. Johnny Cash and June Carter
6. Jerry Lee Lewis and Linda Gail Lewis
7. Nancy Sinatra and Lee Hazelwood
8. Waylon (Jennings) and Jessi (Colter)
9. Loretta Lynn and Conway Twitty
10. Bobbie Gentry and Glen Campbell

GEORGE JONES' DUET PARTNERS

1. Brenda Carter
2. Melba Montgomery
3. Margie Singleton
4. Tammy Wynette
5. Johnny Paycheck
6. Waylon Jennings
7. James Taylor

8. Emmylou Harris
9. Linda Ronstadt
10. Willie Nelson
11. Elvis Costello
12. Dennis and Ray of Dr Hook
13. Pop and Mavis Staples

REDNECK ROCKERS

The 1970s saw the birth of a movement known as 'Redneck Rock', which was based around the city of Austin, Texas. While its roots were in country music of the traditional type (many redneck rockers were disenchanted refugees from Nashville), the genre soon seemed to gain a sound of its own, exemplified by the following acts.

1. Willie Nelson
2. Waylon Jennings

Waylon Jennings

3. Jerry Jeff Walker
4. Billy Joe Shaver
5. Steve Fromholz
6. Michael Murphey
7. B. W. Stevenson
8. Willis Alan Ramsey
9. Kinky Friedman
10. Guy Clark
11. Kenneth Threadgill

12. Townes Van Zandt
13. Doug Sahm
14. Travis Holland
15. Commander Cody and the Lost Planet Airmen
16. Alvin Crow
17. Augie Meyer
18. Hondo Crouch
19. Tompall Glaser
20. Gerry Allen
21. Ray Wylie Hubbard
22. Bobby Bridger
23. Richard Dobson
24. Rusty Wier
25. Jessi Colter
26. Lee Clayton
27. Butch Hancock

THE LOMAX GOLD RECORD COLLECTION

'The first issue of my magazine, *Omaha Rainbow*, appeared in November 1973. Since then I have published as quarterly as possible, reaching issue 28 in November 1981. With issue 17 in the summer of 1978 I began including the Lomax Gold Record Collection. Fifty records are listed in each Collection, among which the top ten or so are listed in some order of merit. Here are the top five from each of the twelve Collections so far published. My personal prejudices shine through – how else could so many of these fine artists hit the high spots?' – Peter O'Brien

1.1 West Texas Waltz – Joe Ely (Honky Tonk Masquerade)
1.2 Old Number Nine – Lee Clayton (Border Affair)
1.3 The Last Hurrah – John Stewart (Fire In The Wind)
1.4 High Rollers – Riders of the Purple Sage (Who Are These Guys?)
1.5 Poncho And Lefty – Townes van Zandt (Live At The Old Quarter)

2.1 Badlands – Bruce Springsteen (Darkness On The Edge Of Town)
2.2 Eighteen Wheels – John Stewart (Fire In The Wind)

2.3 Alkali – Hardin and Russell (Ring Of Bone) Demo

2.4 Old Cheyenne – Ian and Sylvia (The Best Of Ian And Sylvia)

2.5 Baby Ride Easy – Richard Dobson (In Texas Last December)

3.1 Four Strong Winds – Neil Young (Comes A Time)

3.2 Return Of The Grievous Angel – Emmylou Harris (Emmylou Harris With James Burton – Bootleg)

3.3 Lodi – Creedence Clearwater Revival (Green River)

3.4 Rose Water – John Stewart (Wingless Angels)

3.5 Almost Saturday Night – John Fogerty (John Fogerty)

4.1 The Pink And Black Song – Terry Allen (Lubbock On Everything)

4.2 Thoroughfare Gap – Stephen Stills (Thoroughfare Gap)

4.3 Anna On A Memory – John Stewart (Cannons In The Rain)

4.4 Crazy Lemon – Joe Ely (Down On the Drag)

4.5 Romeo Is Bleeding – Tom Waits (Blue Valentine)

Tom Waits

5.1 Lost Her In The Sun – John Stewart (Bombs Away Dream Babies)

5.2 A Little Cocaine – Lee Clayton (Naked Child)

5.3 What Does She See? – Ian Tyson (One Jump Ahead Of The Devil)

5.4 Even Cowgirls Get The Blues – Emmylou Harris (Blue Kentucky Girl)

5.5 Dallas – Jimmie Dale and the Flatlanders (T. For Texas)

6.1 Gold – John Stewart (Bombs Away Dream Babies)

6.2 Starry Eyes – The Records (The Records)

6.3 Powderfinger – Neil Young (Rust Never Sleeps)

6.4 It's Too Late – The Searchers (Searchers)

6.5 I Know I'm Not Wrong – Fleetwood Mac (Tusk)

7.1 Nightman – John Stewart (Bombs Away Dream Babies)

7.2 The Stranger – Richard Dobson (The Big Taste)

7.3 Split And Slide – Butch Hancock (The Wind's Dominion)

7.4 The Free Mexican Airforce – Peter Rowan (Peter Rowan)

7.5 Boxcars – Joe Ely (Honky Tonk Masquerade)

8.1 Texas Number One – Wes McGhee (Air Mail)

8.2 Ashes By Now – Rodney Crowell (But What Will The Neighbours Think?)

8.3 Wind On The River – John Stewart (Dream Babies Go Hollywood)

8.4 Honky Tonk Stuff – Jerry Lee Lewis (When Two Worlds Collide)

8.5 Beer Drinkin' Woman – Ponty Bone (West Texas Squeezebox Boogie)

9.1 Alberta's Child – Ian Tyson (Canadian single)

9.2 Sherry Darling – Bruce Springsteen (The River)

9.3 Baby Ride Easy – Carlene Carter with Dave Edmunds (Musical Shapes)

9.4 That Lovin' You Feelin' Again – Roy Orbison and Emmylou Harris (Roadie)

9.5 Wheels Of Thunder – John Stewart (Dream Babies Go Hollywood)

10.1 The Dream Goes On – Lee Clayton (The Dream Goes On)

10.2 Tunnel Of Love – Dire Straits (Making Movies)

Dire Straits

10.3 That's All Right – Hoyt Axton (Life Machine)

10.4 Swamp Rat – Richard Dobson (American single)

10.5 Wishin' For You – Joe Ely (Musta Notta Gotta Lotta)

11.1 She's Crazy For Leavin' – Guy Clark (The South Coast of Texas)

11.2 Precious To Me – Phil Seymour (Phil Seymour)

11.3 Hard Road – Lucinda Williams (Happy Woman Blues)

11.4 Low And Lonely – Ricky Skaggs (Waitin' For The Sun To Shine)

11.5 Jole Blon – Gary 'US' Bonds (Dedication)

12.1 Joseph Cross – Eric Taylor (Shameless Love)

12.2 Waiting On A Friend – Rolling Stones (Tattoo You)

12.3 Rain – Ian Hunter (Short Back'n'Sides)
12.4 Shame On The Moon – Rodney Crowell (Rodney Crowell)
12.5 Crystelle – Guy Clark (South Coast Of Texas)

Omaha Rainbow, edited by Peter O'Brien, is obtainable from 10 Lesley Court, Harcourt Road, Wallington, Surrey, (UK), and comes highly recommended by the authors.

JOHN STEWART'S GREATEST SONGS

'Give us a John Stewart top twenty,' they said. 'Okay,' I replied without thinking. Since then, every time I've sat down to compile it I've come up with a different list. This is the way it looks at 9.30 pm on 8 December 1981. By the time you read this I'll have changed my mind a hundred more times. No order of merit – I've sweated enough blood already – just a chronological order of release. – *Peter O'Brien*

John Stewart

1. Cody – 'Cody sang to me and I could see Montana in his eyes.'
2. July, You're A Woman – 'I'm drunk out of my mind merely from the fact that you are here.'
3. California Bloodlines – 'There's California bloodlines in my heart.'
4. Mother Country – 'He's sittin' straight and proud and he's drivin' her stone blind.'
5. Willard – 'Willard he's a loner, livin' by the tracks side his home.'
6. Touch Of The Sun – 'You've played one too many beer halls and there ain't nobody come.'
7. Kansas Rain – 'I was standin' in line at the Bank of America. Nobody spoke, they were in the house of God.'
8. Light Come Shine – 'Holy young roller, I've gone and stolen her away from the holy man, his bible and beads.'
9. Durango – 'Well, I never saw Peckinpah, I guess he forgot to call.'
10. Anna On A Memory – 'I see you caught the back wheels, that's how all us stray dogs gonna die.'
11. All Time Woman – 'Mother outlaw's been giving me jaw saying, "Why don't you marry the girl?"'
12. Hung On The Heart – 'We saw the road house lights were burning, we heard the music of the band.'
13. Rose Water – 'Valiums and hearty, an LA party, Topanga music on the radio.'
14. Eighteen Wheels – 'A beehive's laying with her head in his lap, I don't believe she was taking a nap.'
15. The Last Hurrah – 'Loyal friends and front-row dancers, hitch your wagon to a star.'
16. Gold – 'There's people out there turning music into gold.'
17. Lost Her In The Sun – 'Fire up your heart for the wind is getting cold now, it always gets cold for the riders of the night.'
18. Wind On The River – 'Moonlight's alright, radio is all night, seems like heaven to me.'
19. Wheels Of Thunder – 'That old Chevvy was all that I ever need. I had the moves and I knew she had the speed.'
20. Nightman – 'Got me doin' handstands, drummer hit the wambam, yeah!'

'You asshole, O'Brien!' – John Stewart, 18 September 1979. 'You know everything about me there is to know, things I don't even know. I should be asking you what I've been doing for the last twenty years.' – John Stewart, 21 September 1979.

John Stewart began his career as a member of the Kingston Trio, which he left in the late sixties. Since then he has released a series of critically acclaimed, but commercially unsuccessful albums. Nevertheless he remains a strong cult figure among devotees of Americana. The magazine *Omaha Rainbow*, edited by Peter O'Brien, is named after one of his songs and is devoted to the works of John Stewart.

Lyrics all written by John Stewart, published as follows: Nos 1–14: Six Continents Music Publishing Inc (BMI) Interworld Music Ltd (BMI); Nos 15–20: Bugles Publishing/Stigwood Music Inc (BMI)/RSO Publishing/Chappell and Co (BMI).

OMAHA RAINBOW 9   25p

11. CHARTING THE CHARTS

AMERICA'S FIRST SINGLES CHART
(*Billboard*, 20 July 1940)

1. I'll Never Smile Again – Tommy Dorsey
2. The Breeze And I – Jimmy Dorsey
3. Imagination – Glenn Miller
4. Playmates – Kay Kyser
5. Fools Rush In – Glenn Miller
6. Where Was I? – Charlie Barnet
7. Pennsylvania 6–5000 – Glenn Miller
8. Imagination – Tommy Dorsey

Bing Crosby

9. Sierra Sue – Bing Crosby
10. Make Believe Island – Mitchell Ayres

(Courtesy of *Billboard Magazine*)

BRITAIN'S FIRST SINGLES CHART
(*New Musical Express*, 14 November 1952)

1. Here In My Heart – Al Martino
2. You Belong To Me – Jo Stafford
3. Somewhere Along The Way – Nat King Cole
4. Isle Of Innisfree – Bing Crosby
5. Feet Up – Guy Mitchell
6. Half As Much – Rosemary Clooney
7. Forget Me Not – Vera Lynn
   High Noon – Frankie Laine
8. Sugar Bush – Doris Day and Frankie Laine
   Blue Tango – Ray Martin
9. Homing Waltz – Vera Lynn
10. Auf Wiedersehen – Vera Lynn

Vera Lynn

11. Cowpuncher's Cantata – Max Bygraves
    Because You're Mine – Mario Lanza
12. Walking My Baby Back Home – Johnnie Ray

(Courtesy of the *New Musical Express*)

THE BEST-SELLING SINGLES OF 1962 – UK

1. Stranger On The Shore – Acker Bilk
2. I Remember You – Frank Ifield
3. Rock-a-Hula Baby/Can't Help Falling In Love – Elvis Presley
4. Wonderful Land – Shadows
5. Let's Twist Again – Chubby Checker
6. The Young Ones – Cliff Richard

Chubby Checker

7. A Picture Of You – Joe Brown
8. Come Outside – Mike Sarne
9. Good Luck Charm – Elvis Presley
10. I Can't Stop Loving You – Ray Charles
11. Telstar – Tornados
12. Speedy Gonzales – Pat Boone
13. Do You Want To Dance – Cliff Richard
14. Things – Bobby Darin
15. The Loco-Motion – Little Eva
16. Tell Me What He Said – Helen Shapiro
17. Nut Rocker – B. Bumble and the Stingers
18. Roses Are Red – Ronnie Carroll
19. Ginny Come Lately – Brian Hyland
20. Wimoweh – Karl Denver

AMERICA'S BEST-SELLING SINGLES 1962

1. The Twist – Chubby Checker
2. Stranger On The Shore – Acker Bilk
3. Peppermint Twist – Joey Dee
4. Mashed Potato – Dee Dee Sharp
5. Moon River – Henry Mancini
6. I Can't Stop Loving You – Ray Charles
7. You'll Lose A Good Thing – Barbara Lynn
8. The Stripper – David Rose
9. The Wanderer – Dion
10. The Lion Sleeps Tonight – Tokens
11. Johnny Angel – Shelley Fabares
12. The One Who Really Loves You – Mary Wells
13. Ramblin' Rose – Nat 'King' Cole
14. Hey Baby – Bruce Channel
15. Locomotion – Little Eva
16. Duke Of Earl – Gene Chandler
17. Roses Are Red – Bobby Vinton
18. Do You Love Me – Contours
19. Soldier Boy – Shirelles
20. Sherry – Four Seasons

Reproduced courtesy of *Cashbox*

THE BEST-SELLING SINGLES OF 1963 – UK

1. From Me To You – Beatles
2. She Loves You – Beatles
3. In Dreams – Roy Orbison
4. Island Of Dreams – Springfields
5. From A Jack To A King – Ned Miller
6. Deck Of Cards – Wink Martindale
7. How Do You Do It? – Gerry and the Pacemakers
8. Summer Holiday – Cliff Richard
9. Confessin' – Frank Ifield
10. Scarlett O' Hara – Jet Harris and Tony Meehan
11. Can't Get Used To Losing You – Andy Williams
12. Charmaine – Bachelors
13. Please Please Me – Beatles
14. I Like It – Gerry and the Pacemakers
15. Atlantis – Shadows

Acker Bilk

16. Do You Want To Know A Secret? – Billy J. Kramer and the Dakotas
17. Take These Chains From My Heart – Ray Charles
18. Do You Love Me? – Brian Poole and the Tremeloes
19. Sweets For My Sweet – Searchers
20. Foot Tapper – Shadows

AMERICA'S BEST-SELLING SINGLES 1963

1. Limbo Rock – Chubby Checker
2. Go Away Little Girl – Steve Lawrence
3. End Of The World – Skeeter Davis
4. Blue Velvet – Bobby Vinton
5. Telstar – Tornadoes
6. I Will Follow Him – Little Peggy March
7. Rhythm Of The Rain – Cascades
8. Can't Get Used To Losing You – Andy Williams
9. Fingertips – Little Stevie Wonder
10. Return To Sender – Elvis Presley
11. Up On The Roof – Drifters
12. So Much In Love – Tymes
13. He's So Fine – Chiffons
14. Hey Paula – Paul and Paula
15. Big Girls Don't Cry – Four Seasons
16. Surfin' USA – Beach Boys
17. Walk Right In – Rooftop Singers
18. Walk Like A Man – Four Seasons
19. If You Wanna Be Happy – Jimmy Soul
20. Easier Said Than Done – Essex

Reproduced courtesy of *Cashbox*

THE BEST-SELLING SINGLES OF 1964 – UK

1. I Love You Because – Jim Reeves
2. I Won't Forget You – Jim Reeves
3. It's Over – Roy Orbison
4. The Wedding – Julie Rogers
5. Someone Someone – Brian Poole and the Tremeloes
6. I Believe – Bachelors
7. My Boy Lollipop – Millie

8. It's All Over Now – Rolling Stones
9. I Wouldn't Trade You For The World – Bachelors
10. Oh Pretty Woman – Roy Orbison
11. Needles And Pins – Searchers
12. Anyone Who Had A Heart – Cilla Black

Cilla Black

13. A Hard Day's Night – Beatles
14. Have I The Right – Honeycombs
15. Do Wah Diddy Diddy – Manfred Mann
16. Diane – Bachelors
17. You're My World – Cilla Black
18. I'm Into Something Good – Herman's Hermits
19. I Think Of You – Merseybeats
20. Juliet – Four Pennies

AMERICA'S BEST-SELLING SINGLES 1964

1. I Want To Hold Your Hand – Beatles
2. She Loves You – Beatles
3. Hello, Dolly – Louis Armstrong
4. Oh, Pretty Woman – Roy Orbison
5. I Get Around – Beach Boys
6. Louie, Louie – Kingsmen
7. My Guy – Mary Wells

8. Glad All Over – Dave Clark Five
9. Everybody Loves Somebody – Dean Martin
10. Dominique – The Singing Nun
11. There, I've Said It Again – Bobby Vinton
12. Love Me Do – Beatles
13. She's A Fool – Lesley Gore
14. Where Did Our Love Go – Supremes
15. Java – Al Hirt
16. People – Barbra Streisand
17. A Hard Day's Night – Beatles
18. Since I Fell – Lenny Welch
19. Forget Him – Bobby Rydell
20. Under The Boardwalk – Drifters

Reproduced by courtesy of *Cashbox*

THE BEST-SELLING SINGLES OF 1965 – UK

1. I'll Never Find Another You – Seekers
2. Tears – Ken Dodd
3. A Walk In The Black Forest – Horst Jankowski
4. A World Of Our Own – Seekers
5. Crying In The Chapel – Elvis Presley
6. Help! – Beatles
7. I'm Alive – Hollies
8. Zorba's Dance – Marcello Minerbi
9. King Of The Road – Roger Miller
10. The Minute You're Gone – Cliff Richard
11. Mr Tambourine Man – Byrds
12. Eve Of Destruction – Barry McGuire
13. The Clapping Song – Shirley Ellis
14. Long Live Love – Sandie Shaw
15. True Love Ways – Peter and Gordon
16. It's Not Unusual – Tom Jones
    I Got You Babe – Sonny and Cher
18. Almost There – Andy Williams
    Cast Your Fate To The Wind – Sounds Orchestral
20. The Price Of Love – Everly Brothers

NB: Two titles tied for sixteenth place, and two for eighteenth place.

AMERICA'S BEST-SELLING SINGLES 1965

1. Back In My Arms Again – Supremes
2. Wooly Bully – Sam the Sham
3. Mr Lonely – Bobby Vinton
4. I Can't Help Myself – Four Tops
5. Satisfaction – Rolling Stones
6. Downtown – Petula Clark

Petula Clark

7. You've Lost That Lovin' Feelin' – Righteous Brothers
8. Come See About Me – Supremes
9. The 'In' Crowd – Ramsey Lewis
10. You Were On My Mind – We Five
11. Help! – Beatles
12. Crying In The Chapel – Elvis Presley
13. Love Potion Number 9 – Searchers
14. I Got You Babe – Sonny and Cher
15. This Diamond Ring – Gary Lewis and the Playboys
16. My Girl – Temptations
17. King Of The Road – Roger Miller
18. Hang On Sloopy – McCoys
19. I Feel Fine – Beatles
20. The Birds And The Bees – Jewel Akens

Reproduced courtesy of *Cashbox*

THE BEST-SELLING SINGLES OF 1966 – UK

1. Distant Drums – Jim Reeves
2. Strangers In The Night – Frank Sinatra
3. Spanish Flea – Herb Alpert and the Tijuana Brass
4. Hold Tight – Dave Dee, Dozy, Beaky, Mick and Tich
5. Sloop John B. – Beach Boys
6. Mama – Dave Berry
7. These Boots Are Made For Walkin' – Nancy Sinatra
8. God Only Knows – Beach Boys
9. A Groovy Kind Of Love – Mindbenders
10. Sunny Afternoon – Kinks
11. When A Man Loves A Woman – Percy Sledge
12. Too Soon To Know – Roy Orbison
13. Yellow Submarine/Eleanor Rigby – Beatles
13. Monday Monday – Mamas and the Papas
15. Black Is Black – Los Bravos
16. You Don't Have To Say You Love Me – Dusty Springfield
17. River Deep, Mountain High – Ike and Tina Turner

Ike and Tina Turner

The More I See You – Chris Montez
19. With A Girl Like You – Troggs
20. You Were On My Mind – Crispian St Peters

NB: Two titles tied for seventeenth place.

AMERICA'S BEST-SELLING SINGLES 1966

1. Ballad Of The Green Berets – Staff Sergeant Barry Sadler
2. California Dreamin' – The Mamas and the Papas
3. Sounds Of Silence – Simon and Garfunkel
4. Sunny – Bobby Hebb
5. Strangers In The Night – Frank Sinatra
6. You Can't Hurry Love – Supremes
7. A Groovy King Of Love – Mindbenders
8. I Got You – James Brown
9. Little Red Riding Hood – Sam the Sham
10. See You In September – Happenings
11. Good Lovin' – Young Rascals
12. We Can Work It Out – Beatles
13. Uptight – Stevie Wonder
14. You Don't Have To Say You Love Me – Dusty Springfield
15. Kicks – Paul Revere and the Raiders
16. Lightnin' Strikes – Lou Christie
17. Cherish – Association
18. Soul And Inspiration – Righteous Brothers
19. Hanky Panky – Tommy James and the Shondells
20. 96 Tears – ? (Question Mark) and the Mysterians

Reproduced courtesy of *Cashbox*

THE BEST-SELLING SINGLES OF 1967 – UK

1. Release Me – Engelbert Humperdinck
2. There Goes My Everything – Engelbert Humperdinck

Engelbert Humperdinck

3. The Last Waltz – Engelbert Humperdinck
4. Just Loving You – Anita Harris
5. San Francisco (Be Sure To Wear Flowers In Your Hair) – Scott McKenzie
6. Puppet On A String – Sandie Shaw
7. I'll Never Fall In Love Again – Tom Jones
8. There Must Be A Way – Frankie Vaughan
9. A Whiter Shade Of Pale – Procol Harum
10. I'm A Believer – Monkees
11. Somethin' Stupid – Frank and Nancy Sinatra
12. Dedicated To The One I Love – Mamas and the Papas
13. It Must Be Him – Vikki Carr
14. Excerpt From A Teenage Opera – Keith West
15. Massachusetts – Bee Gees
16. Silence Is Golden – Tremeloes
17. Edelweiss – Vince Hill
18. All You Need Is Love – Beatles
19. This Is My Song – Petula Clark
20. If I Were A Rich Man – Topol

AMERICA'S BEST-SELLING SINGLES 1967

1. The Letter – Box Tops
2. Light My Fire – Doors
3. Can't Take My Eyes Off You – Frankie Valli
4. Ode To Billie Joe – Bobbie Gentry
5. To Sir With Love – Lulu
6. Happy Together – Turtles
7. Windy – Association
8. I'm A Believer – Monkees
9. Groovin' – Young Rascals
10. Respect – Aretha Franklin
11. Georgy Girl – Seekers
12. I Think We're Alone Now – Tommy James and the Shondells
13. Something Stupid – Frank and Nancy Sinatra
14. Soul Man – Sam and Dave
15. Come Back When You Grow Up – Bobby Vee
16. Sweet Soul Music – Arthur Conley
17. Ruby Tuesday – Rolling Stones
18. Kind Of A Drag – Buckinghams
19. A Little Bit Of Soul – Music Explosion
20. I Got Rhythm – Happenings

Reproduced courtesy of *Cashbox*

THE BEST-SELLING SINGLES OF 1968 – UK

1. What A Wonderful World – Louis Armstrong
2. I Pretend – Des O'Connor
3. Those Were The Days – Mary Hopkin
4. Help Yourself – Tom Jones
5. Young Girl – Union Gap featuring Gary Puckett
6. Delilah – Tom Jones
7. Little Arrows – Leapy Lee
8. Baby Come Back – Equals
9. The Good, The Bad And The Ugly – Hugo Montenegro
10. Jesamine – Casuals
11. She Wears My Ring – Solomon King
    Hey Jude – Beatles

13. If I Only Had Time – John Rowles
14. This Guy's In Love With You – Herb Alpert
15. Simon Says – 1910 Fruitgum Company
16. Honey – Bobby Goldsboro
17. A Man Without Love – Engelbert Humperdinck
18. Fire – Crazy World Of Arthur Brown
19. I've Gotta Get A Message To You – Bee Gees
20. Do It Again – Beach Boys
    Can't Take My Eyes Off You – Andy Williams

Andy Williams

The Son Of Hickory Holler's Tramp – O. C. Smith

NB: Two titles tied for eleventh place, and three titles tied for twentieth place

AMERICA'S BEST-SELLING SINGLES 1968

1. Hey Jude – Beatles
2. Love Is Blue – Paul Mauriat
3. Young Girl – Union Gap featuring Gary Puckett

4. The Dock Of The Bay – Otis Redding
5. Mrs Robinson – Simon and Garfunkel
6. Honey – Bobby Goldsboro
7. People Got To Be Free – Rascals
8. Green Tambourine – Lemon Pipers
9. This Guy's In Love With You – Herb Alpert
10. Tighten Up – Archie Bell
11. Yummy, Yummy, Yummy – Ohio Express
12. Harper Valley PTA – Jeannie C. Riley
13. Judy In Disguise – John Fred and his Playboy Band
14. Little Green Apples – O. C. Smith
15. Hello, I Love You – Doors
16. I've Gotta Get A Message To You – Bee Gees
17. A Beautiful Morning – Rascals
18. Cry Like A Baby – Box Tops
19. The Ballad Of Bonnie And Clyde – Georgie Fame
20. I Wish It Would Rain – Temptations

Reproduced courtesy of *Cashbox*

THE BEST-SELLING SINGLES OF 1969 – UK

1. My Way – Frank Sinatra
2. Je T'Aime . . . Moi Non Plus – Jane Birkin and Serge Gainsbourg
3. Gentle On My Mind – Dean Martin
4. Honky Tonk Women – Rolling Stones
5. Nobody's Child – Karen Young
6. Saved By The Bell – Robin Gibb
7. Please Don't Go – Donald Peers
8. Get Back – Beatles
9. I'll Never Fall In Love Again – Bobbie Gentry
10. Dizzy – Tommy Roe
11. Albatross – Fleetwood Mac
12. In The Ghetto – Elvis Presley
13. I Heard It Through The Grapevine – Marvin Gaye
14. Sugar Sugar – Archies
15. Bad Moon Rising – Creedence Clearwater Revival
16. Make Me An Island – Joe Dolan

17. Where Do You Go To My Lovely – Peter Sarstedt
18. My Cherie Amour – Stevie Wonder
19. Time Is Tight – Booker T. and the M.G.s
20. Don't Forget To Remember – Bee Gees

AMERICA'S BEST-SELLING SINGLES 1969

1. Sugar Sugar – Archies
2. Honky Tonk Women – Rolling Stones
3. Aquarius – Fifth Dimension

Fifth Dimension

4. I Heard It Through The Grapevine – Marvin Gaye
5. Everyday People – Sly and the Family Stone
6. Dizzy – Tommy Roe
7. I Can't Get Next To You – Temptations
8. Crimson And Clover – Tommy James
9. Build Me Up Buttercup – Foundations
10. Hair – Cowsills
11. In The Year 2525 (Exordium And Terminus) – Zager and Evans
12. Easy To Be Hard – Three Dog Night
13. Wichita Lineman – Glen Campbell
14. Get Back – Beatles
15. Time Of The Season – Zombies
16. One – Three Dog Night
17. Crystal Blue Persuasion – Tommy James and the Shondells

18. Touch Me – Doors
19. Green River – Creedence Clearwater Revival
20. Jean – Oliver

Reproduced courtesy of *Cashbox*

THE BEST-SELLING SINGLES OF 1970 – UK

1. The Wonder Of You – Elvis Presley
2. Yellow River – Christie
3. In The Summertime – Mungo Jerry

Ray Dorset of Mungo Jerry

4. Band Of Gold – Freda Payne
5. Something – Shirley Bassey
6. Wanderin' Star – Lee Marvin
7. Spirit In The Sky – Norman Greenbaum
8. Two Little Boys – Rolf Harris
9. All Right Now – Free
10. Cottonfields – Beach Boys

Music Week listed only ten singles in its survey of 1970

AMERICA'S BEST-SELLING SINGLES 1970

1. Spirit In The Sky – Norman Greenbaum

2. ABC – Jackson 5
3. Band Of Gold – Freda Payne
4. Get Ready – Rare Earth
5. Bridge Over Troubled Water – Simon and Garfunkel
6. Venus – Shocking Blue
7. American Woman – Guess Who
8. Which Way You Goin' Billy – Poppy Family
9. Let It Be – Beatles
10. Mama Told Me Not To Come – Three Dog Night
11. Ball Of Confusion – Temptations
12. The Love You Save – Jackson 5
13. Raindrops Keep Falling On My Head – B. J. Thomas
14. Cracklin' Rosie – Neil Diamond
15. Spill The Wine – Eric Burdon
16. (They Long To Be) Close To You – Carpenters
17. Hey There Lonely Girl – Eddie Holman
18. War – Edwin Starr
19. Lay Down (Candles In The Rain) – Melanie
20. Instant Karma (We All Shine On) – John Lennon, Yoko Ono and the Plastic Ono Band

Reproduced courtesy of *Cashbox*

THE BEST-SELLING SINGLES OF 1971 – UK

1. My Sweet Lord – George Harrison
2. Maggie May – Rod Stewart
3. Chirpy Chirpy Cheep Cheep – Middle Of The Road
4. Knock Three Times – Dawn
5. Hot Love – T. Rex
6. The Pushbike Song – Mixtures
7. Never Ending Song Of Love – New Seekers
8. I'm Still Waiting – Diana Ross
9. Hey Girl, Don't Bother Me – Tams
10. Get It On – T. Rex

Music Week listed only ten singles in its survey of 1971

AMERICA'S BEST-SELLING SINGLES 1971

1. Joy To The World – Three Dog Night
2. It's Too Late – Carole King
3. Indian Reservation – Raiders
4. How Can You Mend A Broken Heart – Bee Gees
5. She's A Lady – Tom Jones
6. Rose Garden – Lynn Anderson
7. Just My Imagination – Temptations
8. Go Away Little Girl – Donny Osmond
9. One Bad Apple – Osmond Brothers
10. Take Me Home Country Roads – John Denver
11. Never Can Say Goodbye – Jackson 5
12. Draggin' The Line – Tommy James
13. Doesn't Somebody Want To Be Wanted – Partridge Family

Partridge Family

14. Treat Her Like A Lady – Cornelius Brothers and Sister Rose
15. Want Ads – Honey Cone
16. Don't Pull Your Love – Hamilton, Joe Frank and Reynolds
17. Signs – Five Man Electrical Band
18. Knock Three Times – Dawn
19. Smiling Faces Sometimes – Undisputed Truth
20. Put Your Hand In The Hand – Ocean

Reproduced courtesy of *Cashbox*

THE BEST-SELLING SINGLES OF 1972 – UK

1. Amazing Grace – Royal Scots Dragoon Guards
2. Mouldy Old Dough – Lieutenant Pigeon
3. Puppy Love – Donny Osmond
4. Without You – Nilsson
5. I'd Like To Teach The World To Sing – New Seekers
6. Son Of My Father – Chicory Tip
7. Rock And Roll (Parts 1 and 2) – Gary Glitter
8. Metal Guru – T. Rex
9. Mother Of Mine – Neil Reid
10. Telegram Sam – T. Rex

11. American Pie – Don McLean
12. Mama Weer All Crazee Now – Slade
13. School's Out – Alice Cooper
14. You Wear It Well – Rod Stewart
15. Beg, Steal Or Borrow – New Seekers
16. Vincent – Don McLean
17. Clair – Gilbert O'Sullivan
18. My Ding-A-Ling – Chuck Berry
19. How Can I Be Sure – David Cassidy
20. Sylvia's Mother – Dr Hook and the Medicine Show

AMERICA'S BEST-SELLING SINGLES 1972

1. American Pie – Don McLean
2. Alone Again (Naturally) – Gilbert O'Sullivan
3. Brand New Key – Melanie
4. Daddy, Don't You Walk So Fast – Wayne Newton
5. Without You – Nilsson
6. I Gotcha – Joe Tex
7. Let's Stay Together – Al Green
8. If Loving You Is Wrong (I Don't Wanna Be Right) – Luther Ingram
9. Brandy (You're A Fine Girl) – Looking Glass
10. The Lion Sleeps Tonight – Robert John
11. Heart Of Gold – Neil Young
12. Family Affair – Sly and the Family Stone
13. Rockin' Robin – Michael Jackson
14. Lean On Me – Bill Withers
15. Nice To Be With You – Gallery
16. Slippin' Into Darkness – War
17. Baby Don't Get Hooked On Me – Mac Davis
18. A Horse With No Name – America
19. First Time Ever I Saw Your Face – Roberta Flack
20. Long Cool Woman (In A Black Dress) – Hollies

Reproduced courtesy of *Cashbox*

THE BEST-SELLING SINGLES OF 1973 – UK

1. Tie A Yellow Ribbon Round The Ole Oak Tree – Dawn featuring Tony Orlando
2. Eye Level – Simon Park
3. Welcome Home – Peters and Lee
4. Blockbuster – Sweet
5. Cum On Feel The Noise – Slade
6. See My Baby Jive – Wizzard
7. I'm The Leader Of The Gang (I Am) – Gary Glitter
8. I Love You, Love Me Love – Gary Glitter

9. The Twelfth Of Never – Donny Osmond
10. Spanish Eyes – Al Martino
11. Daydreamer/The Puppy Song – David Cassidy
12. Long Haired Lover From Liverpool – Little Jimmy Osmond
13. Skweeze Me Pleeze Me – Slade
14. And I Love You So – Perry Como
15. Hello Hello I'm Back Again – Gary Glitter
16. Get Down – Gilbert O'Sullivan
17. Ballroom Blitz – Sweet
18. Do You Wanna Touch Me (Oh Yeah) – Gary Glitter
19. Young Love – Donny Osmond
20. Rubber Bullets – 10CC

AMERICA'S BEST-SELLING SINGLES 1973

1. Tie A Yellow Ribbon Round The Ol' Oak Tree – Dawn featuring Tony Orlando

Dawn and Tony Orlando

2. Bad, Bad Leroy Brown – Jim Croce
3. Delta Dawn – Helen Reddy
4. Crocodile Rock – Elton John
5. Touch Me In The Morning – Diana Ross
6. My Love – Paul McCartney and Wings
7. You're So Vain – Carly Simon
8. Playground In My Mind – Clint Holmes
9. Me And Mrs Jones – Billy Paul
10. Shambala – Three Dog Night
11. Let's Get It On – Marvin Gaye
12. Love Train – O'Jays
13. Clair – Gilbert O'Sullivan
14. Last Song – Edward Bear
15. Midnight Train To Georgia – Gladys Knight and the Pips
16. Half-Breed – Cher

Cher

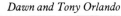

17. Say, Has Anybody Seen My Sweet Gypsy Rose – Dawn featuring Tony Orlando
18. Drift Away – Dobie Gray
19. Brother Louie – Stories
20. Will It Go Round In Circles – Billy Preston

Reproduced courtesy of *Cashbox*

THE BEST-SELLING SINGLES OF 1974 – UK

1. Tiger Feet – Mud
2. Seasons In The Sun – Terry Jacks
3. Billy, Don't Be A Hero – Paper Lace
4. When Will I See You Again – Three Degrees
5. Rock Your Baby – George McCrae
6. Gonna Make You A Star – David Essex
7. She – Charles Aznavour
8. Kung Fu Fighting – Carl Douglas
9. Everything I Own – Ken Boothe
10. Sugar Baby Love – Rubettes
11. Devil Gate Drive – Suzi Quatro
12. Love Me For A Reason – Osmonds
13. Jealous Mind – Alvin Stardust
14. The Air That I Breathe – Hollies
15. Annie's Song – John Denver
16. Waterloo – Abba
17. Wombling Song – Wombles
18. You Make Me Feel Brand New – Stylistics
19. The Most Beautiful Girl – Charlie Rich
20. Y Viva Espana – Sylvia

AMERICA'S BEST-SELLING SINGLES 1974

1. Show And Tell – Al Wilson
2. Come And Get Your Love – Redbone
3. The Most Beautiful Girl – Charlie Rich
4. Rock Me Gently – Andy Kim
5. The Way We Were – Barbra Streisand
6. Sunshine On My Shoulders – John Denver
7. You Make Me Feel Brand New – Stylistics
8. Rock On – David Essex
9. Seasons In The Sun – Terry Jacks
10. The Joker – Steve Miller Band
11. You Haven't Done Nothing – Stevie Wonder
12. Bennie And The Jets – Elton John
13. The Locomotion – Grand Funk Railroad
14. Love's Theme – Love Unlimited

15. Spiders And Snakes – Jim Stafford
16. Nothing From Nothing – Billy Preston
17. TSOP – MFSB
18. You're Sixteen – Ringo Starr
19. The Night Chicago Died – Paper Lace
20. Top Of The World – Carpenters

Reproduced courtesy of *Cashbox*

THE BEST-SELLING SINGLES OF 1975 – UK

1. Bye Bye Baby – Bay City Rollers
2. Sailing – Rod Stewart

Rod Stewart

3. I Can't Give You Anything (But My Love) – Stylistics
4. Whispering Grass – Don Estelle and Windsor Davies
5. Stand By Your Man – Tammy Wynette
6. Give A Little Love – Bay City Rollers
7. Hold Me Close – David Essex
8. The Last Farewell – Roger Whittaker
9. I Only Have Eyes For You – Art Garfunkel

10. Tears On My Pillow – Johnny Nash
11. I'm Not In Love – 10CC
12. Barbados – Typically Tropical
13. If – Telly Savalas
14. There Goes My First Love – Drifters
15. Three Steps To Heaven – Showaddywaddy
16. The Hustle – Van McCoy
17. Space Oddity – David Bowie
18. January – Pilot
19. Funky Moped/Magic Roundabout – Jasper Carrott
20. Make Me Smile (Come Up And See Me) – Steve Harley and Cockney Rebel

AMERICA'S BEST-SELLING SINGLES 1975

1. Love Will Keep Us Together – Captain and Tennille
2. Rhinestone Cowboy – Glen Campbell
3. Boogie On Reggae Woman – Stevie Wonder
4. Pick Up The Pieces – Average White Band

Average White Band

5. Fame – David Bowie
6. At Seventeen – Janis Ian
7. Shinin' Star – Earth, Wind and Fire
8. Thank God, I'm A Country Boy – John Denver
9. Lady Marmalade – Labelle
10. Island Girl – Elton John
11. Kung Fu Fighting – Carl Douglas

12. My Eyes Adored You – Frankie Valli
13. Black Water – Doobie Brothers
14. Why Can't We Be Friends – War
15. One Of These Nights – Eagles
16. Wasted Days And Wasted Nights – Freddy Fender
17. Mandy – Barry Manilow
18. The Hustle – Van McCoy
19. Have You Never Been Mellow – Olivia Newton-John
20. Laughter In The Rain – Neil Sedaka

Reproduced courtesy of *Cashbox*

THE BEST-SELLING SINGLES OF 1976 – UK

1. Save Your Kisses For Me – Brotherhood of Man
2. Don't Go Breaking My Heart – Elton John and Kiki Dee
3. Mississippi – Pussycat
4. Dancing Queen – Abba
5. A Little Bit More – Dr Hook
6. If You Leave Me Now – Chicago
7. Fernando – Abba
8. I Love To Love – Tina Charles
9. The Roussos Phenomenon (EP) – Demis Roussos

Demis Roussos

10. December '63 (Oh What A Night) – Four Seasons
11. Under The Moon Of Love – Showaddywaddy
12. You To Me Are Everything – Real Thing

13. Forever And Ever – Slik
14. Sailing – Rod Stewart
15. Young Hearts Run Free – Candi Staton
16. Combine Harvester (Brand New Key) – Wurzels
17. When Forever Has Gone – Demis Roussos
18. Jungle Rock – Hank Mizell
19. Can't Get By Without You – Real Thing
20. You Make Me Feel Like Dancing – Leo Sayer

AMERICA'S BEST-SELLING SINGLES 1976

1. Disco Lady – Johnnie Taylor
2. Play That Funky Music – Wild Cherry
3. Kiss And Say Goodbye – Manhattans
4. Disco Duck – Rick Dees and his Cast of Idiots
5. Don't Go Breaking My Heart – Elton John/Kiki Dee
6. A Fifth Of Beethoven – Walter Murphy and the Big Apple Band
7. Afternoon Delight – Starland Vocal Band
8. Tonight's The Night (Gonna Be Alright) – Rod Stewart
9. Silly Love Songs – Wings
10. Shake Your Booty – KC and the Sunshine Band
11. Love Machine – Miracles
12. 50 Ways To Leave Your Lover – Paul Simon

Paul Simon

13. Love Hangover – Diana Ross
14. If You Leave Me Now – Chicago
15. Rock 'n' Me – Steve Miller Band
16. Boogie Fever – Sylvers
17. Dream Weaver – Gary Wright
18. Misty Blue – Dorothy Moore
19. Welcome Back – John Sebastian
20. You'll Never Find Another Love Like Mine – Lou Rawls

Reproduced courtesy of *Cashbox*

THE BEST-SELLING SINGLES OF 1977 – UK

1. Mull Of Kintyre/Girls School – Wings
2. Don't Give Up On Us – David Soul
3. Don't Cry For Me Argentina – Julie Covington
4. When I Need You – Leo Sayer
5. Silver Lady – David Soul
6. Knowing Me, Knowing You – Abba
7. I Feel Love – Donna Summer
8. Way Down – Elvis Presley
9. So You Win Again – Hot Chocolate
10. Angelo – Brotherhood of Man
11. Chanson D'Amour – Manhattan Transfer
12. Yes Sir, I Can Boogie – Baccara
13. Black Is Black – La Belle Epoque
14. Fanfare For The Common Man – Emerson, Lake and Palmer
15. Ma Baker – Boney M
16. Name Of The Game – Abba
17. Rockin' All Over The World – Status Quo
18. Love Theme From *A Star Is Born* ('Evergreen') – Barbra Streisand
19. How Deep Is Your Love – Bee Gees
20. Lucille – Kenny Rogers

AMERICA'S BEST-SELLING SINGLES 1977

1. You Light Up My Life – Debby Boone
2. I Just Want To Be Your Everything – Andy Gibb
3. Dancing Queen – Abba
4. Undercover Angel – Alan O'Day
5. Torn Between Two Lovers – Mary MacGregor
6. Love Theme From *A Star Is Born* (Evergreen) – Barbra Streisand
7. I Like Dreaming – Kenny Nolan
8. Higher And Higher – Rita Coolidge
9. Swayin' To The Music (Slow Dancing) – Johnny Rivers
10. Theme From *Star Wars* – Meco
11. The Things We Do For Love – 10CC
12. Weekend In New England – Barry Manilow

Barry Manilow

13. Best Of My Love – Emotions
14. Nobody Does It Better – Carly Simon
15. I'm Your Boogie Man – KC and the Sunshine Band
16. When I Need You – Leo Sayer
17. Don't Leave Me This Way – Thelma Houston
18. Angel In Your Arms – Hot
19. Carry On Wayward Son – Kansas
20. Southern Nights – Glen Campbell

Reproduced courtesy of *Cashbox*

THE BEST-SELLING SINGLES OF 1978 – UK

1. Rivers Of Babylon/Brown Girl In The Ring – Boney M
2. You're The One That I Want – John Travolta and Olivia Newton-John
3. Summer Nights – John Travolta and Olivia Newton-John
4. Three Times A Lady – Commodores
5. The Smurf Song – Father Abraham and the Smurfs
6. Night Fever – Bee Gees
7. Take A Chance On Me – Abba
8. Matchstalk Men And Matchstalk Cats And Dogs – Brian and Michael
9. Rat Trap – Boomtown Rats
10. Dreadlock Holiday – 10CC
11. Wuthering Heights – Kate Bush

Kate Bush

12. Sandy – John Travolta
13. Rasputin – Boney M
14. Substitute – Clout
15. Denis (Denee) – Blondie
16. Baker Street – Gerry Rafferty
17. Figaro – Brotherhood of Man
18. Come Back My Love – Darts
19. Love Don't Live Here Anymore – Rose Royce
20. It's Raining – Darts

AMERICA'S BEST-SELLING SINGLES 1978

1. Night Fever – Bee Gees
2. Stayin' Alive – Bee Gees
3. Shadow Dancing – Andy Gibb
4. Kiss You All Over – Exile
5. Three Times A Lady – Commodores
6. Hot Child In The City – Nick Gilder
7. Boogie Oogie Oogie – A Taste of Honey
8. Emotion – Samantha Sang
9. You're The One That I Want – John Travolta and Olivia Newton-John
10. Miss You – Rolling Stones
11. Grease – Frankie Valli
12. Baker Street – Gerry Rafferty
13. Can't Smile Without You – Barry Manilow
14. Baby Come Back – Player
15. Short People – Randy Newman
16. Lay Down Sally – Eric Clapton
17. It's A Heartache – Bonnie Tyler
18. Just The Way You Are – Billy Joel
19. Sometimes When We Touch – Dan Hill
20. You Needed Me – Anne Murray

Reproduced courtesy of *Cashbox*

THE BEST-SELLING SINGLES OF 1979 – UK

1. Bright Eyes – Art Garfunkel
2. Heart Of Glass – Blondie
3. We Don't Talk Anymore – Cliff Richard
4. I Don't Like Mondays – Boomtown Rats
5. When You're In Love With A Beautiful Woman – Dr Hook
6. I Will Survive – Gloria Gaynor
7. Are 'Friends' Electric? – Tubeway Army
8. Dance Away – Roxy Music
9. Sunday Girl – Blondie
10. One Day At A Time – Lena Martell
11. Message In A Bottle – Police

The Police

12. Pop Muzik – M
13. Hit Me With Your Rhythm Stick – Ian Dury and the Blockheads
14. Oliver's Army – Elvis Costello and the Attractions
15. Tragedy – Bee Gees
16. Chiquitita – Abba
17. Video Killed The Radio Star – Buggles
18. Cars – Gary Numan
19. Every Day Hurts – Sad Cafe
20. Ring My Bell – Anita Ward

Sad Cafe

AMERICA'S BEST-SELLING SINGLES 1979

1. Le Freak – Chic
2. My Sharona – Knack
3. Da Ya Think I'm Sexy – Rod Stewart
4. YMCA – Village People
5. What A Fool Believes – Doobie Brothers
6. Ring My Bell – Anita Ward
7. Bad Girls – Donna Summer
8. Too Much Heaven – Bee Gees
9. Reunited – Peaches and Herb
10. I Will Survive – Gloria Gaynor
11. Heart Of Glass – Blondie
12. Good Times – Chic
13. Sad Eyes – Robert John
14. Hot Stuff – Donna Summer
15. Pop Muzik – M
16. Fire – Pointer Sisters
17. Don't Stop 'Til You Get Enough – Michael Jackson
18. Rise – Herb Alpert
19. Tragedy – Bee Gees
20. Knock On Wood – Amii Stewart

Reproduced courtesy of *Cashbox*

THE BEST-SELLING SINGLES OF 1980 – UK

1. Don't Stand So Close To Me – Police
2. Woman In Love – Barbra Streisand
3. Feels Like I'm In Love – Kelly Marie
4. Super Trouper – Abba
5. D.I.S.C.O. – Ottawan
6. The Tide Is High – Blondie
7. Geno – Dexy's Midnight Runners
8. Together We Are Beautiful – Fern Kinney
9. Coward Of The County – Kenny Rogers
10. (Just Like) Starting Over – John Lennon
11. Working My Way Back To You/Forgive Me Girl (medley) – Detroit Spinners
12. 9 To 5 – Sheena Easton
13. Baggy Trousers – Madness
14. Ashes To Ashes – David Bowie
15. Theme From *MASH* – Mash
16. Going Underground – Jam
17. Crying – Don McLean
18. The Winner Takes It All – Abba
19. Dance Yourself Dizzy – Liquid Gold
20. No-one Quite Like Grandma – St Winifred's School Choir

THE BEST-SELLING SINGLES OF THE FIFTIES – UK

1. Rock Around The Clock – Bill Haley and His Comets (1954)
2. Diana – Paul Anka (1957)
3. Mary's Boy Child – Harry Belafonte (1957)
4. What Do You Want To Make Those Eyes At Me For – Emile Ford and the Checkmates (1959)
5. Jailhouse Rock – Elvis Presley (1958)
6. What Do You Want – Adam Faith (1959)
7. Living Doll – Cliff Richard (1959)
8. All Shook Up – Elvis Presley (1957)
9. Love Letters In The Sand – Pat Boone (1957)
10. It Doesn't Matter Anymore – Buddy Holly (1959)

ONE HUNDRED BEST-SELLING SINGLES OF THE SIXTIES – UK

Based almost entirely on actual sales figures, the following is the most accurate guide to the best-selling singles of the sixties ever published. It's no accident that this list is more comprehensive than *The Rock Lists Album*'s survey of the best-selling singles of the fifties or the seventies; simply, the sixties represented the golden era of popular music.

1. She Loves You – Beatles (1963)
2. I Want To Hold Your Hand – Beatles (1963)
3. Tears – Ken Dodd (1965)
4. Can't Buy Me Love – Beatles (1964)
5. I Feel Fine – Beatles (1964)

St Winifred's School Choir

6. The Carnival Is Over – Seekers (1965)
7. We Can Work It Out – Beatles (1965)
8. Release Me – Engelbert Humperdinck (1967)
9. It's Now Or Never – Elvis Presley (1960)
10. Green, Green Grass Of Home – Tom Jones (1966)
11. The Last Waltz – Engelbert Humperdinck (1967)
12. I Remember You – Frank Ifield (1962)

Frank Ifield

13. Stranger On The Shore – Mr Acker Bilk with the Leon Young String Chorale (1961)
14. The Young Ones – Cliff Richard and the Shadows (1962)
15. Sugar Sugar – Archies (1969)
16. The Next Time/Bachelor Boy – Cliff Richard and the Shadows (1962)
17. Telstar – Tornadoes (1962)
18. Help! – Beatles (1965)
19. Two Little Boys – Rolf Harris (1969)
20. Glad All Over – Dave Clark Five (1963)
21. Needles And Pins – Searchers (1964)
22. Anyone Who Had A Heart – Cilla Black (1964)
23. Lovesick Blues – Frank Ifield (1962)

24. Hey Jude – Beatles (1968)
25. You'll Never Walk Alone – Gerry and the Pacemakers (1963)
26. I Love You Because – Jim Reeves (1964)
27. There Goes My Everything – Engelbert Humperdinck (1967)
28. I Won't Forget You – Jim Reeves (1964)
29. A Hard Day's Night – Beatles (1964)
30. The Last Time – Rolling Stones (1965)
31. I'll Never Find Another You – Seekers (1965)
32. Are You Sure – Allisons (1961)
33. Distant Drums – Jim Reeves (1966)

Jim Reeves

34. Are You Lonesome Tonight – Elvis Presley (1961)
35. From Me To You – Beatles (1963)
36. Hello Goodbye – Beatles (1967)
37. I'm A Believer – Monkees (1967)
38. Those Were The Days – Mary Hopkin (1968)
39. Wooden Heart – Elvis Presley (1961)
40. Return To Sender – Elvis Presley (1962)
41. Oh Pretty Woman – Roy Orbison (1964)
42. Twist And Shout (EP) – Beatles (1963)
43. Can't Help Falling In Love/Rock A Hula Baby – Elvis Presley (1962)
44. Do Wah Diddy Diddy – Manfred Mann (1964)

45. Space Oddity – David Bowie (1969)
46. I Got You Babe – Sonny and Cher (1965)
47. Lily The Pink – Scaffold (1968)
48. A Whiter Shade Of Pale – Procol Harum (1967)
49. Just Loving You – Anita Harris (1967)
50. Magical Mystery Tour (Double EP) – Beatles (1967)
51. My Old Man's A Dustman – Lonnie Donegan (1960)
52. (I Can't Get No) Satisfaction – Rolling Stones (1965)
53. My Boy Lollipop – Millie (1964)
54. Bobby's Girl – Susan Maughan (1962)
55. I Believe – Bachelors (1964)
56. Little Children – Billy J. Kramer and the Dakotas (1964)
57. Bits And Pieces – Dave Clark Five (1964)
58. You're My World – Cilla Black (1964)
59. Ruby, Don't Take Your Love To Town – Kenny Rogers (1969)
60. My Way – Frank Sinatra (1969)
61. Ticket To Ride – Beatles (1965)
62. The Wedding – Julie Rogers (1964)
63. Get Back – Beatles (1969)
64. Strangers In The Night – Frank Sinatra (1966)
65. Surrender – Elvis Presley (1961)
66. Honey – Bobby Goldsboro (1968)
67. Have I The Right – Honeycombs (1964)
68. All You Need Is Love – Beatles (1976)
69. What A Wonderful World/Cabaret – Louis Armstrong (1968)
70. Wonderful Land – Shadows (1962)
71. A World Without Love – Peter and Gordon (1964)
72. It's Not Unusual – Tom Jones (1965)
73. Cinderella Rockefella – Esther and Abi Ofarim (1968)
74. Puppet On A String – Sandie Shaw (1967)
75. Paperback Writer – Beatles (1966)
76. Diane – Bachelors (1964)
77. Delilah – Tom Jones (1968)
78. Penny Lane/Strawberry Fields Forever – Beatles (1967)

79. Walkin' Back To Happiness – Helen Shapiro (1961)
80. Apache – Shadows (1960)
81. Yellow Submarine/Eleanor Rigby – Beatles (1966)
82. It's Over – Roy Orbison (1964)
83. House Of The Rising Sun – Animals (1964)
84. Go Now – Moody Blues (1964)
85. This Is My Song – Petula Clark (1967)
86. These Boots Are Made For Walking – Nancy Sinatra (1966)

Nancy Sinatra

87. Honky Tonk Women – Rolling Stones (1969)
88. I'm Into Something Good – Herman's Hermits (1964)
89. I Can't Stop Loving You – Ray Charles (1962)
90. Somethin' Stupid – Nancy Sinatra and Frank Sinatra (1967)
91. Juliet – Four Pennies (1964)
92. March Of The Siamese Children – Kenny Ball and His Jazzmen (1962)
93. Mr Tambourine Man – Byrds (1965)
94. Good Luck Charm – Elvis Presley (1962)
95. Silence Is Golden – Tremeloes (1967)
96. Massachusetts – Bee Gees (1967)
97. Yeh Yeh – Georgie Fame and the Blue Flames (1964)
98. The Good, The Bad And The Ugly – Hugo Montenegro (1968)

99. Young Girl – Union Gap featuring Gary Puckett (1968)
100. Crying In The Chapel – Elvis Presley (1965)

TOP 100 SINGLES OF THE SEVENTIES (UK)

Compiled by the BMRB from Chart panel sales 1970–79.

1. Mull Of Kintyre/Girls School – Wings
2. Rivers Of Babylon/Brown Girl In The Ring – Boney M
3. You're The One That I Want – Olivia Newton-John and John Travolta
4. Sailing – Rod Stewart
5. Save Your Kisses For Me – Brotherhood of Man
6. I'd Like To Teach The World To Sing – New Seekers
7. Summer Nights – John Travolta and Olivia Newton-John
8. Don't Give Up On Us – David Soul

David Soul

9. Bohemian Rhapsody – Queen
10. Under The Moon Of Love – Showaddywaddy
11. Mississippi – Pussycat
12. My Sweet Lord – George Harrison
13. Bright Eyes – Art Garfunkel
14. Don't Go Breaking My Heart – Elton John/Kiki Dee
15. Amazing Grace – Royal Scots Dragoon Guards
16. Mary's Boy Child – Boney M
17. Tie A Yellow Ribbon – Dawn
18. If You Leave Me Now – Chicago
19. YMCA – Village People

Village People

20. Don't Cry For Me Argentina – Julie Covington
21. Mouldy Old Dough – Lieutenant Pigeon
22. Dancing Queen – Abba
23. Puppy Love – Donny Osmond
24. Without You – Nilsson
25. Floral Dance – Brighouse and Rastrick Band
26. Eye Level – Simon Park Orchestra
27. A Little Bit More – Dr Hook
28. When I Need You – Leo Sayer
29. I Love You, Love Me Love – Gary Glitter
30. How Deep Is Your Love – Bee Gees
31. Silver Lady – David Soul
32. Heart Of Glass – Blondie
33. Knowing Me, Knowing You – Abba
34. I Feel Love – Donna Summer
35. We Don't Talk Anymore – Cliff Richard
36. Way Down – Elvis Presley
37. Bye Bye Baby – Bay City Rollers
38. Long Haired Lover From Liverpool – Little Jimmy Osmond
39. In The Summertime – Mungo Jerry
40. Welcome Home – Peters and Lee

41. Fernando – Abba
42. Hit Me With Your Rhythm Stick – Ian Dury and the Blockheads
43. Three Times A Lady – Commodores
44. So You Win Again – Hot Chocolate
45. Smurf Song – Father Abraham
46. Reason To Believe/Maggie May – Rod Stewart
47. Yes Sir, I Can Boogie – Baccara
48. I Don't Like Monday – Boomtown Rats
49. Angelo – Brotherhood of Man
50. When A Child Is Born – Johnny Mathis

Johnny Mathis

51. Chanson D'Amour – Manhattan Transfer
52. The Wonder Of You – Elvis Presley
53. When You're In Love – Dr Hook
54. I Will Survive – Gloria Gaynor
55. Are Friends Electric – Tubeway Army
56. Chirpy Chirpy Cheep Cheep – Middle of the Road
57. Night Fever – Bee Gees
58. Dance Away – Roxy Music
59. Ernie (The Fastest Milkman In The West) – Benny Hill
60. Rockin' All Over The World – Status Quo
61. Black Is Black – La Belle Epoque
62. Blockbuster – Sweet
63. Sunday Girl – Blondie

64. My Ding-a-ling – Chuck Berry
65. Amazing Grace – Judy Collins
66. One Day At A Time – Lena Martell
67. Merry Xmas Everybody – Slade
68. Name Of The Game – Abba
69. I Can't Give You Anything (But My Love) – Stylistics
70. Rat Trap – Boomtown Rats
71. Fanfare For The Common Man – Emerson, Lake and Palmer
72. Whispering Grass – Windsor Davis and Don Estelle
73. I Love To Love – Tina Charles
74. Sideshow – Barry Biggs
75. Bridge Over Troubled Water – Simon and Garfunkel
76. Ma Baker – Boney M
77. Wandrin' Star/I Talk To the Trees – Lee Marvin and Clint Eastwood
78. Love Theme From *A Star Is Borne*: Evergreen – Barbra Streisand
79. Tiger Feet – Mud
80. Knock Three Times – Dawn
81. Hot Love – T. Rex
82. Stand By Your Man – Tammy Wynette
83. Message In A Bottle – Police
84. Grandad – Clive Dunn
85. The Roussos Phenomenon (EP) – Demis Roussos
86. Take A Chance On Me – Abba
87. We Are The Champions – Queen
88. Matchstalk Men And Matchstalk Cats And Dogs – Brian and Michael
89. Pop Muzik – M
90. Gonna Make You A Star – David Essex

DAVID ESSEX DECCA

91. Mother Of Mine – Neil Reid
92. Lucille – Kenny Rogers
93. Son Of My Father – Chicory Tip
94. Magic Fly – Space
95. December '63 – Four Seasons
96. Oliver's Army – Elvis Costello and the Attractions

Elvis Costello

Terry Jacks

97. Seasons In The Sun – Terry Jacks
98. Cum On Feel The Noise – Slade
99. Tragedy – Bee Gees
100. See My Baby Jive – Wizzard

Courtesy of *Music Week*.

AMERICA'S TOP FIFTY SINGLES OF THE SEVENTIES

The following was compiled by Watermark Incorporated from the weekly 'Hot One Hundred' of *Billboard* magazine 1970–79.

1. You Light Up My Life – Debby Boone

2. Bridge Over Troubled Water – Simon and Garfunkel
3. Joy To The World – Three Dog Night
4. The First Time Ever I Saw Your Face – Roberta Flack
5. Alone Again Naturally – Gilbert O'Sullivan
6. Tonight's The Night – Rod Stewart
7. American Pie – Don McLean
8. How Deep Is Your Love – The Bee Gees
9. Stayin' Alive – The Bee Gees
10. My Sharona – The Knack
11. One Bad Apple – Osmonds
12. Shadow Dancing – Andy Gibb
13. Maggie May/Reason To Believe – Rod Stewart
14. It's Too Late – Carole King
15. My Sweet Lord – George Harrison
16. Night Fever – The Bee Gees
17. Silly Love Songs – Wings
18. Le Freak – Chic
19. I'll Be There – Jackson Five

Jackson Five

20. Best Of My Love – The Emotions
21. How Can You Mend A Broken Heart – The Bee Gees
22. A Horse With No Name – America
23. Close To You – The Carpenters
24. Bad Girls – Donna Summer
25. Reunited – Peaches and Herb
26. I Can See Clearly Now – Johnny Nash

27. Tie A Yellow Ribbon Round The Ole Oak Tree – Dawn
28. My Love – Wings
29. You're So Vain – Carly Simon
30. Ain't No Mountain High Enough – Diana Ross
31. Raindrops Keep Falling On My Head – B. J. Thomas
32. Love Will Keep Us Together – The Captain and Tennille
33. Hot Stuff – Donna Summer
34. Without You – Nilsson
35. Da Ya Think I'm Sexy – Rod Stewart
36. Crocodile Rock – Elton John
37. I Will Survive – Gloria Gaynor
38. American Woman/No Sugar Tonight – Three Dog Night
39. Let It Be – The Beatles
40. I Just Wanna Be Your Everything – Andy Gibb
41. I Honestly Love You – Olivia Newton-John
42. December '63 (Oh What A Night) – The Four Seasons
43. Three Times A Lady – The Commodores
44. Don't Go Breaking My Heart – Elton John and Kiki Dee
45. Me And Mrs Jones – Billy Paul
46. I Think I Love You – The Partridge Family
47. The Way We Were – Barbra Streisand
48. Fifty Ways To Leave Your Lover – Paul Simon
49. Kiss You All Over – Exile
50. Family Affair – Sly and the Family Stone

Nilsson

Gloria Gaynor

The Four Seasons

SINGLES THAT TOPPED BOTH BRITISH AND AMERICAN CHARTS

Bill Haley

Peter and Gordon

The Rolling Stones

Artist	Title	Year
Perez Prado	Cherry Pink And Apple Blossom White	1955
Bill Haley and His Comets	Rock Around The Clock	1955
Tennessee Ernie Ford	Sixteen Tons	1955
Dean Martin	Memories Are Made Of This	1956
Kay Starr	Rock And Roll Waltz	1956
Guy Mitchell	Singing The Blues	1956
Tab Hunter	Young Love	1957
Andy Williams	Butterfly	1957
Elvis Presley	All Shook Up	1957
Elvis Presley	Jailhouse Rock	1957
Everly Brothers	All I Have To Do Is Dream	1958
Tommy Edwards	It's All In The Game	1958
Conway Twitty	It's Only Make Believe	1958
Platters	Smoke Gets In Your Eyes	1959
Bobby Darin	Mack The Knife	1959
Johnny Preston	Running Bear	1960
Everly Brothers	Cathy's Clown	1960
Elvis Presley	It's Now Or Never	1960
Elvis Presley	Are You Lonesome Tonight?	1960
Elvis Presley	Surrender	1961
Marcels	Blue Moon	1961
Del Shannon	Runaway	1961
Highwaymen	Michael	1961
Elvis Presley	Good Luck Charm	1962
Ray Charles	I Can't Stop Loving You	1962
Tornados	Telstar	1962
Beatles	I Want To Hold Your Hand	1964
Beatles	She Loves You	1964
Beatles	Can't Buy Me Love	1964
Peter and Gordon	World Without Love	1964
Beatles	A Hard Day's Night	1964
Animals	House Of The Rising Sun	1964
Roy Orbison	Oh Pretty Woman	1964
Manfred Mann	Do Wah Diddy Diddy	1964
Supremes	Baby Love	1964
Beatles	I Feel Fine	1964
Righteous Brothers	You've Lost That Lovin' Feeling	1965
Beatles	Ticket To Ride	1965
Byrds	Mr Tambourine Man	1965
Rolling Stones	Satisfaction	1965
Sonny and Cher	I Got You Babe	1965
Beatles	Help	1965
Rolling Stones	Get Off My Cloud	1965
Beatles	We Can Work It Out	1966
Nancy Sinatra	These Boots Are Made For Walking	1966
Rolling Stones	Paint It Black	1966
Frank Sinatra	Strangers In The Night	1966

Beatles	Paperback Writer	1966
Four Tops	Reach Out I'll Be There	1966
Beach Boys	Good Vibrations	1966
Monkees	I'm A Believer	1966
Frank and Nancy Sinatra	Something Stupid	1967
Beatles	All You Need Is Love	1967
Beatles	Hello, Goodbye	1967
Beatles	Hey Jude	1968
Marvin Gaye	I Heard It Through The Grapevine	1968
Tommy Roe	Dizzy	1969
Beatles	Get Back	1969
Zager and Evans	In The Year 2525	1969
Rolling Stones	Honky Tonk Women	1969
Archies	Sugar Sugar	1969
Simon and Garfunkel	Bridge Over Troubled Water	1970
Smokey Robinson and the Miracles	Tears Of A Clown	1970
George Harrison	My Sweet Lord	1970
Dawn	Knock Three Times	1971
Rod Stewart	Maggie May	1971
Nilsson	Without You	1972
Chuck Berry	My Ding-a-ling	1972
Dawn	Tie A Yellow Ribbon Round The Ole Oak Tree	1973
Terry Jacks	Seasons In The Sun	1974
Ray Stevens	The Streak	1974
George McCrae	Rock Your Baby	1974
John Denver	Annie's Song	1974
Carl Douglas	Kung Fu Fighting	1974
Four Seasons	December '63 (Oh, What A Night)	1976
Elton John and Kiki Dee	Don't Go Breaking My Heart	1976
Chicago	If You Leave Me Now	1976
David Soul	Don't Give Up On Us	1977
Leo Sayer	When I Need You	1977
Bee Gees	Night Fever	1978
Olivia Newton-John and John Travolta	You're The One That I Want	1978
Commodores	Three Times A Lady	1978
Rod Stewart	Da Ya Think I'm Sexy	1978
Blondie	Heart Of Glass	1979
Bee Gees	Tragedy	1979
Gloria Gaynor	I Will Survive	1979
Anita Ward	Ring My Bell	1979
Pink Floyd	Another Brick In The Wall (Part II)	1979
Blondie	Call Me	1980
Barbra Streisand	Woman In Love	1980
John Lennon	(Just Like) Starting Over	1980
Blondie	The Tide Is High	1981
Paul McCartney and Stevie Wonder	Ebony And Ivory	1982
Human League	Don't You Want Me	1982
Survivor	Eye Of The Tiger (Theme From *Rocky III*)	1982

Simon and Garfunkel

Carl Douglas
The Human League

AMERICAN NUMBER ONE SINGLES BY BRITISH ARTISTS

To qualify for inclusion in this list, acts must be at least 50% British.

Auf Wiederseh'n Sweetheart – Vera Lynn (4 July 1952)
Stranger On The Shore – Mr Acker Bilk (26 May 1962)
The Stripper – David Rose (7 July 1962)
Telstar – Tornadoes (22 December 1962)
I Want To Hold Your Hand – Beatles (1 February 1964)
She Loves You – Beatles (21 March 1964)

The Beatles

Can't Buy Me Love – Beatles (4 April 1964)
Love Me Do – Beatles (30 May 1964)
A World Without Love – Peter and Gordon (27 June 1964)
A Hard Day's Night – Beatles (1 August 1964)
The House Of The Rising Sun – Animals (5 September 1964)
Do Wah Diddy Diddy – Manfred Mann (17 October 1964)
I Feel Fine – Beatles (26 December 1964)
Downtown – Petula Clark (23 January 1965)
Eight Days A Week – Beatles (13 March 1965)
I'm Telling You Now – Freddie and the Dreamers (10 April 1965)
Game Of Love – Wayne Fontana and the Mindbenders (24 April 1965)

Mrs Brown You've Got A Lovely Daughter – Herman's Hermits (1 May 1965)
Ticket To Ride – Beatles (22 May 1965)
(I Can't Get No) Satisfaction – Rolling Stones (10 July 1965)
I'm Henry VIII, I Am – Herman's Hermits (7 August 1965)
Help! – Beatles (4 September 1965)
Yesterday – Beatles (9 October 1965)
Get Off Of My Cloud – Rolling Stones (6 November 1965)
Over And Over – Dave Clark Five (25 December 1965)
We Can Work It Out – Beatles (8 January 1966)
My Love – Petula Clark (5 February 1966)
Paint It, Black – Rolling Stones (11 June 1966)
Paperback Writer – Beatles (25 June 1966)
Wild Thing – Troggs (30 July 1966)
Sunshine Superman – Donovan (3 September 1966)
Winchester Cathedral – New Vaudeville Band (3 December 1966)
Ruby Tuesday – Rolling Stones (4 March 1967)
Penny Lane – Beatles (18 March 1967)
All You Need Is Love – Beatles (19 August 1967)
To Sir, With Love – Lulu (21 October 1967)
Hello, Goodbye – Beatles (30 December 1967)
Hey Jude – Beatles (28 September 1968)
Get Back – Beatles (24 May 1969)
Honky Tonk Women – Rolling Stones (23 August 1969)
Come Together/Something – Beatles (29 November 1969)
Let It Be – Beatles (11 April 1970)
The Long And Winding Road – Beatles (13 June 1970)
My Sweet Lord – George Harrison (26 December 1970)
Brown Sugar – Rolling Stones (29 May 1971)
How Can You Mend A Broken Heart – Bee Gees (7 August 1971)
Uncle Albert – Admiral Halsey – Paul and Linda McCartney (4 September 1971)

Maggie May – Rod Stewart (2 October 1971)
Crocodile Rock – Elton John (3 February 1973)
My Love – Paul McCartney and Wings (2 June 1973)
Give Me Love (Give Me Peace On Earth) – George Harrison (30 June 1973)
Angie – Rolling Stones (20 October 1973)
Photograph – Ringo Starr (24 November 1973)
You're 16 – Ringo Starr (26 January 1974)
Bennie & The Jets – Elton John (13 April 1974)
Band On The Run – Paul McCartney and Wings (8 June 1974)
The Night Chicago Died – Paper Lace (17 August 1974)
I Shot The Sheriff – Eric Clapton (19 September 1974)
I Honestly Love You – Olivia Newton-John (5 October 1974)

Olivia Newton-John

Whatever Gets You Thru' The Night – John Lennon (16 November 1974)
Lucy In The Sky With Diamonds – Elton John (4 January 1975)

Pick Up The Pieces – Average White Band (22 February 1975)

Have You Never Been Mellow – Olivia Newton-John (8 March 1975)

Philadelphia Freedom – Elton John (12 April 1975)

Listen To What The Man Said – Paul McCartney and Wings (19 July 1975)

Jive Talkin' – Bee Gees (9 August 1975)

Fame – David Bowie (20 September 1975)

Island Girl – Elton John (1 November 1975)

Saturday Night – Bay City Rollers (3 January 1976)

Silly Love Songs – Wings (22 May 1976)

Don't Go Breaking My Heart – Elton John and Kiki Dee (7 August 1976)

You Should Be Dancing – Bee Gees (4 September 1976)

Tonight's The Night (Gonna Be Alright) – Rod Stewart (13 November 1976)

You Make Me Feel Like Dancing – Leo Sayer (15 January 1977)

Blinded By The Light – Manfred Mann's Earth Band (19 February 1977)

When I Need You – Leo Sayer (14 May 1977)

Dreams – Fleetwood Mac (18 June 1977)

I Just Wanna Be Your Everything – Andy Gibb (30 July 1977)

How Deep Is Your Love – Bee Gees (24 December 1977)

Stayin' Alive – Bee Gees (4 February 1978)

(Love Is) Thicker Than Water – Andy Gibb (4 March 1978)

Night Fever – Bee Gees (18 March 1978)

With A Little Luck – Wings (20 May 1978)

You're The One That I Want – Olivia Newton-John and John Travolta (10 June 1978)

Shadow Dancing – Andy Gibb (17 June 1978)

Miss You – Rolling Stones (5 August 1978)

Hot Child In The City – Nick Gilder (28 October 1978)

Too Much Heaven – Bee Gees (6 January 1979)

Da Ya Think I'm Sexy – Rod Stewart (10 February 1979)

Tragedy – Bee Gees (24 March 1979)

Love You Inside Out – Bee Gees (9 June 1979)

Pop Muzik – M (3 November 1979)

Escape (The Pina Colada Song) – Rupert Holmes (22 December 1979)

Rupert Holmes

Crazy Little Thing Called Love – Queen (23 February 1980)

Another Brick In The Wall (Part II) – Pink Floyd (22 March 1980)

Coming Up (Live in Glasgow) – Paul McCartney and Wings (28 June 1980)

Magic – Olivia Newton-John (2 August 1980)

Another One Bites The Dust – Queen (4 October 1980)

(Just Like) Starting Over – John Lennon (3 January 1981)

Morning Train (9 To 5) – Sheena Easton (2 May 1981)

Physical – Olivia Newton-John (1 November 1981)

Ebony And Ivory – Paul McCartney and Stevie Wonder (15 May 1982)

Don't You Want Me – Human League (30 June 1982)

Why some artists are included.

● David Rose was born in London and lived there until he was four years old. He now lives in America.

● Nick Gilder, now a resident of Canada, was also born in London and lived there until he was ten years old.

● Rupert Holmes was born in Northwich in the county of Cheshire, England of Anglo-American parents. His professional name recalls his English childhood memories of Rupert Bear (a cartoon character) and Sherlock Holmes.

● Olivia Newton-John, the Bee Gees and Andy Gibb were all British-born and Aussie-raised.

● Three of Fleetwood Mac's five members are British.

And others aren't.

● Gilbert O'Sullivan and Carl Douglas are usually presumed to be British. In fact O'Sullivan is from Waterford in the Republic of Ireland and Douglas hails from Jamaica.

John Lennon

The Young Rascals

Archie Bell and the Drells
Sly Stone

AMERICAN NUMBER ONE SINGLES WHICH FAILED TO MAKE THE UK CHARTS

Artist	Title	Year
Dave 'Baby' Cortez	The Happy Organ	1955
Wilbert Harrison	Kansas City	1955
Fleetwoods	Mr Blue	1958
Larry Verne	Mr Custer	1958
Bert Kaempfert	Wonderland By Night	1959
Lawrence Welk	Calcutta	1959
Bobby Lewis	Tossin' And Turnin'	1959
Joe Dowell	Wooden Heart	1960
Marvelettes	Please Mr Postman	1961
Gene Chandler	Duke Of Earl	1961
David Rose Orchestra	The Stripper	1961
Steve Lawrence	Go Away Little Girl	1961
Little Peggy March	I Will Follow Him	1961
Stevie Wonder	Fingertips Part 2	1962
Bobby Vinton	Blue Velvet	1962
Bobby Vinton	Mr Lonely	1963
Gary Lewis and the Playboys	This Diamond Ring	1963
Beatles	Eight Days A Week	1963
Herman's Hermits	Mrs Brown, You've Got A Lovely Daughter	1963
Herman's Hermits	I'm Henry VIII, I Am	1964
Young Rascals	Good Lovin'	1965
Association	Cherish	1965*
Johnny Rivers	Poor Side Of Town	1965
Buckinghams	Kind Of A Drag	1965
Association	Windy	1966
Lulu	To Sir With Love	1966
Strawberry Alarm Clock	Incense And Peppermints	1966
Archie Bell and the Drells	Tighten Up	1967
Hugh Masakela	Grazing In The Grass	1967
Rascals	People Got To Be Free	1967†
Tommy James and the Shondells	Crimson And Clover	1967
Henry Mancini	Love Theme From 'Romeo And Juliet'	1968
Sly and the Family Stone	Thank You (Falettin Me Be Mice Elf Agin)	1968
Beatles	Long And Winding Road	1968
Osmonds	One Bad Apple	1969
Janis Joplin	Me And Bobby McGee	1969
Honey Cone	Want Ads	1970
Raiders	Indian Reservation	1970*
Bee Gees	How Can You Mend A Broken Heart	1971
Paul McCartney	Uncle Albert/Admiral Halsey	1971
Donny Osmond	Go Away Little Girl	1971
Sammy Davis Jr.	Candy Man	1971
Looking Glass	Brandy (You're A Fine Girl)	1971
Three Dog Night	Black And White	1971*

Artist	Title	Year
Helen Reddy	I Am Woman	1971
Vicki Lawrence	The Night The Lights Went Out In Georgia	1972
Billy Preston	Will It Go Round In Circles	1972
Jim Croce	Bad, Bad Leroy Brown	1972
Maureen McGovern	The Morning After (Song From *The Poseidon Adventure*)	1972 1973
Stories	Brother Louie	1973
Helen Reddy	Delta Dawn	1973
Grand Funk Railroad	We're An American Band	1973
Cher	Half Breed	1973
Jim Croce	Time In A Bottle	1973
Steve Miller	The Joker	1973
Al Wilson	Show And Tell	1973
John Denver	Sunshine On My Shoulder	1973
Blue Swede	Hooked On A Feeling	1974
Grand Funk	The Loco-motion	1974
Bo Donaldson and the Heywoods	Billy Don't Be A Hero	1974
Billy Preston	Nothing From Nothing	1974
Harry Chapin	Cat's In The Cradle	1974
Ohio Players	Fire	1974
Linda Ronstadt	You're No Good	1974
Eagles	Best Of My Love	1974
Olivia Newton-John	Have You Never Been Mellow	1975
Doobie Brothers	Black Water	1975
B. J. Thomas	(Hey Won't You Play) Another Somebody Done Somebody Wrong Song	1975 1975
Tony Orlando and Dawn	He Don't Love You (Like I Love You)	1975
Freddy Fender	Before The Next Teardrop Falls	1975
John Denver	Thank God I'm A Country Boy	1975
America	Sister Golden Hair	1975
Hamilton, Joe Frank and Reynolds	Fallin' In Love	1975
John Denver	I'm Sorry	1975
Neil Sedaka	Bad Blood	1975
Staple Singers	Let's Do It Again	1975
Bay City Rollers	Saturday Night	1975
Barry Manilow	I Write The Songs	1975
Ohio Players	Love Rollercoaster	1976
Rhythm Heritage	Theme From *S.W.A.T.*	1976
John Sebastian	Welcome Back	1976
Sylvers	Boogie Fever	1976
Daryl Hall and John Oates	Rich Girl	1976
Bill Conti	Gonna Fly Now (Theme From *Rocky*)	1976
Shaun Cassidy	Da Doo Ron Ron	1977
Barry Manilow	Looks Like We Made It	1977
Andy Gibb	(Love Is) Thicker Than Water	1977
Nick Gilder	Hot Child In The City	1977
Air Supply	The One That You Love	1978

BRITISH NUMBER ONE SINGLES WHICH FAILED TO MAKE THE AMERICAN CHART

1. She Wears Red Feathers – Guy Mitchell (1953)
2. Broken Wings – Stargazers (1953)
3. (How Much Is) That Doggie In The Window – Lita Roza (1953)
4. Look At That Girl – Guy Mitchell (1953)
5. Answer Me – David Whitfield (1953)
6. Answer Me – Frankie Laine (1953)
7. I See The Moon – Stargazers (1954)
8. Such A Night – Johnnie Ray (1954)
9. My Son, My Son – Vera Lynn (1954)
10. Let's Have Another Party – Winifred Atwell (1954)
11. Finger Of Suspicion – Dickie Valentine (1955)
12. Softly, Softly – Ruby Murray (1955)
13. Give Me Your Word – Tennessee Ernie Ford (1955)
14. Cherry Pink And Apple Blossom White – Eddie Calvert (1955)
15. Unchained Melody – Jimmy Young (1955)
16. Dreamboat – Alma Cogan (1955)
17. Rose Marie – Slim Whitman (1955)
18. The Man From Laramie – Jimmy Young (1955)
19. Hernando's Hideaway – Johnson Brothers (1955)
20. Christmas Alphabet – Dickie Valentine (1955)
21. Poor People Of Paris – Winifred Atwell (1956)
22. No Other Love – Ronnie Hilton (1956)
23. Singing The Blues – Tommy Steele (1957)

Notes

† Not released as A side of a UK single.
* Not released as a single in UK.

24. Garden Of Eden – Frankie Vaughan (1957)
25. Cumberland Gap – Lonnie Donegan (1957)
26. Gamblin' Man/Putting On the Style – Lonnie Donegan (1957)
27. The Story Of My Life – Michael Holliday (1958)
28. Hoots Mon – Lord Rockingham's XI (1958)
29. The Day That The Rains Came – Jane Morgan (1959)
30. As I Love You – Shirley Bassey (1959)
31. Side Saddle – Russ Conway (1959)
32. Roulette – Russ Conway (1959)
33. Only Sixteen – Craig Douglas (1959)
34. Travellin' Light – Cliff Richard and the Shadows (1959)
35. What Do You Want – Adam Faith (1959)
36. What Do You Want To Make Those Eyes At Me For – Emile Ford and the Checkmates (1959)
37. Starry Eyed – Michael Holliday (1960)
38. Why – Anthony Newley (1960)
39. Poor Me – Adam Faith (1960)
40. My Old Man's A Dustman – Lonnie Donegan (1960)
41. Three Steps To Heaven – Eddie Cochran (1960)
42. Please Don't Tease – Cliff Richard and the Shadows (1960)
43. Shakin' All Over – Johnny Kidd and the Pirates (1960)
44. Apache – Shadows (1960)
45. Tell Laura I Love Her – Ricky Valance (1960)
46. I Love You – Cliff Richard and the Shadows (1960)
47. Sailor – Petula Clark (1961)
48. Wooden Heart – Elvis Presley (1961)
49. You're Driving Me Crazy – Temperance Seven (1961)
50. Well I Ask You – Eden Kane (1961)
51. You Don't Know – Helen Shapiro (1961)
52. Johnny, Remember Me – John Leyton (1961)

Helen Shapiro

53. Reach For The Stars/Climb Ev'ry Mountain – Shirley Bassey (1961)
54. Kon-Tiki – Shadows (1961)
55. Tower Of Strength – Frankie Vaughan (1961)
56. Moon River – Danny Williams (1961)
57. The Young Ones – Cliff Richard and the Shadows (1962)
58. Wonderful Land – Shadows (1962)
59. Come Outside – Mike Sarne (1962)
60. Dance On – Shadows (1963)

61. Diamonds – Jet Harris and Tony Meehan (1963)
62. Wayward Wind – Frank Ifield (1963)
63. Summer Holiday – Cliff Richard and the Shadows (1963)
64. Foot Tapper – Shadows (1963)
65. Sweets For My Sweet – Searchers (1963)
66. Do You Love Me – Brian Poole and the Tremeloes (1963)
67. Anyone Who Had A Heart – Cilla Black (1964)
68. Juliet – Four Pennies (1964)
69. Little Red Rooster – Rolling Stones (1964)
70. The Minute You're Gone – Cliff Richard (1965)
71. Where Are You Now (My Love) – Jackie Trent (1965)
72. I'm Alive – Hollies (1965)
73. Tears – Ken Dodd (1965)
74. The Carnival Is Over – Seekers (1965)
75. Michelle – Overlanders (1966)
76. Out Of Time – Chris Farlowe (1966)
77. All Or Nothing – Small Faces (1966)
78. Puppet On A String – Sandie Shaw (1967)
79. Everlasting Love – Love Affair (1968)
80. Legend Of Xanadu – Dave Dee, Dozy, Beaky, Mick and Tich (1968)
81. What A Wonderful World/Cabaret – Louis Armstrong (1968)
82. I Pretend – Des O'Connor (1968)
83. Lily The Pink – Scaffold (1968)
84. Ob-La-Di, Ob-La-Da – Marmalade (1969)
85. Albatross – Fleetwood Mac (1969)
86. Blackberry Way – Move (1969)
87. (If Paradise Is) Half As Nice – Amen Corner (1969)
88. I'll Never Fall In Love Again – Bobby Gentry (1969)
89. Two Little Boys – Rolf Harris (1969)
90. Wand'rin' Star – Lee Marvin (1970)
91. All Kinds Of Everything – Dana (1970)
92. Back Home – England World Cup Squad (1970)

93. Voodoo Chile – Jimi Hendrix Experience (1970)
94. Grandad – Clive Dunn (1971)
95. Baby Jump – Mungo Jerry (1971)
96. Chirpy Chirpy Cheep Cheep – Middle of the Road (1971)
97. Coz I Luv You – Slade (1971)
98. Ernie (The Fastest Milkman In The West) – Benny Hill (1971)
99. Metal Guru – T. Rex (1972)
100. Mouldy Old Dough – Lieutenant Pigeon (1973)
101. See My Baby Jive – Wizzard (1973)
102. Skweeze Me Pleeze Me – Slade (1973)
103. Welcome Home – Peters and Lee (1973)

Peters and Lee

104. I'm The Leader Of The Gang (I Am) – Gary Glitter (1973)
105. Angel Fingers – Wizzard (1973)
106. Eye Level – Simon Park Orchestra (1973)
107. Daydreamer/The Puppy Song – David Cassidy (1973)

108. I Love You, Love Me Love – Gary Glitter (1973)
109. Merry Xmas Everybody – Slade (1973)
110. You Won't Find Another Fool Like Me – New Seekers (1974)
111. Tiger Feet – Mud (1974)
112. Devil Gate Drive – Suzi Quatro (1974)
113. Jealous Mind – Alvin Stardust (1974)
114. Always Yours – Gary Glitter (1974)
115. She – Charles Aznavour (1974)
116. Everything I Own – Ken Boothe (1974)
117. Gonna Make You A Star – David Essex (1974)
118. Lonely This Christmas – Mud (1974)
119. Down, Down – Status Quo (1975)

Status Quo

120. If – Telly Savalas (1975)
121. Bye Bye Baby – Bay City Rollers (1975)
122. Oh Boy – Mud (1975)
123. Whispering Grass – Windsor Davies and Don Estelle (1975)
124. Tears On My Pillow – Johnny Nash (1975)
125. Give A Little Love – Bay City Rollers (1975)
126. Barbados – Typically Tropical (1975)
127. Hold Me Close – David Essex (1975)
128. D.I.V.O.R.C.E. – Billy Connolly (1975)
129. Forever And Ever – Slik (1976)
130. I Love To Love – Tina Charles (1976)
131. No Charge – J. J. Barrie (1976)

132. Combine Harvester (Brand New Key) – Wurzels (1976)
133. The Roussos Phenomenon (EP) – Demis Roussos (1976)
134. Mississippi – Pussycat (1976)
135. Under The Moon Of Love – Showaddywaddy (1976)
136. When A Child Is Born (Soleado) – Johnny Mathis (1976)
137. Don't Cry For Me Argentina – Julie Covington (1977)
138. Chanson D'Amour – Manhattan Transfer (1977)
139. Angelo – Brotherhood of Man (1977)
140. Yes Sir, I Can Boogie – Baccara (1977)
141. Up Town Top Ranking – Althia and Donna (1978)
142. Figaro – Brotherhood Of Man (1978)
143. Wuthering Heights – Kate Bush (1978)
144. Matchstalk Man And Matchstalk Cats And Dogs – Brian and Michael (1978)
145. Rat Trap – Boomtown Rats (1978)

Boomtown Rats

146. Hit Me With Your Rhythm Stick – Ian Dury and the Blockheads (1979)
147. Bright Eyes – Art Garfunkel (1979)
148. Sunday Girl – Blondie (1979)
149. Are 'Friends' Electric – Gary Numan (1979)
150. I Don't Like Mondays – Boomtown Rats (1979)
151. One Day At A Time – Lena Martell (1979)

152. Walking On The Moon – Police (1979)
153. Specials AKA (Live EP) – Specials (1980)
154. Together We Are Beautiful – Fern Kinney (1980)
155. Going Underground – Jam (1980)

The Jam

156. Geno – Dexy's Midnight Runners (1980)
157. What's Another Year – Johnny Logan (1980)
158. Theme From *MASH* – Mash (1980)
159. Use It Up And Wear It Out – Odyssey (1980)
160. Start – Jam (1980)
161. Feels Like I'm In Love – Kelly Marie (1980)
162. No One Quite Like Grandma – St Winifred's School Choir (1980)
163. Jealous Guy – Roxy Music (1981)
164. This Ole House – Shakin' Stevens (1981)
165. Making Your Mind Up – Bucks Fizz (1981)
166. Stand And Deliver – Adam and the Ants (1981)
167. Ghost Town – Specials (1981)
168. Green Door – Shakin' Stevens (1981)
169. Japanese Boy – Aneka (1981)
170. Prince Charming – Adam and the Ants (1981)

171. Begin The Beguine (Volver A Empezar) – Julio Iglesias (1981)
172. The Land Of Make Believe – Bucks Fizz (1982)
173. Oh Julie – Shakin' Stevens (1982)
174. The Model – Kraftwerk (1982)
175. Town Called Malice/Precious – Jam (1982)
176. The Lion Sleeps Tonight – Tight Fit (1982)
177. Seven Tears – Goombay Dance Band (1982)
178. My Camera Never Lies – Bucks Fizz (1982)
179. A Little Peace – Nicole (1982)
180. House Of Fun – Madness (1982)

Madness

181. Goody Two Shoes – Adam Ant (1982)
182. Happy Talk – Captain Sensible (1982)

MOST WEEKS AT NUMBER ONE – US SINGLES CHART

By Artist

Weeks
85 Elvis Presley (18 records)
59 Beatles (20)
45 Bing Crosby (8)
42 Perry Como (8)
32 Jimmy Dorsey (7)
31 Glenn Miller (7)
27 Bee Gees (9)
26 Vaughn Monroe (3)
22 Supremes (12)

The Supremes

22 Harry James (4)
22 Patti Page (3)
21 Pat Boone (6)
21 Sammy Kaye (5)
20 Tommy Dorsey (3)
20 Les Paul and Mary Ford (2)

By Disc

Weeks
13 Frenesi – Artie Shaw (1940)
   I've Heard That Song Before – Harry James (1943)
   Goodnight Irene – Gordon Jenkins (1953)
12 I'll Never Smile Again – Tommy Dorsey (1940)
   Paper Doll – Mills Brothers (1943)
   Heartaches – Ted Weems (1947)
   Near You – Francis Craig (1947)
11 Riders In The Sky – Vaughn Monroe (1949)
   Third Man Theme – Anton Karas (1950)
   Cry – Johnnie Ray (1951)
   Vaya Con Dios – Les Paul and Mary Ford (1953)
   White Christmas – Bing Crosby (1942)
   Hound Dog/Don't Be Cruel (1956)

10 Amapola – Jimmy Dorsey (1941)
Moonlight Cocktail – Glenn Miller (1942)
Till The End Of Time – Bing Crosby (1945)
The Gypsy – Ink Spots (1946)
Ballerina – Vaughn Monroe (1947)
Buttons And Bows – Dinah Shore (1948)
Where Is Your Heart – Percy Faith (1953)
Cherry Pink And Apple Blossom White – Perez Prado (1955)
You Light Up My Life – Debby Boone (1977)
Physical – Olivia Newton-John (1981–82)

MOST WEEKS AT NUMBER ONE – UK SINGLES CHART

By Artist

No. of Weeks
73 Elvis Presley (17 records)
65 Beatles (17 records)
35 Cliff Richard (10 records)
32 Frankie Laine (4 records)
31 Abba (9 records)
20 Slade (6 records)
19 Everly Brothers (4 records)
18 Rolling Stones (8 records)
17 Frank Ifield (4 records)
16 Shadows (5 records)
16 T. Rex (4 records)
16 John Travolta and Olivia Newton-John (2 records)

By Disc

Weeks
18 I Believe – Frankie Laine (1953)
11 Rose Marie – Slim Whitman (1955)
10 Cara Mia – David Whitfield (1954)
 9 Here In My Heart – Al Martino (1952)
Oh Mein Papa – Eddie Calvert (1954)
Secret Love – Doris Day (1954)
Diana – Paul Anka (1957)
Bohemian Rhapsody – Queen (1975)
Mull Of Kintyre/Girl's School – Wings (1977)

You're The One That I Want – John Travolta and Olivia Newton-John (1978)

MOST WEEKS AT NUMBER ONE AUSTRALIA

Singles

Hey Jude/ Revolution – Beatles	1968	15 weeks
Fernando – Abba	1976	15 weeks
Mamma Mia – Abba	1975	12 weeks
Shakin' All Over/Que Sera Sera – Normie Rowe and the Playboys	1965	11 weeks
Tom Dooley – Kingston Trio	1958	10 weeks
My Sweet Lord – George Harrison	1971	10 weeks
Tie A Yellow Ribbon Round The Old Oak Tree – Dawn	1973	10 weeks
Farewell Aunty Jack – Grahame Bond	1974	10 weeks
Mull Of Kintyre – Wings	1977	10 weeks

MOST NUMBER ONE SINGLES – US

Based on *Billboard* 1940–1982

20 Beatles (1964–70)
18 Elvis Presley (1956–69)
12 Supremes (1964–69)
10 Perry Como (1945–58)
 9 Bee Gees (1971–79)
 8 Bing Crosby (1940–45)
Rolling Stones (1965–78)
 7 Glenn Miller (1941–43)
Jimmy Dorsey (1941–44)
Paul McCartney/Wings (1971–80)
 6 Pat Boone (1955–61)
Stevie Wonder (1963–77)

• The Beatles and the Bee Gees jointly hold the record for most consecutive Number Ones – six.
• Bing Crosby's total excludes the 1944 No. 1 'Don't Fence Me In', a joint effort also featuring the Andrews Sisters.
• In addition to fronting all twelve Number One singles by the Supremes, Diana Ross has notched a further five solo chart-toppers (1970–1980) plus one jointly with Lionel Richie (1981).
• Honourable mention: Elton John has hit the summit five times as a solo artist and once with Kiki Dee.

Elton John

MOST HITS – UK SINGLES CHART

102 Elvis Presley
 78 Cliff Richard
 35 Stevie Wonder
 33 Frank Sinatra
 31 David Bowie
Shadows
Diana Ross
 30 Lonnie Donegan
Rolling Stones
 29. Elton John
Frankie Vaughan
Hollies
 28 Nat 'King' Cole
Everly Brothers
Roy Orbison
Beatles

27 Petula Clark
  Billy Fury
  Who
  Hot Chocolate

Hot Chocolate

26 Pat Boone
  Tom Jones
  Shirley Bassey
  Beach Boys

NB: Totals exclude collaborations with other artists

MOST HITS – US SINGLES CHART
1940–82

Unlike its British counterpart, this list takes account of hits resulting from the pairing of two usually quite separate acts. For example, Bing Crosby's collaborative efforts with the Andrews Sisters formed an integral part of his early output and have been added to his solo hits.

Artist (Hits)	First – last Hit
1. Elvis Presley (147)	1956–1977
2. Perry Como (103)	1944–1974
3. Frank Sinatra (96)	1943–1979
4. James Brown (92)	1959–1977
5. Nat 'King' Cole (78)	1944–1966
6. Ray Charles (73)	1957–1975
7. Bing Crosby (69)	1940–1960
8. Patti Page (68)	1948–1968
9. Beatles (68)	1964–1982
10. Fats Domino (66)	1955–1968
11. Pat Boone (60)	1955–1969
12. Eddie Fisher (48)	1950–1967

MOST WEEKS ON CHART – US SINGLES

Weeks
72 White Christmas – Bing Crosby (1942–62)
43 Rock Around The Clock – Bill Haley and his Comets (1955, 1974)
40 I Go Crazy – Paul Davis (1978)
39 The Twist – Chubby Checker (1960, 1961)
   Wonderful! Wonderful! – Johnny Mathis (1957)
   Honky Tonk – Bill Doggett (1956)
38 Blue Tango – Leroy Anderson (1952)
   So Rare – Jimmy Dorsey (1957)
   Why Me – Kris Kristofferson (1973)
37 The Wayward Wind – Gogi Grant (1956)
   Monster Mash – Bobby 'Boris' Pickett and the Crypt-Kickers (1962, 1970, 1973)

Ray Charles

34 Be My Love – Mario Lanza (1950)
   The Loveliest Night Of The Year – Mario Lanza (1951)
   Love Letters In The Sand – Pat Boone (1957)
   It's Not For Me To Say – Johnny Mathis (1957)
   Around The World – Victor Young (1957)
33 How Deep Is Your Love – Bee Gees (1977)
32 Twelfth Street Rag – Pee Wee Hunt (1948)
   Around The World – Mantovani (1957)
   Feelings – Morris Albert (1975)
   Baby Come Back – Player (1978)
   Jessie's Girl – Rick Springfield (1981)

NB: Paul Davis' 'I Go Crazy' holds the record for most consecutive weeks on the chart.

MOST WEEKS ON CHART – UK SINGLES

Weeks
122 My Way – Frank Sinatra (1969, 1970, 1971)
67 Amazing Grace – Judy Collins (1970, 1971, 1972)
57 Rock Around The Clock – Bill Haley and his Comets (1955, 1956, 1957, 1968, 1974)
56 Release Me – Engelbert Humperdinck (1967)
55 Stranger On The Shore – Acker Bilk (1961)
47 I Love You Because – Jim Reeves (1964, 1971)
44 Let's Twist Again – Chubby Checker (1961, 1962, 1975)
41 Deck Of Cards – Wink Martindale (1959, 1960, 1963, 1973)
40 Rivers Of Babylon/Brown Girl In The Ring – Boney M (1978)
   Tie A Yellow Ribbon Round The Old Oak Tree – Dawn featuring Tony Orlando (1973, 1974)
   A Scottish Soldier – Andy Stewart (1961)

39 He'll Have To Go – Jim Reeves (1960, 1971)

38 Somewhere My Love – Mike Sammes Singers (1966, 1967)

36 I Believe – Frankie Laine (1953)
I Pretend – Des O'Connor (1968)

35 And I Love You So – Perry Como (1973, 1974)
Hound Dog – Elvis Presley (1956, 1971)
Albatross – Fleetwood Mac (1968, 1973)
Let's Dance – Chris Montez (1962, 1972, 1979)

34 Heartbreak Hotel – Elvis Presley (1956, 1971)
Je T'Aime . . . Moi Non Plus – Jane Birkin and Serge Gainsbourg (1969, 1974)
Chirpy Chirpy Cheep Cheep – Middle of the Road (1971)
Leader Of The Pack – Shangri-Las (1965, 1972, 1976)
Nights In White Satin – Moody Blues (1967, 1972, 1979)

33 She Loves You – Beatles (1963, 1964)

MOST WEEKS ON CHART – AUSTRALIAN SINGLES CHART

Weeks

42 She Loves You – Beatles (1963)

37 Moon River – Jerry Butler (1961)

33 Fernando – Abba (1976)

32 Mamma Mia – Abba (1975)

31 I Was Made For Loving You – Kiss (1979)

30 A Pub With No Beer – Slim Dusty (1958)

29 Mississippi – Pussycat (1976)
Arrividerci Roma – Vic Damone (1958)
Around The World – Bing Crosby (1957)
Around The World – Victor Young (1957)

28 Exodus – Ferrante and Teicher (1961)
Song Of Joy – Miguel Rios (1970)

MOST WEEKS AT NUMBER ONE – JAPANESE SINGLES CHART

Weeks

21 Ozashiki Kouta – Kasuko Matsuo and the Mahina Stars (1964)

19 Yumewa Yoru Hiraku – Soni Mari and Midorikuwa Ako (1966)

18 Tokyo Blues – Nishida Sachiko (1964)

17 Tokyo Olympic Song – Haruo Minami (1964)
Koi No Kisetsu – Pinky and the Killers (1968)
Onna No Michi – Shiro Miya and Rinkara Trio (1972)

16 Kimo To Itsumademo – Yuko Kayama (1965)
Onna Gokoro Nu Uta – Bob Satake (1965)

15 Kuroneko No Tango – Osamu Minagawa (1969)

14 Aishiti, Aishiti, Aishichattanoya – Myuki Tashiro and the Mahina Stars (1965)
Yuhi Ga Naiteiru – The Spiders (1966)

Western artists rarely make an impression on the Japanese charts. To remedy this situation the Japanese music journal *Music Labo* has a separate international chart each week. This chart is open only to foreign acts. Should their sales warrant it, international hits are crossed over into the main chart. In 1981 the Nolans became the first non-indigenous act to top this chart for four years with 'Sexy Dancer', the Japanese title for 'I'm In The Mood For Dancing'.

SINGLES WHICH HAVE LEAPT FROM OUTSIDE THE TOP TEN TO NUMBER ONE IN A SINGLE WEEK – UK

33–1 Happy Talk – Captain Sensible (3 July 1982)

27–1 Hey Jude – Beatles (14 September 1968)

22–1 Green Door – Shakin' Stevens (1 August 1981)

21–1 (Just Like) Starting Over – John Lennon (20 December 1980)

19–1 (If Paradise Is) Half As Nice – Amen Corner (15 February 1969)
Love Me For A Reason – Osmonds (31 August 1974)

17–1 Get Off Of My Cloud – Rolling Stones (6 November 1965)

16–1 I Hear You Knocking – Dave Edmunds (28 November 1970)
Chirpy Chirpy Cheep Cheep – Middle Of The Road (19 June 1971)
Young Love – Donny Osmond (25 August 1973)
Dancing Queen – Abba (4 September 1976)

15–1 I Don't Like Mondays – Boomtown Rats (28 July 1979)
Too Much Too Young – Specials (2 February 1980)

14–1 Eye Level – Simon Park Orchestra (29 September 1973)

13–1 In The Summertime – Mungo Jerry (13 June 1970)

12–1 Love Grows – Edison Lighthouse (31 January 1970)

11–1 Sixteen Tons – Tennessee Ernie Ford (20 January 1956)
(There's) Always Something There To Remind Me – Sandie Shaw (22 October 1964)

Sandie Shaw

Michelle – Overlanders (27 January 1966)
Lady Madonna – Beatles (27 March 1968)
Sugar Sugar – Archies (25 October 1969)
She – Charles Aznavour (29 June 1974)
Summer Nights – John Travolta and Olivia Newton-John (17 June 1978)

HIGHEST NEW ENTRIES – US SINGLES CHART

The American singles chart is a much slower moving animal than its British counterpart and new entries debuting higher than No. 30 are rare indeed. The following is a complete list of records which made their initial American chart appearance at No. 20 or higher.

No. 6   Let It Be – Beatles (21 March 1970)

No. 7   The Purple People Eater – Sheb Wooley (24 May 1958)

No. 7   Wear My Ring Around Your Neck – Elvis Presley (12 April 1958)

No. 10   Hey Jude – Beatles (14 September 1968)

No. 10   Get Back – Beatles (10 May 1969)

No. 12   Love Me Tender – Elvis Presley (10 October 1956)

No. 12   Mrs Brown You've Got A Lovely Daughter – Herman's Hermits (17 April 1965)

No. 15   Jailhouse Rock – Elvis Presley (5 October 1957)

No. 15   Hard Headed Woman – Elvis Presley (21 June 1958)

No. 18   Poor Little Fool – Ricky Nelson (28 June 1958)

No. 20   Something – Beatles (18 October 1959)

No. 20   Imagine – John Lennon (23 October 1971)

GREATEST MONOPOLY – US SINGLES CHART

In the 42-year history of the American singles chart, two acts have managed to place more than eight songs on the chart simultaneously.

On 19 December 1956, 'Paralyzed', 'Old Shep' and 'Poor Boy' joined 'Don't Be Cruel', 'Hound Dog', 'Love Me Tender', 'Anyway You Want Me (That's How I Will Be)', 'Love Me' and 'When My Blue Moon Turns To Gold Again' to give Elvis Presley a total of nine concurrent hits. Presley's record stood for more than seven years until, inevitably, it was beaten by the Beatles.

The Beatles' first US hit was 'I Want To Hold Your Hand', which debuted at No. 45 on 18 January 1964. Just fourteen days later it was number one. Then the floodgates opened with Beatles releases almost every other day. Joining Capitol, the Beatles' official American licensees, in the avalanche of product were Swan, Vee Jay and Tollie, all of which reissued singles previously leased from Capitol. MGM and Atco also weighed in with recordings taken from the Beatles' German sessions with Tony Sheridan in 1961.

By 28 March 1964, the Beatles had ten records in the American singles chart. The following week their tally increased to twelve, including the entire top five – a feat without precedent. But Beatlemania reached its absolute peak on 11 April when the Fabs occupied no less than 14 slots on the hot hundred, spearheading a full scale assault on the US charts by British artists.

Here's a complete breakdown of that magical period when four lads from Liverpool took the American chart by the scruff of the neck:

	Mar 28	Apr 4	Apr 11
She Loves You	1	3	4
I Want To Hold Your Hand	2	4	7
Twist And Shout	3	2	2
Please Please Me	4	5	9
I Saw Her Standing There	26	31	38
Can't Buy Me Love	27	1	1
From Me To You	50	41	52
All My Loving	71	58	50
Roll Over Beethoven	75	68	78
Do You Want To Know A Secret	78	46	14
You Can't Do That	–	65	48
Thank You Girl	–	79	61
There's A Place	–	–	74
Love Me Do	–	–	81

The Beatles also established the all-time record for number of hits in a calendar year in 1964 scoring a total of 30 – well clear of the previous record of seventeen established by Elvis Presley in 1956.

ALWAYS THE BRIDESMAID, NEVER THE BRIDE (UK)

Artists with most UK hit singles who've never had a number one.

1. Stevie Wonder (32 hits)*
2. Nat 'King' Cole (28)
3. Elton John (27)
   Billy Fury (27)
5. Who (24)
6. Electric Light Orchestra (23)
7. Brenda Lee (22)
8. Duane Eddy (21)
   Gene Pitney (21)
10. Fats Domino (20)
    Gladys Knight (20)

* Stevie Wonder finally topped the British singles chart in April 1982 with 'Ebony And Ivory', his duet with Paul McCartney. As a solo artist, however, his tally of 32 hits without a number one still stands.

ALWAYS A BRIDESMAID, NEVER THE BRIDE (US)

A surprising number of artists have logged a large number of hits without ever reaching number one. The all-time champion is James Brown who notched 92 hits between 1959 and 1977 but reached the top ten only five times with a highest position of number three.

Johnny Cash

Brown's records were a permanent fixture on jukeboxes in America's black ghettoes but rarely received airplay on the white dominated radio networks. Thus their sales potential was seldom fully realized.

In common with many black acts Brown was forced to release more singles than his white contemporaries in order to maximize his earning capacity. This may – or may not – explain why so many black acts accumulated hits at a fast rate, and why nine out of our top ten 'bridesmaids' are black.

Number of Hits	Highest Position Attained	
92	3	James Brown
66	2	Fats Domino
54	4	Jackie Wilson
49	2	Brook Benton
48	2	Johnny Cash
39	4	Impressions
39	4	Jerry Butler
38	6	Wilson Pickett
37	20	Bobby Bland
34	15	B. B. King

UK NUMBER ONE SINGLES BY FEMALE SOLOISTS

1953 You Belong To Me – Jo Stafford
     Comes A-Long A-Love – Kay Starr
     (How Much Is) That Doggie In The Window – Lita Roza
1954 Secret Love – Doris Day
     Little Things Mean A Lot – Kitty Kallen
     My Son, My Son – Vera Lynn
     This Ole House – Rosemary Clooney
1955 Mambo Italiano – Rosemary Clooney
     Softly, Softly – Ruby Murray
     Dreamboat – Alma Cogan
1956 Rock And Roll Waltz – Kay Starr
     Whatever Will Be, Will Be – Doris Day
     Lay Down Your Arms – Anne Shelton

Doris Day

1958 Who's Sorry Now – Connie Francis
     Carolina Moon/Stupid Cupid – Connie Francis
1959 The Day That The Rains Came – Jane Morgan
     As I Love You – Shirley Bassey
1961 Sailor – Petula Clark
     You Don't Know – Helen Shapiro
     Reach For The Stars/Climb Ev'ry Mountain – Shirley Bassey
     Walking Back To Happiness – Helen Shapiro
1964 Anyone Who Had A Heart – Cilla Black
     You're My World – Cilla Black
     (There's) Always Something There To Remind Me – Sandie Shaw
1965 Where Are You Now (My Love) – Jackie Trent
     Long Live Love – Sandie Shaw
1966 These Boots Are Made For Walking – Nancy Sinatra
     You Don't Have To Say You Love Me – Dusty Springfield
1967 This Is My Song – Petula Clark
     Puppet On A String – Sandie Shaw
1968 Those Were The Days – Mary Hopkin
1969 I'll Never Fall In Love Again – Bobbie Gentry

1970 All Kinds Of Everything – Dana
Band Of Gold – Freda Payne
1971 I'm Still Waiting – Diana Ross
1973 Can The Can – Suzi Quatro
1974 Devil Gate Drive – Suzi Quatro
1975 Stand By Your Man – Tammy Wynette
1976 I Love To Love – Tina Charles
1977 Don't Cry For Me Argentina – Julie Covington
Free – Deniece Williams
I Feel Love – Donna Summer

Donna Summer

1978 Wuthering Heights – Kate Bush
1979 I Will Survive – Gloria Gaynor
Ring My Bell – Anita Ward
One Day At A Time – Lena Martell
1980 Together We Are Beautiful – Fern Kinney
Feels Like I'm In Love – Kelly Marie
Woman In Love – Barbra Streisand
1981 Japanese Boy – Aneka
1982 A Little Peace – Nicole
I've Never Been To Me – Charlene
Fame – Irene Cara

UK CHART-TOPPING SINGLES BY DUOS

1. All I Have To Do Is Dream – Everly Brothers (1958)
2. When – Kalin Twins (1958)
3. Cathy's Clown – Everly Brothers (1960)
4. Walk Right Back/Ebony Eyes – Everly Brothers (1961)
5. Temptation – Everly Brothers (1961)
6. Diamonds – Jet Harris and Tony Meehan (1963)

Jet Harris and Tony Meehan

7. World Without Love – Peter and Gordon (1964)
8. You've Lost That Lovin' Feelin' – Righteous Brothers (1965)
9. I Got You Babe – Sonny and Cher (1965)
10. Something Stupid – Frank and Nancy Sinatra (1967)
11. Cinderella Rockefella – Esther and Abi Ofarim (1968)
12. In The Year 2525 – Zager and Evans (1969)
13. Je T'Aime Moi Non Plus – Jane Birkin and Serge Gainsbourg (1969)
14. Bridge Over Troubled Water – Simon and Garfunkel (1970)
15. Double Barrel – Dave and Ansil Collins (1971)
16. Welcome Home – Peters and Lee (1973)
17. Whispering Grass – Windsor Davies and Don Estelle (1975)
18. Barbados – Typically Tropical (1975)
19. Don't Go Breaking My Heart – Elton John and Kiki Dee (1976)
20. Yes Sir, I Can Boogie – Baccara (1977)
21. Uptown Top Ranking – Althia and Donna (1978)
22. Matchstalk Men And Matchstalk Cats And Dogs – Brian and Michael (1978)
23. You're The One That I Want – John Travolta and Olivia Newton-John (1978)
24. Summer Nights – John Travolta and Olivia Newton-John (1978)
25. Video Killed The Radio Star – Buggles (1979)
26. Tainted Love – Soft Cell (1981)
27. Ebony And Ivory – Paul McCartney and Stevie Wonder (1982)

SCOTTISH CHART-TOPPERS (UK SINGLES CHART)

Despite their eligibility to top the British chart from its inception, it was 17 years before an act from north of Hadrian's Wall managed to reach Number One.

1. Ob-La-Di, Ob-La-Da – Marmalade (1 January 1969)
2. Chirpy Chirpy Cheep Cheep – Middle of the Road (19 June 1971)
3. Amazing Grace – Royal Scots Dragoon Guards (15 April 1972)
4. January – Pilot (1 February 1975)
5. Bye Bye Baby – Bay City Rollers (22 March 1975)

Bay City Rollers

6. Give A Little Love – Bay City Rollers (19 July 1975)
7. D.I.V.O.R.C.E. – Billy Connolly (22 November 1975)
8. Forever And Ever – Slik (14 February 1976)
9. One Day At A Time – Lena Martell (27 October 1979)
10. Japanese Boy – Aneka (29 August 1981)

INSTRUMENTAL CHART-TOPPERS (UK SINGLES CHART)

1. Moulin Rouge – Mantovani (14 August 1953)
2. Oh, Mein Papa – Eddie Calvert (8 January 1954)
3. Let's Have Another Party – Winifred Atwell (3 December 1954)
4. Cherry Pink And Apple Blossom White – Perez Prado (29 April 1955)
5. Cherry Pink And Apple Blossom White – Eddie Calvert (27 May 1955)
6. Poor People Of Paris – Winifred Atwell (13 April 1956)
7. Hoots Mon – Lord Rockingham's XI (28 November 1958)
8. Side Saddle – Russ Conway (27 March 1959)
9. Roulette – Russ Conway (19 June 1959)
10. Apache – Shadows (25 August 1960)
11. On The Rebound – Floyd Cramer (18 May 1961)
12. Kon-tiki – Shadows (5 October 1961)

The Shadows

13. Wonderful Land – Shadows (22 March 1962)
14. Nut Rocker – B. Bumble and the Stingers (17 May 1962)
15. Telstar – Tornados (4 October 1962)
16. Dance On – Shadows (24 January 1963)
17. Diamonds – Jet Harris and Tony Meehan (31 January 1963)
18. Foot Tapper – Shadows (28 March 1963)
19. The Good, The Bad And The Ugly – Hugo Montenegro (13 November 1968)
20. Albatross – Fleetwood Mac (29 January 1969)
21. Amazing Grace – Royal Scots Dragoon Guards (15 April 1972)
22. Mouldy Old Dough – Lieutenant Pigeon (14 October 1972)
23. Eye Level – Simon Park Orchestra (29 September 1973)

Gary U.S. Bonds

HELLO, HELLO – I'M BACK AGAIN

Recording acts which bounced back to score a British hit single after more than twelve years away from the charts.

DIVISION ONE – Those who did it with new recordings.

		Final chart appearance before 'dry' spell	Date of chart return	
1.	Gary 'US' Bonds	14 October 1961	31 May 1981	(19 years 228 days)
2.	Paul Evans	31 March 1960	16 December 1978	(18 years 244 days)
3.	Bing Crosby	30 August 1957	9 August 1975	(17 years 344 days)
4.	Slim Whitman	5 July 1957	5 October 1974	(17 years 92 days)
5.	Mike Berry	23 May 1963	2 August 1980	(17 years 71 days)
6.	Dee Clark	2 October 1959	11 October 1975	(16 years 9 days)
7.	Billy Fury	15 September 1966	4 September 1982	(15 years 350 days)
8.	Trini Lopez	4 May 1967	19 December 1981	(14 years 209 days)
9.	Danny Williams	14 March 1963	30 July 1977	(14 years 135 days)
10.	Acker Bilk	21 March 1963	21 August 1976	(13 years 153 days)
11.	Marianne Faithful	16 March 1967	24 November 1979	(12 years 253 days)
12.	Little Richard	16 July 1964	2 July 1977	(12 years 251 days)
13.	Exciters	21 February 1963	4 October 1975	(12 years 225 days)
14.	Paul Anka	16 August 1962	28 September 1974	(12 years 43 days)

DIVISION TWO – Those who did it with reissues of previous hits.

1.	Glenn Miller	12 March 1954	24 January 1976	(21 years 318 days)
2.	Teddy Bears	3 April 1959	14 April 1979	(20 years 11 days)
3.	Danny and the Juniors	18 April 1958	10 July 1976	(18 years 83 days)
4.	Goons	6 November 1956	21 July 1973	(16 years 257 days)
5.	Johnny Tillotson	6 June 1963	14 April 1979	(15 years 312 days)
6.	Dion	3 May 1962	22 May 1976	(14 years 19 days)
7.	Fats Domino	12 December 1963	24 April 1976	(13 years 232 days)
8.	Shirley Ellis	29 July 1965	8 July 1978	(12 years 344 days)
9.	Bobby Darin	29 December 1966	14 April 1979	(12 years 259 days)
10.	Chubby Checker	21 November 1963	29 November 1975	(12 years 8 days)

INSTRUMENTALS WHICH TOPPED THE AMERICAN SINGLES CHART

Artist	Title	Year
Perez Prado	Cherry Pink And Apple Blossom White	1955
Les Baxter	Unchained Melody	1955
Roger Williams	Autumn Leaves	1955
Nelson Riddle	Lisboa Antigua	1956
Les Baxter	Poor People Of Paris	1956
Morris Stoloff	Moonglow and Theme From *Picnic*	1956
Perez Prado	Patricia	1958
Dave 'Baby' Cortez	The Happy Organ	1959
Santo and Johnny	Sleepwalk	1959
Percy Faith	Theme From *A Summer Place*	1960
Bert Kaempfert	Wonderland By Night	1961
Lawrence Welk	Calcutta	1961
Acker Bilk	Stranger On The Shore	1962
David Rose	The Stripper	1962
Tornados	Telstar	1962
Paul Mauriat	Love Is Blue	1968
Hugh Masekela	Grazing In The Grass	1968
Henry Mancini	Love Theme From *Romeo And Juliet*	1969
Edgar Winter	Frankenstein	1973
Love Unlimited Orchestra	Love's Theme	1974
Average White Band	Pick Up The Pieces	1975
Rhythm Heritage	Theme From *S.W.A.T.*	1976
Walter Murphy	A Fifth Of Beethoven	1976
Meco	*Star Wars* Theme	1977
Herb Alpert	Rise	1979
Vangelis	Chariots Of Fire	1982

Dion

THE ULTIMATE ONE-HIT WONDERS: ACTS WHICH MADE NUMBER ONE WITH THEIR FIRST HIT BUT NEVER MADE THE CHARTS AGAIN

America
1. Pistol-Packin' Mama – Al Dexter (1943)
2. Theme From 'The Third Man' – Anton Karas (1950)
3. It's In The Book – Johnny Standley (1952)
4. I Saw Mommy Kissing Santa Claus – Jimmy Boyd (1952)
5. Let Me Go, Lover – Joan Weber (1954)
6. Moonglow And Theme From *Picnic* – Morris Stoloff conducting the Columbia Pictures Orchestra (1956)
7. He's Got The Whole World (In His Hands) – Laurie London (1958)
8. Little Star – Elegants (1958)
9. Get A Job – Silhouettes (1958)
10. Alley-Oop – Hollywood Argyles (1960)
11. Dominique – The Singing Nun (Soeur Sourire) (1963)
12. In The Year 2525 (Exordium And Terminus) – Zager and Evans (1969)
13. Gonna Fly Now (Theme From *Rocky*) – Bill Conti (1977)

All the above artists reached Number One with the songs mentioned. As of May 1982 none had managed to score a follow-up hit – not even a single week at No. 100.

Britain
1. Little Things Mean A Lot – Kitty Kallen (1954)
2. It's Almost Tomorrow – Dreamweavers (1956)
3. When – Kalin Twins (1958)
4. Here Comes Summer – Jerry Keller (1959)
5. Tell Laura I Love Her – Ricky Valance (1960)
6. Nut Rocker – B. Bumble and the Stingers (1962)
7. Michelle – Overlanders (1966)
8. Fire – Crazy World of Arthur Brown (1968)
9. In The Year 2525 (Exordium And Terminus) – Zager and Evans (1969)
10. Je T'Aime . . . Moi Non Plus – Jane Birkin and Serge Gainsbourg (1969)
11. Sugar Sugar – Archies (1969)
12. Wand'rin' Star – Lee Marvin (1970)
13. Spirit In The Sky – Norman Greenbaum (1970)
14. Woodstock – Matthews' Southern Comfort (1970)
15. Grandad – Clive Dunn (1971)
16. Eye Level – Simon Park Orchestra (1973)
17. Barbados – Typically Tropical (1975)
18. No Charge – J. J. Barrie (1976)
19. Float On – Floaters (1977)
20. Uptown Top Ranking – Althia and Donna (1978)
21. Matchstalk Men And Matchstalk Cats And Dogs – Brian and Michael (1978)
22. Ring My Bell – Anita Ward (1979)
23. One Day At A Time – Lena Martell (1979)
24. Together We Are Beautiful – Fern Kinney (1980)
25. What's Another Year – Johnny Logan (1980)
26. Theme From MASH – Mash (1980)
27. No One Quite Like Grandma – St Winifred's School Choir (1980)
28. Shaddap You Face – Joe Dolce Music Theatre (1981)

NB: In cases where part of a potential one hit wonder has scored hits in his/her own right (eg Dave Stewart was half of a chart-topping collaboration with the otherwise uncharted Barbara Gaskin but also had a hit with Colin Blunstone) the record has been excluded.

THE TWENTY BEST-SELLING SINGLES IN AUSTRALIA – 1981

1. Counting The Beat – Swingers
2. Stars On 45 – Stars On 45
3. Antmusic – Adam and the Ants
4. Jealous Guy – Roxy Music
5. Devo Live (12 in. EP) – Devo
6. Bette Davis Eyes – Kim Carnes
7. Nine To Five (Morning Train) – Sheena Easton

Sheena Easton

8. Endless Love – Diana Ross and Lionel Richie
9. Who Can It Be Now – Men At Work
10. Kids In America – Kim Wilde
11. This Ole House – Shakin' Stevens
12. Turn Me Loose – Loverboy
13. Start Me Up – Rolling Stones
14. You Weren't In Love With Me – Billy Field
15. Jessie's Girl – Rick Springfield
16. Duncan – Slim Dusty
17. Girls Can Get It – Dr Hook
18. (Just Like) Starting Over – John Lennon
19. You Drive Me Crazy – Shakin' Stevens
20. Keep On Loving You – REO Speedwagon

20 BEST-SELLING SINGLES IN THE NETHERLANDS – 1981

1. How 'Bout Us – Champaign
2. Why Tell Me Why – Anita Meijer
3. Stars On 45 – Stars On 45
4. Every Little Thing She Does Is Magic – The Police
5. Pretend – Alvin Stardust
6. One Day In Your Life – Michael Jackson
7. Shine Up – Doris D and the Pins
8. Making Your Mind Up – Bucks Fizz
9. Vienna – Ultravox
10. Dance On – Doris D and the Pins
11. In The Air Tonight – Phil Collins
12. I've Seen That Face Before – Grace Jones
13. Can You Feel It – Jacksons
14. For Your Eyes Only – Sheena Easton
15. Don't Stop The Music – Yarbrough and Peoples
16. Angel Of Mine – Frank Duval and Orchestra
17. This Ole House – Shakin' Stevens
18. De Verzonken Stad – Frank en Mirella
19. 'N Beetje Verliefd – Andre Hazes
20. Without Your Love – Roger Daltrey

List supplied courtesy of *Stichting Neder-landse Top 40.*)

THE FIRST AMERICAN ALBUM CHART

1. Collection Of Favourites – King Cole Trio
2. Glenn Miller And Orchestra – Glenn Miller and Orchestra
3. Meet Me In St Louis – Judy Garland
4. Songs Of Norway – Original New York Cast
5. Three Caballeros – Charles Wolcott and Orchestra

Printed in *Billboard* magazine on 15 March 1945.

AMERICA'S BEST-SELLING ALBUMS 1962

1. West Side Story – Original Soundtrack
2. Camelot – Original Cast
3. Blue Hawaii – Elvis Presley
4. Joan Baez Volume 2 – Joan Baez
5. Modern Sounds In Country and Western Music – Ray Charles
6. Peter, Paul And Mary – Peter, Paul and Mary
7. Your Twist Party – Chubby Checker
8. Judy At Carnegie – Judy Garland
9. Time Out – Dave Brubeck
10. Doin' The Twist At The Peppermint Lounge – Joey Dee
11. Twist – Chubby Checker
12. Moon River – Andy Williams
13. Breakfast At Tiffany's – Original Soundtrack
14. Stranger On The Shore – Acker Bilk
15. The Stripper – David Rose
16. College Concert – Kingston Trio
17. A Song For Young Love – Lettermen
18. Music Man – Original Soundtrack
19. Flower Drum Song – Original Soundtrack
20. Pot Luck – Elvis Presley

Reproduced courtesy of *Cashbox*.

AMERICA'S BEST-SELLING ALBUMS 1963

1. West Side Story – Original Soundtrack
2. Peter, Paul And Mary – Peter, Paul and Mary
3. Movin' – Peter, Paul and Mary
4. Joan Baez In Concert – Joan Baez
5. I Left My Heart In San Francisco – Tony Bennett
6. Moon River – Andy Williams
7. Lawrence Of Arabia – Original Soundtrack
8. Pot Luck – Elvis Presley
9. Days Of Wine And Roses – Andy Williams
10. Barbra Streisand Album – Barbra Streisand
11. Bye Bye Birdie – Original Soundtrack
12. Jazz Samba – Stan Getz
13. How The West Was Won – Original Soundtrack
14. I Wanna Be Around – Tony Bennett
15. Roy Orbison's Greatest Hits – Roy Orbison
16. Surfin' USA – Beach Boys
17. Oliver! – Original Soundtrack
18. Kingston Trio Number 16 – Kingston Trio
19. Songs I Sing On The Jackie Gleason Show – Frank Fontaine
20. Think Ethnic – Smothers Brothers

Reproduced courtesy of *Cashbox*.

THE BEST-SELLING ALBUMS OF 1964 – UK

Record Retailer's year-end surveys did not list albums until 1964.

1. West Side Story – Original Soundtrack
2. With The Beatles – Beatles
3. The Rolling Stones – Rolling Stones
4. Please Please Me – Beatles
5. A Hard Day's Night – Beatles
6. In Dreams – Roy Orbison
7. The Bachelors And Sixteen Great Songs – Bachelors
8. Wonderful Life – Cliff Richard
9. Stay With The Hollies – Hollies
10. Meet The Searchers – Searchers
11. How Do You Do It – Gerry and the Pacemakers
12. Dance With The Shadows – Shadows
13. Moonlight And Roses – Jim Reeves
14. Freddie And The Dreamers – Freddie and The Dreamers
15. Gentleman Jim – Jim Reeves
16. Shadows' Greatest Hits – Shadows
17. Kissin' Cousins – Elvis Presley
18. Born Free – Frank Ifield
19. A Girl Called Dusty – Dusty Springfield
20. It's The Searchers – Searchers

AMERICA'S BEST-SELLING ALBUMS 1964

1. Meet The Beatles – Beatles
2. Honey In The Horn – Al Hirt
3. West Side Story – Original Soundtrack
4. Second Barbra Streisand Album – Barbra Streisand
5. Blowin' In The Wind – Peter, Paul and Mary
6. Hello Dolly – Original Soundtrack
7. The Barbra Streisand Album – Barbra Streisand
8. Peter, Paul And Mary – Peter, Paul And Mary
9. Louie, Louie – Kingsmen
10. Catch A Rising Star – John Gary
11. Movin' – Peter, Paul and Mary
12. Pink Panther – Henry Mancini
13. Charade – Henry Mancini
14. Funny Girl – Original Cast
15. Hello Dolly – Louis Armstrong
16. Introducing The Beatles – Beatles
17. Days Of Wine And Roses – Andy Williams
18. Ramblin' – New Christy Minstrels
19. Shut Down Volume 2 – Beach Boys
20. Cotton Candy – Al Hirt

Reproduced courtesy of *Cashbox*.

THE BEST-SELLING ALBUMS OF 1965 – UK

1. Beatles For Sale – Beatles
2. Mary Poppins – Original Soundtrack
3. Sound Of Music – Original Soundtrack
4. Freewheelin' – Bob Dylan
5. Rolling Stones Volume 2 – Rolling Stones
6. Bringing It All Back Home – Bob Dylan
7. 13 Lucky Shades Of Val Doonican – Val Doonican
8. Help! – Beatles
9. Almost There – Andy Williams
10. My Fair Lady – Original Soundtrack
11. Joan Baez In Concert Volume 5 – Joan Baez
12. The Bachelors And Sixteen Great Songs – Bachelors
13. The Best Of Jim Reeves – Jim Reeves
14. West Side Story – Original Soundtrack
15. Animal Tracks – Animals
16. Kinks – Kinks
17. A Hard Day's Night – Beatles
18. Burt Bacharach, Hitmaker – Burt Bacharach
19. Sound Of The Shadows – Shadows
20. Kinda Kinks – Kinks

AMERICA'S BEST-SELLING ALBUMS 1965

1. Mary Poppins – Original Soundtrack
2. My Fair Lady – Original Soundtrack
3. Fiddler On The Roof – Original Cast
4. Where Did Our Love Go? – Supremes
5. Goldfinger – Original Soundtrack
6. People – Barbra Streisand
7. Sound Of Music – Original Soundtrack
8. Beatles '65 – Beatles
9. Beach Boys In Concert – Beach Boys
10. Dear Heart – Andy Williams
11. Beach Boys Today – Beach Boys
12. Bringing It All Back Home – Bob Dylan
13. Introducing Herman's Hermits – Herman's Hermits
14. Best Of Al Hirt – Al Hirt
15. Rolling Stones Now – Rolling Stones
16. The Return Of Roger Miller – Roger Miller
17. A Song Will Rise – Peter, Paul and Mary
18. My Name Is Barbra – Barbra Streisand
19. Blue Midnight – Bert Kaempfert
20. Hello Dolly – Original Cast

Reproduced courtesy of *Cashbox*.

THE BEST-SELLING ALBUMS OF 1966 – UK

Record Retailer's year-end survey in 1966 did not include best-selling albums.

AMERICA'S BEST-SELLING ALBUMS 1966

1. Sound Of Music – Original Soundtrack
2. Whipped Cream And Other Delights – Herb Alpert and the Tijuana Brass
3. Going Places – Herb Alpert
4. Dr Zhivago – Original Soundtrack
5. South Of The Border – Herb Alpert
6. The Best Of Herman's Hermits – Herman's Hermits
7. The Best Of The Animals – Animals
8. What Now My Love – Herb Alpert
9. Lonely Bull – Herb Alpert
10. Why Is There Air? – Bill Cosby
11. Fiddler On The Roof – Original Cast
12. If You Can Believe Your Eyes And Ears – Mamas and the Papas
13. Big Hits (High Tide And Green Grass) – Rolling Stones
14. My Name Is Barbra, Two – Barbra Streisand
15. September Of My Years – Frank Sinatra
16. Rubber Soul – Beatles
17. Wonderfulness – Bill Cosby
18. Greatest Hits – Dave Clark Five
19. Strangers In The Night – Frank Sinatra

Dave Clark Five

20. Spanish Eyes – Al Martino

Reproduced courtesy of *Cashbox*.

THE BEST-SELLING ALBUMS OF 1967 – UK

1. The Sound Of Music – Original Soundtrack
2. The Best Of The Beach Boys Volume 1 – Beach Boys
3. Dr Zhivago – Original Soundtrack
4. Going Places – Herb Alpert
5. The Monkees – Monkees
6. Sgt Pepper's Lonely Hearts Club Band – Beatles
7. Fiddler On The Roof – Original London Cast
8. Come The Day – Seekers
9. Four Tops Live – Four Tops
10. A Drop Of The Hard Stuff – Dubliners
11. Green, Green Grass Of Home – Tom Jones
12. Release Me – Engelbert Humperdinck
13. Are You Experienced? – Jimi Hendrix Experience
14. This Is James Last – James Last
15. Hand Clappin', Foot Stompin', Funky Butt – Live! – Geno Washington

Record Retailer's year-end survey in 1967 listed only fifteen albums.

Tom Jones

AMERICA'S BEST-SELLING ALBUMS 1967

1. Dr Zhivago – Original Soundtrack
2. Sound Of Music – Original Soundtrack
3. A Man And A Woman – Original Soundtrack
4. More Of The Monkees – Monkees
5. Sgt Pepper's Lonely Hearts Club Band – Beatles
6. Surrealistic Pillow – Jefferson Airplane
7. SRO – Herb Alpert
8. The Monkees – Monkees
9. Monkees Headquarters – Monkees
10. Doors – Doors
11. Sounds Like – Herb Alpert
12. Revenge – Bill Cosby
13. Never Loved A Man – Aretha Franklin
14. Deliver – Mamas and the Papas
15. Best Of Lovin' Spoonful – Lovin' Spoonful
16. Born Free – Andy Williams
17. Collections – Young Rascals

The Young Rascals

18. Whipped Cream And Other Delights – Herb Alpert and the Tijuana Brass
19. Wonderfulness – Herb Alpert
20. Release Me – Engelbert Humperdinck

Reproduced courtesy of *Cashbox*.

THE BEST-SELLING ALBUMS OF 1968 – UK

1. The Sound Of Music – Original Soundtrack
2. Tom Jones Live At The Talk Of Town – Tom Jones
3. Greatest Hits – Diana Ross and the Supremes
4. Greatest Hits – Four Tops
5. The Best Of The Beach Boys Volume 1 – Beach Boys
6. 13 Smash Hits – Tom Jones
7. Jungle Book – Original Soundtrack
8. The History Of Otis Redding – Otis Redding
9. Peter Green's Fleetwood Mac – Fleetwood Mac
10. John Wesley Harding – Bob Dylan
11. British Motown Chartbusters – Various
12. Bookends – Simon and Garfunkel
13. Delilah – Tom Jones
14. Greatest Hits – Hollies
15. Otis Blue – Otis Redding

Record Retailer's year-end survey in 1968 listed only fifteen albums.

AMERICA'S BEST-SELLING ALBUMS 1968

1. Disraeli Gears – Cream
2. The Graduate – Original Soundtrack
3. Are You Experienced? – Jimi Hendrix Experience
4. Bookends – Simon and Garfunkel
5. Look Around – Sergio Mendes
6. Parsley, Sage, Rosemary And Thyme – Simon and Garfunkel
7. Lady Soul – Aretha Franklin
8. Best Of The Brass – Herb Alpert
9. Magical Mystery Tour – Beatles
10. Blooming Hits – Paul Mauriat
11. Honey – Bobby Goldsboro
12. Wheels Of Fire – Cream
13. Dr Zhivago – Original Soundtrack
14. Time Peace – The Rascals Greatest Hits – Rascals
15. The Good, The Bad And The Ugly – Original Soundtrack
16. Axis – Bold As Love – Jimi Hendrix
17. Aretha Now – Aretha Franklin
18. To Russell, My Brother, Whom I Slept With – Bill Cosby
19. Herb Alpert's Ninth – Herb Alpert
20. Realization – Johnny Rivers

Reproduced courtesy of *Cashbox*.

THE BEST-SELLING ALBUMS OF 1969 – UK

1. The Best Of The Seekers – Seekers
2. The Sound Of Music – Original Soundtrack
3. His Orchestra, His Chorus, His Singers, His Sound – Ray Conniff
4. Abbey Road – Beatles
5. Johnny Cash At San Quentin – Johnny Cash
6. Oliver – Original Soundtrack
7. According To My Heart – Jim Reeves
8. Goodbye – Mary Hopkin
9. Nashville Skyline – Bob Dylan
10. Diana Ross And The Supremes Join The Temptations – Diana Ross and the Supremes with the Temptations
11. Motown Chartbusters Volume 3 – Various

12. Hair – Original Cast (London)
    The World Of Mantovani Volume 1 –
    Mantovani
14. World Of Val Doonican – Val
    Doonican
15. On The Threshold Of A Dream –
    Moody Blues
    The World of Mantovani Volume 2 –
    Mantovani
17. The Beatles (white album) – Beatles
18. Flaming Star – Elvis Presley
19. Stand Up – Jethro Tull
20. This Is Tom Jones – Tom Jones

Two records tied for twelfth and fifteenth places.

AMERICA'S BEST-SELLING ALBUMS 1969

1. Hair – Original Cast
2. In-A-Gadda-Da-Vida – Iron
   Butterfly
3. Blood Sweat And Tears – Blood
   Sweat and Tears
4. The Beatles (White Album) – Beatles
5. Donovan's Greatest Hits – Donovan
6. Led Zeppelin Volume 1 – Led
   Zeppelin
7. Romeo And Juliet – Original
   Soundtrack
8. Wichita Lineman – Glen Campbell

Glen Campbell

9. Bayou Country – Creedence
   Clearwater Revival
10. Funny Girl – Original Soundtrack
11. The Association's Greatest Hits –
    Association
12. Nashville Skyline – Bob Dylan
13. Gentle On My Mind – Glen
    Campbell
14. The Soft Parade – Doors
15. Age Of Aquarius – Fifth Dimension
16. This Is Tom Jones – Tom Jones
17. Crosby, Stills And Nash – Crosby,
    Stills and Nash
18. Johnny Cash At San Quentin –
    Johnny Cash
19. Oliver – Original Soundtrack
20. Cheap Thrills – Big Brother and the
    Holding Company

Reproduced courtesy of *Cashbox*.

THE BEST-SELLING ALBUMS OF 1970 – UK

1. Bridge Over Troubled Water – Simon
   and Garfunkel
2. Led Zeppelin II – Led Zeppelin
3. Easy Rider – Original Soundtrack
4. Paint Your Wagon – Original
   Soundtrack
5. Motown Chartbusters Volume 3 –
   Various
6. Abbey Road – Beatles
7. Let It Be – Beatles
8. Deep Purple In Rock – Deep Purple
9. McCartney – Paul McCartney
10. Andy Williams' Greatest Hits – Andy
    Williams
11. Johnny Cash At San Quentin –
    Johnny Cash
12. A Question Of Balance – Moody
    Blues
13. The Sound Of Music – Original
    Soundtrack
14. Paranoid – Black Sabbath
15. Motown Chartbusters Volume 4 –
    Various
16. Cosmo's Factory – Creedence
    Clearwater Revival
17. Tom Jones Live In Las Vegas – Tom
    Jones

Paul McCartney

18. Let It Bleed – Rolling Stones
19. Fire And Water – Free
20. Black Sabbath – Black Sabbath

AMERICA'S BEST-SELLING ALBUMS 1970

1. Chicago – Chicago
2. Déjà Vu – Crosby, Stills, Nash and
   Young
3. Bridge Over Troubled Water – Simon
   and Garfunkel
4. Woodstock – Original Soundtrack
5. Abbey Road – Beatles
6. Santana – Santana
7. Led Zeppelin II – Led Zeppelin
8. Joe Cocker – Joe Cocker
9. McCartney – Paul McCartney
10. Easy Rider – Original Soundtrack
11. Music From Butch Cassidy And The
    Sundance Kid – Burt Bacharach
12. Live At Leeds – The Who
13. American Woman – Guess Who
14. Let It Be – Beatles
15. Get Ready – Rare Earth

16. Willy And The Poor Boys – Creedence Clearwater Revival
17. Sweet Baby James – James Taylor
18. Raindrops Keep Falling On My Head – B. J. Thomas
19. Tom Jones Live At Las Vegas – Tom Jones
20. Hair – Original Cast

Reproduced courtesy of *Cashbox*.

THE BEST-SELLING ALBUMS OF 1971 – UK

1. Bridge Over Troubled Water – Simon and Garfunkel
2. Every Picture Tells A Story – Rod Stewart
3. Sticky Fingers – Rolling Stones
4. Motown Chartbusters Volume 5 – Various
5. Electric Warrior – T. Rex
6. Mud Slide Slim And The Blue Horizon – James Taylor
7. Every Good Boy Deserves Favour – Moody Blues
8. Andy Williams' Greatest Hits – Andy Williams
9. Ram – Paul and Linda McCartney
10. Tapestry – Carole King

Music Week listed only ten albums in its year-end survey of 1971.

AMERICA'S BEST-SELLING ALBUMS 1971

1. Jesus Christ Superstar – A Rock Opera – Various
2. Tapestry – Carole King
3. Tea For The Tillerman – Cat Stevens
4. Mud Slide Slim – James Taylor
5. Sticky Fingers – Rolling Stones
6. Pearl – Janis Joplin
7. Abraxas – Santana
8. Carpenters – Carpenters
9. Ram – Paul and Linda McCartney
10. Golden Bisquits – Three Dog Night
11. Up To Date – Partridge Family
12. Love Story – Original Soundtrack

13. Close To You – Carpenters
14. Aqualung – Jethro Tull
15. 4 Way Street – Crosby, Stills, Nash and Young
16. Every Picture Tells A Story – Rod Stewart
17. Chicago III – Chicago
18. Paranoid – Black Sabbath
19. The Partridge Family Album – Partridge Family
20. Pendulum – Creedence Clearwater Revival

Reproduced courtesy of *Cashbox*.

THE BEST-SELLING ALBUMS OF 1972 – UK

1. Twenty-two Dynamic Hits – Various
2. 20 All Time Hits Of The Fifties – Various
3. Simon And Garfunkel's Greatest Hits – Simon and Garfunkel
4. Never A Dull Moment – Rod Stewart
5. Twenty Fantastic Hits – Various
6. Bridge Over Troubled Water – Simon and Garfunkel
7. Fog On The Tyne – Lindisfarne
8. Slade Alive – Slade
9. Twenty-five Rockin' And Rollin' Greats – Various
10. American Pie – Don McLean

Music Week again listed only ten albums in its year-end survey of 1972.

AMERICA'S BEST-SELLING ALBUMS 1972

1. Tapestry – Carole King
2. Music – Carole King
3. Harvest – Neil Young
4. American Pie – Don McLean
5. Teaser And The Firecat – Cat Stevens
6. Let's Stay Together – Al Green
7. Concert For Bangla Desh – George Harrison and Various Artists
8. Fragile – Yes
9. America – America
10. Led Zeppelin IV – Led Zeppelin

The Rolling Stones

11. Hot Rocks 1964–1971 – Rolling Stones
12. Thick As A Brick – Jethro Tull
13. Honky Chateau – Elton John
14. Paul Simon – Paul Simon
15. Chicago At Carnegie Hall – Chicago
16. Eat A Peach – Allman Brothers
17. First Take – Roberta Flack
18. Baby I'm A Want You – Bread
19. Nilsson Schmilsson – Nilsson
20. Exile On Main Street – Rolling Stones

Reproduced courtesy of *Cashbox*.

THE BEST-SELLING ALBUMS OF 1973 – UK

1. Aladdin Sane – David Bowie
2. Simon And Garfunkel's Greatest Hits – Simon and Garfunkel
3. Don't Shoot Me, I'm Only The Piano Player – Elton John
4. We Can Make It – Peters And Lee
5. The Beatles 1967–70 – Beatles
6. The Dark Side Of The Moon – Pink Floyd
7. Back To Front – Gilbert O'Sullivan
8. Hunky Dory – David Bowie
9. The Beatles 1962–66 – Beatles
10. And I Love You So – Perry Como
11. The Rise And Fall Of Ziggy Stardust – David Bowie
12. Now And Then – Carpenters
13. Pin Ups – David Bowie
14. Bridge Over Troubled Water – Simon and Garfunkel
15. Sing It Again Rod – Rod Stewart
16. Clockwork Orange – Original Soundtrack

17. Billion Dollar Babies – Alice Cooper
18. Goat's Head Soup – Rolling Stones
19. Slayed – Slade
20. For Your Pleasure – Roxy Music

AMERICA'S BEST-SELLING ALBUMS 1973

1. The Dark Side Of The Moon – Pink Floyd
2. Houses Of The Holy – Led Zeppelin
3. Diamond Girl – Seals and Crofts
4. The World Is A Ghetto – War
5. Seventh Sojourn – Moody Blues
6. The Captain And Me – Doobie Brothers
7. Life And Times – Jim Croce
8. Talking Book – Stevie Wonder
9. Rocky Mountain High – John Denver
10. Chicago IV – Chicago
11. No Secrets – Carly Simon
12. Rhymes And Reasons – Carole King
13. They Only Come Out At Night – Edgar Winter Group
14. Lady Sings The Blues – Diana Ross (Soundtrack)
15. Billion Dollar Babies – Alice Cooper
16. Catch Bull At Four – Cat Stevens
17. Made In Japan – Deep Purple

Deep Purple

18. The Best Of Bread – Bread
19. I'm Still In Love With You – Al Green
20. Now And Then – Carpenters

Reproduced courtesy of *Cashbox*.

THE BEST-SELLING ALBUMS OF 1974 – UK

1. The Singles 1969–1973 – Carpenters
2. Band On The Run – Wings
3. Tubular Bells – Mike Oldfield
4. Elvis Presley's 40 Greatest Hits – Elvis Presley
5. The Dark Side Of The Moon – Pink Floyd
6. Goodbye Yellow Brick Road – Elton John
7. And I Love You So – Perry Como
8. Rollin' – Bay City Rollers
9. Simon And Garfunkel's Greatest Hits – Simon and Garfunkel
10. Old, New, Borrowed And Blue – Slade
11. Another Time, Another Place – Bryan Ferry
12. Hergest Ridge – Mike Oldfield
13. Super Bad – Various
14. Diamond Dogs – David Bowie

David Bowie

15. Caribou – Elton John
16. Journey To The Centre Of The Earth – Rick Wakeman

17. Elton John's Greatest Hits – Elton John
18. Diana And Marvin – Diana Ross and Marvin Gaye
19. Smiler – Rod Stewart
20. Scott Joplin Piano Rags – Joshua Rifkin

AMERICA'S BEST-SELLING ALBUMS 1974

1. John Denver's Greatest Hits – John Denver
2. Band On The Run – Paul McCartney and Wings
3. Goodbye Yellow Brick Road – Elton John
4. The Singles 1969–1973 – Carpenters
5. Bachman Turner Overdrive Volume 2 – Bachman Turner Overdrive
6. Don't Mess Around With Jim – Jim Croce
7. The Sting – Original Soundtrack
8. Chicago VII – Chicago
9. Innervisions – Stevie Wonder
10. Behind Closed Doors – Charlie Rich
11. Back Home Again – John Denver
12. Caribou – Elton John
13. American Graffiti – Original Soundtrack
14. Court And Spark – Joni Mitchell
15. Sundown – Gordon Lightfoot
16. Shinin' On – Grand Funk
17. Tubular Bells – Mike Oldfield
18. The Joker – Steve Miller Band
19. Hot Cakes – Carly Simon
20. If You Love Me, Let Me Know – Olivia Newton-John

Reproduced courtesy of *Cashbox*.

THE BEST-SELLING ALBUMS OF 1975 – UK

1. The Best Of The Stylistics – Stylistics
2. Once Upon A Star – Bay City Rollers
3. Atlantic Crossing – Rod Stewart
4. Horizon – Carpenters
5. 40 Golden Greats – Jim Reeves
6. 40 Greatest Hits – Elvis Presley

7. Tubular Bells – Mike Oldfield
8. Greatest Hits – Elton John
9. Venus And Mars – Wings
10. The Singles 1969–1973 – Carpenters
11. 40 Greatest Hits – Perry Como
12. Captain F.ntastic And The Brown Dirt Cowboy – Elton John
13. Greatest Hits – Simon and Garfunkel
14. 20 Greatest Hits – Tom Jones
15. His Greatest Hits – Engelbert Humperdinck
16. Rollin' – Bay City Rollers
17. Original Soundtrack – 10CC
18. Favourites – Peters and Lee
19. The Dark Side Of The Moon – Pink Floyd
20. Get Dancing – Various

AMERICA'S BEST-SELLING ALBUMS 1975

1. Elton John's Greatest Hits – Elton John
2. Captain Fantastic And The Brown Dirt Cowboy – Elton John
3. That's The Way Of The World – Earth, Wind And Fire
4. Have You Never Been Mellow – Olivia Newton-John
5. Rock Of The Westies – Elton John
6. One Of These Nights – Eagles
7. Average White Band – Average White Band
8. Windsong – John Denver
9. Not Fragile – Bachman Turner Overdrive
10. Red Octopus – Jefferson Starship
11. Back Home Again – John Denver
12. Physical Graffiti – Led Zeppelin
13. Tommy – Original Soundtrack
14. Wish You Were Here – Pink Floyd
15. War Child – Jethro Tull
16. Fire – Ohio Players
17. The Heat Is On – Isley Brothers
18. Chicago VIII – Chicago
19. Heart Like A Wheel – Linda Ronstadt
20. Welcome To My Nightmare – Alice Cooper

Reproduced courtesy of *Cashbox*.

THE BEST-SELLING ALBUMS OF 1976 – UK

1. Greatest Hits – Abba
2. 20 Golden Greats – Beach Boys
3. Forever And Ever – Demis Roussos
4. Wings At The Speed Of Sound – Wings
5. A Night On The Town – Rod Stewart
6. Live In London – John Denver
7. Laughter And Tears – Neil Sedaka
8. Their Greatest Hits 1971–1975 – Eagles
9. 20 Golden Greats – Glen Campbell
10. The Very Best Of Slim Whitman – Slim Whitman
11. The Best Of Roy Orbison – Roy Orbison
12. A Night At The Opera – Queen
13. Desire – Bob Dylan
14. Greatest Hits Volume 2 – Diana Ross
15. Instrumental Gold – Various
16. Frampton Comes Alive – Peter Frampton
17. Changesonebowie – David Bowie
18. Rock Follies – Julie Covington, Rula Lenska, Charlotte Cornwell and Sue Lloyd-Davies
19. How Dare You – 10CC
20. The Best Of Gladys Knight And The Pips – Gladys Knight and the Pips

AMERICA'S BEST-SELLING ALBUMS 1976

1. Frampton Comes Alive – Peter Frampton
2. Their Greatest Hits – Eagles
3. Fleetwood Mac – Fleetwood Mac
4. Songs In The Key Of Life – Stevie Wonder
5. History – America's Greatest Hits – America
6. Wings At The Speed Of Sound – Wings
7. Gratitude – Earth, Wind and Fire
8. Breezin' – George Benson
9. A Night At The Opera – Queen
10. Dreamweaver – Gary Wright
11. Song Of Joy – Captain and Tennille

Captain and Tennille

12. Rocks – Aerosmith
13. KC And The Sunshine Band – KC and the Sunshine Band
14. Silk Degrees – Boz Scaggs
15. Spirit – Earth, Wind and Fire
16. Chicago X – Chicago
17. Fly Like An Eagle – Steve Miller Band
18. Spitfire – Jefferson Starship
19. Boston – Boston
20. Look Out For Number One – Brothers Johnson

Reproduced courtesy of *Cashbox*.

THE BEST-SELLING ALBUMS OF 1977 – UK

1. Arrival – Abba
2. 20 Golden Greats – Shadows
3. 20 Golden Greats – Diana Ross and the Supremes
4. A Star Is Born – Original Soundtrack (Kris Kristofferson and Barbra Streisand)
5. Rumours – Fleetwood Mac
6. Hotel California – Eagles
7. The Sound Of Bread – Bread
8. Endless Flight – Leo Sayer
9. Greatest Hits – Abba
10. The Johnny Mathis Collection – Johnny Mathis
11. Animals – Pink Floyd
12. Never Mind The Bollocks – Here's The Sex Pistols – Sex Pistols

Leo Sayer

13. Portrait of Sinatra, Forty Songs From The Life Of A Man – Frank Sinatra
14. Disco Fever – Various
15. A New World Record – Electric Light Orchestra
16. Going For The One – Yes
17. All Time Greats – Connie Francis
18. Red River Valley – Slim Whitman
19. Songs In The Key Of Life – Stevie Wonder
20. Oxygene – Jean Michel Jarre

AMERICA'S BEST-SELLING ALBUMS 1977

1. Rumours – Fleetwood Mac
2. Hotel California – Eagles
3. Boston – Boston
4. Songs In The Key Of Life – Stevie Wonder
5. Frampton Comes Alive – Peter Frampton
6. *Star Wars* – Original Soundtrack
7. *A Star Is Born* – Original Soundtrack (Barbra Streisand and Kris Kristofferson)
8. Commodores – Commodores
9. Fly Like An Eagle – Steve Miller Band
10. Foreigner – Foreigner
11. I'm In You – Peter Frampton
12. Wings Over America – Wings
13. Night Moves – Bob Seger

The Eagles

14. Leftoverture – Kansas
15. CSN – Crosby, Stills and Nash
16. Shaun Cassidy – Shaun Cassidy
17. Book Of Dreams – Steve Miller Band
18. JT – James Taylor
19. Greatest Hits – Linda Ronstadt
20. Live At The Palladium – Marvin Gaye

Reproduced courtesy of *Cashbox*.

THE BEST-SELLING ALBUMS OF 1978 – UK

1. Saturday Night Fever – Various
2. Grease – Various
3. The Album – Abba
4. Nightflight To Venus – Boney M
5. 20 Golden Greats – Nat 'King' Cole
6. Rumours – Fleetwood Mac
7. Out Of The Blue – Electric Light Orchestra
8. 20 Golden Greats – Buddy Holly and the Crickets
9. The Kick Inside – Kate Bush
10. Images – Don Williams
11. War Of The Worlds – Various
12. And Then There Were Three – Genesis

13. Classic Rock – London Symphony Orchestra
14. New Boots And Panties – Ian Dury and the Blockheads
15. Live And Dangerous – Thin Lizzy
16. Reflections – Andy Williams
17. The Sound Of Bread – Bread
18. Street Legal – Bob Dylan
19. The Stud – Various
20. 20 Golden Greats – Hollies

AMERICA'S BEST-SELLING ALBUMS 1978

1. Saturday Night Fever – Bee Gees and Various Artists
2. The Stranger – Billy Joel
3. Grease – Various Artists
4. Some Girls – Rolling Stones
5. Double Vision – Foreigner
6. Running On Empty – Jackson Browne
7. Point Of No Return – Kansas
8. Slowhand – Eric Clapton
9. Rumours – Fleetwood Mac
10. Natural High – Commodores
11. Stranger In Town – Bob Seger and the Silver Bullet Band
12. Aja – Steely Dan
13. News Of The World – Queen
14. Even Now – Barry Manilow
15. Footloose And Fancy Free – Rod Stewart
16. Don't Look Back – Boston
17. All 'n' All – Earth, Wind and Fire
18. London Town – Wings
19. The Grand Illusion – Styx
20. Simple Dreams – Linda Ronstadt

Reproduced courtesy of *Cashbox*.

THE BEST-SELLING ALBUMS OF 1979 – UK

1. Parallel Lines – Blondie
2. Discovery – Electric Light Orchestra
3. The Very Best Of Leo Sayer – Leo Sayer
4. Breakfast In America – Supertramp
5. Voulez Vous – Abba

6. Greatest Hits Volume 2 – Barbra Streisand
7. Spirits Having Flown – Bee Gees
8. Greatest Hits Volume 2 – Abba
9. Reggatta De Blanc – Police
10. Manilow Magic – Barry Manilow
11. Greatest Hits – Rod Stewart
12. Last The Whole Night Long – James Last
13. Armed Forces – Elvis Costello and the Attractions
14. Outlandos D'Amour – Police
15. The Best Disco Album In The World – Various
16. Replicas – Tubeway Army
17. I Am – Earth, Wind and Fire
18. C'Est Chic – Chic
19. Dire Straits – Dire Straits
20. Manifesto – Roxy Music

AMERICA'S BEST-SELLING ALBUMS 1979

1. Breakfast In America – Supertramp
2. Bad Girls – Donna Summer
3. Minute By Minute – Doobie Brothers
4. 52nd Street – Billy Joel
5. Cheap Trick At Budokan – Cheap Trick
6. Spirits Having Flown – Bee Gees
7. Blondes Have More Fun – Rod Stewart
8. Get The Knack – Knack
9. Candy-O – Cars
10. In Through The Out Door – Led Zeppelin
11. 2 Hot! – Peaches and Herb
12. Desolation Angels – Bad Company
13. I Am – Earth, Wind and Fire
14. Midnight Magic – Commodores
15. Dire Straits – Dire Straits
16. Briefcase Full Of Blues – Blues Brothers
17. Rickie Lee Jones – Rickie Lee Jones
18. Off The Wall – Michael Jackson
19. Discovery – Electric Light Orchestra
20. C'est Chic – Chic

Reproduced courtesy of *Cashbox*.

THE BEST-SELLING ALBUMS OF 1980 – UK

1. Super Trouper – Abba
2. Zenyatta Mondatta – Police
3. Greatest Hits – Rose Royce
4. Guilty – Barbra Streisand
5. Pretenders – Pretenders
6. Reggatta De Blanc – Police
7. Flesh And Blood – Roxy Music
8. Manilow Magic – Barry Manilow
9. Off The Wall – Michael Jackson
10. Duke – Genesis
11. Sky 2 – Sky
12. Double Fantasy – John Lennon and Yoko Ono

Boney M

13. One Step Beyond – Madness
14. 12 Gold Bars – Status Quo
15. String Of Hits – Shadows
16. Last Dance – Various (Motown)
17. Greatest Hits Volume 2 – Abba
18. Outlandos D'Amour – Police
19. The Magic Of Boney M – Boney M
20. Scary Monsters And Super Creeps – David Bowie

MOST WEEKS AT NUMBER ONE – UK ALBUM CHART

83 South Pacific – Original Soundtrack (1958–61)
69 Sound Of Music – Original Soundtrack (1965–68)
34 Bridge Over Troubled Water – Simon and Garfunkel (1970–71)
30 Please Please Me – Beatles (1963)
27 Sgt Pepper's Lonely Hearts Club Band – Beatles (1967)
22 GI Blues – Elvis Presley (1961)
21 With The Beatles – Beatles (1963–64)
21 A Hard Day's Night – Beatles (1964)
21 Abba's Greatest Hits – Abba (1976–77)
18 Blue Hawaii – Elvis Presley (1962)
18 Saturday Night Fever – Original Soundtrack (1978)
17 Abbey Road – Beatles (1969–70)
17 The Singles 1969–1973 – Carpenters (1974)

MOST WEEKS AT NUMBER ONE – US ALBUM CHART

67 South Pacific – Original Cast (1949)
54 West Side Story – Original Soundtrack (1962)
31 Calypso – Harry Belafonte (1956)
   South Pacific – Original Soundtrack (1958)
   Rumours – Fleetwood Mac (1977)
25 Al Jolson Album Volume 1 – Al Jolson (1947)
24 Saturday Night Fever – Original Movie Soundtrack (1978)

MOST WEEKS IN TOP TEN – US ALBUM CHART

1. Sound Of Music – Soundtrack (109 weeks)
2. Dr Zhivago – Soundtrack (71 weeks)
3. Whipped Cream And Other Delights – Herb Alpert and the Tijuana Brass (61 weeks)
4. Rumours – Fleetwood Mac (52 weeks)

Frampton Comes Alive – Peter
Frampton (52 weeks)
6. Blood Sweat And Tears – Blood,
Sweat and Tears (50 weeks)
7. In-A-Gadda-Da-Vida – Iron
Butterfly (49 weeks)
8. Mary Poppins – Original Soundtrack
(48 weeks)
Goin' Places – Herb Alpert and the
Tijuana Brass (48 weeks)
10. Tapestry – Carole King (46 weeks)

List donated by Paul Grein of *Billboard*.

MOST WEEKS ON CHART – UK ALBUMS

1.	The Sound Of Music – Original Soundtrack	365 weeks
2.	South Pacific – Original Soundtrack	306 weeks
3.	Bridge Over Troubled Water – Simon and Garfunkel	291 weeks
4.	The Dark Side Of The Moon – Pink Floyd	275 weeks
5.	Greatest Hits – Simon and Garfunkel	263 weeks
6.	Tubular Bells – Mike Oldfield	242 weeks
7.	Bat Out Of Hell – Meat Loaf	237 weeks
8.	Rumours – Fleetwood Mac	230 weeks

QUALIFICATION: 200 weeks on chart.

'Bat Out Of Hell' and 'Rumours' were still
adding to their 'weeks on chart' totals at the
end of November 1982.

HIGHEST NEW ENTRIES – US ALBUM CHART

No. 1
Captain Fantastic And The Brown Dirt
Cowboy – Elton John
(7 June 1975)

Rock Of The Westies – Elton John
(8 November 1975)

Songs In The Key Of Life – Stevie
Wonder
(16 October 1976)

Stevie Wonder

No. 2
Windsong – John Denver
(4 October 1975)

Presence – Led Zeppelin
(24 April 1976)

(Compiled by Paul Grein, of *Billboard*
Magazine.)

THE TWENTY BEST-SELLING ALBUMS IN AUSTRALIA – 1981

1. Double Fantasy – John Lennon and
Yoko Ono
2. Sirocco – Australian Crawl
3. Back In Black – AC/DC
4. Bad Habits – Billy Field
5. Makin' Movies – Dire Straits
6. Icehouse – Icehouse
7. Face Value – Phil Collins
8. Hotter Than July – Stevie Wonder
9. Christopher Cross – Christopher
Cross
10. Corroboree – Split Enz
11. Zenyatta Mondatta – Police
12. Tattoo You – Rolling Stones
13. Greatest Hits – Dr Hook
14. The Jazz Singer – Neil Diamond
15. Arc Of A Diver – Steve Winwood
16. Beatles Ballads – Beatles
17. Bella Donna – Stevie Nicks
18. Time – Electric Light Orchestra
19. Stars On 45 – Stars On 45
20. Devo Live (12in EP) – Devo

Note: Due to a substantial price increase
while it was in the singles chart, 'Devo
Live' ceased to be eligible for inclusion.
However, its new price was steep enough
for it to qualify as an honorary album. It
therefore features in both year-end listings.

Abba

NORWAY'S BEST-SELLING ALBUMS OF ALL TIME

1. I Smurfland – Geir Borrenson
2. Grease – Original Soundtrack
3. The Album – Abba
4. Greatest Hits – Smokie
5. Saturday Night Fever – Original
Soundtrack
6. Arrival – Abba
7. Brakara – Prima Vera
8. Abba – Abba
9. Hotel California – Eagles
10. Spirits Having Flown – Bee Gees

12. ROCK REFERENCE

ABBREVIATIONS

There are a number of familiar sets of initials in everyday use in the music business but in some cases their meaning is not clear. The following list may help . . .

Record Companies
1. EMI – Electrical and Musical Industries
2. WEA – Warner/Reprise, Elektra/Asylum, Atlantic
3. CBS – Columbia Broadcasting Systems
4. RSO – Robert Stigwood Organization
5. A&M – (Herb) Alpert and (Jerry) Moss
6. MCA – Music Corporation of America
7. RCA – Recording Corporation of America
8. ABC – American Broadcasting Corporation
9. DJM – Dick James Music
10. SGC – Screen Gems Columbia

Other Musical Terms
1. A&R – Artistes and Repertoire
2. dbs – decibels
3. DI – Direct Injection
4. R&B – Rhythm and Blues
5. C&W – Country and Western
6. MGs (Booker T and . . .) – Memphis Group
7. BMRB – British Market Research Bureau
8. AM – Amplitude Modulation
9. FM – Frequency Modulation
10. VHF – Very High Frequency
11. MOR – Middle of the Road
12. AOR – Adult Orientated Rock
13. PA – Personal Appearance or Public Address (system)

REAL NAMES OF ROCK STARS

1.	David Bowie	David Jones
2.	Gary Glitter	Paul Gadd

Paul Gadd aka Gary Glitter

3.	Joe Strummer	John Mellor
4.	Rat Scabies	Chris Miller
5.	Chubby Checker	Ernest Evans
6.	Cliff Richard	Harry Webb
7.	Gary Numan	Gary Webb
8.	The Big Bopper	J. P. Richardson
9.	Bob Dylan	Robert Zimmerman
10.	Bobby Vee	Robert Velline
11.	Gary 'US' Bonds	Gary Anderson
12.	Captain Sensible	Ray Burns
13.	Tom Verlaine	Tom Miller
14.	Richard Hell	Richard Meyers
15.	Sting	Gordon Sumner
16.	Shakin' Stevens	Michael Barrett
17.	Captain Beefheart	Don Van Vliet
18.	Gene Vincent	Eugene Vincent Craddock
19.	King Curtis	Curtis Ousley
20.	Elvis Costello	Declan P. McManus

MORE REAL NAMES

1.	Ray Charles	Ray Charles Robinson
2.	Billy Fury	Ronald Wycherley
3.	Marty Wilde	Reginald Smith
4.	Georgie Fame	Clive Powell
5.	Peter Green	Peter Greenbaum
6.	Len Barry	Leonard Borisoff
7.	Carole King	Carole Klein
8.	Sid Vicious	John Ritchie
9.	Freddy Cannon	Freddy Piciarello
10.	Mickie Most	Michael Hayes
11.	Freddie Mercury	Freddie Bulsara
12.	Van Morrison	George Ivan Morrison
13.	Tenpole Tudor	Edward Tudorpole
14.	Ben E. King	Benjamin Nelson
15.	Connie Francis	Constance Franconero
16.	Little Richard	Richard Penniman
17.	Lulu	Marie Lawrie
18.	Peggy Lee	Norma Egstrom
19.	Dusty Springfield	Mary O'Brien
20.	Brenda Lee	Brenda Mae Tarpley

THE RETURN OF REAL NAMES

1.	Ringo Starr	Richard Starkey
2.	David Bowie	David Jones
3.	Sheena Easton	Sheena Orr
4.	Johnny Rotten	John Lydon
5.	John Denver	John Deutschendorf
6.	Crystal Gayle	Brenda Crystal Webb
7.	Loretta Lynn	Loretta Webb
8.	Marc Bolan	Mark Feld
9.	Buddy Holly	Charles Hardin Holley
10.	Kiki Dee	Pauline Matthews
11.	Rick Derringer	Richard Zehringer
12.	Meat Loaf	Marvin Lee Aday
13.	Tammy Wynette	Wynette Pugh

14. Tom Jones	Thomas Jones Woodward
15. Engelbert Humperdinck	Arnold Dorsey
16. Allan Clarke	Harold Clarke
17. Alvin Stardust	Bernard Jewry
18. Poly Styrene	Marion Elliott
19. Bobby Darin	Walden Robert Cassotto
20. Manfred Mann	Michael Lubowitz

REAL NAMES MEET GODZILLA

1. Dion	Dion DiMucci
2. Paul Jones	Paul Pond
3. Stevie Wonder	Steveland Judkins (or Hardaway or Morris)
4. Billy J. Kramer	William Howard Ashton
5. Little Eva	Eva Narcissus Boyd
6. The Captain and Tennille	Daryl Dragon and Toni Tennille
7. Tony Sheridan	Anthony McGinnity
8. Del Shannon	Charles Westover
9. Conway Twitty	Harold Jenkins
10. Bobby Rydell	Robert Ridarelli
11. Doris Day	Doris Kappelhoff

Bobby Rydell

12. Frankie Valli	Frank Castelluccio
13. Russ Conway	Trevor Stanford
14. Frankie Avalon	Frank Avallone
15. Fabian	Fabiano Forte
16. Les Paul	Lester Polfus
17. Peter Tork	Peter Thorkelson
18. Kim Wilde	Kim Smith
19. Lou Christie	Lugee Sacco
20. Connie Stevens	Concerta Ann

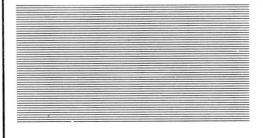

Smokie

CHANGE OF NAME, CHANGE OF FORTUNE

Twenty groups who made it only after changing their original moniker, but without changing their personnel substantially.

Original Name	*New Name*
1. Primettes	Supremes
2. Primes	Temptations
3. Matadors	Miracles
4. Four Aims	Four Tops
5. Del Phis	Martha and the Vandellas
6. Del Rios	Tavares
7. Big Thing	Chicago
8. Detours/High Numbers	Who
9. TW4	Styx
10. Soft White Underbelly	Blue Oyster Cult
11. Beefeaters/Jet Set	Byrds
12. Pud	Doobie Brothers
13. Spectres	Status Quo
14. Earth	Black Sabbath
15. Kindness	Smokie
16. Abdabs	Pink Floyd
17. Hawks	The Band
18. Carl and the Passions	Beach Boys
19. Golliwogs	Creedence Clearwater Revival
20. Ambrose Slade	Slade

SONGWRITING ALIASES

Well known songwriters use pseudonyms for a variety of reasons, both personal and legal. In the former category, Paul McCartney metamorphized into Bernard Webb to write the Peter and Gordon hit 'Woman'. He later explained that he had done so in order to gauge reaction to the song without the added impetus it would have gained if it had been tagged a McCartney composition. Other songwriters have developed *alter egos* to divert publishing rights on new songs from publisher A to publisher B. The reasons for this are usually financial and need not concern us here, since none of the songwriters listed below assumed their second identities for such a reason.

Real or generally used name	Alias	Best known composition under alias
Paul McCartney	Bernard Webb	Woman (Peter and Gordon)
Jerry Ragavoy	Norman Meade	Time Is On My Side (Rolling Stones)
Chuck Berry	E. Anderson	
Tony Hatch	Anthony	Let It Rock (Chuck Berry)
Jerry Leiber and Mike Stoller	Elmo Glick	Forget Him (Bobby Rydell) Stand By Me (Ben E. King)
Lou Adler, Herb Alpert and Sam Cooke	Barbara Campbell	Only Sixteen (Sam Cooke)
Graham Nash, Allan Clarke and Tony Hicks	L. Ransford	We're Through (Hollies)
Elton John and Bernie Taupin	Ann Orson and Carte Blanche	Don't Go Breaking My Heart (Elton John and Kiki Dee)
Mick Jagger and Keith Richard	Nanker Phelge	Play With Fire (Rolling Stones)

Tony Hatch
Jonathan King

ALIASES UNDER WHICH KENNETH KING HAS HAD BRITISH HITS

Kenneth King, for his sins, is better known as Jonathan King but has assumed numerous other identities in successful attempts to infiltrate the radio airwaves and score hits. His successful aliases, and the biggest hit scored under each, are:

Jonathan King	Everyone's Gone To the Moon
Sakkarin	Sugar Sugar
Bubblerock	(I Can't Get No) Satisfaction
One Hundred Ton and a Feather	It Only Takes A Minute
Weathermen	It's The Same Old Song
53rd and 3rd	Chick A Boom
Sound 9418	In The Mood
Father Abraphart and the Smurps	Lick A Smurp For Christmas (All Fall Down)
Shag	Loop Di Love

King has also recorded as Count Giovanni, Nemo, and Sean Hoff and the Shotguns and has, at various times, claimed to be the Angelettes and the Piglets, both hitmaking British girl groups. Whilst acknowledging that King wrote and produced the hits of both groups we find it hard to believe that he could achieve falsettos of such authenticity and have thus excluded them from the above list. There is probably more truth in the rumour that King supplied most of the vocals for 'Keep On Dancing', the Bay City Rollers' introductory British smash.

RECORDING ALIASES

1. Eivets Rednow – Stevie Wonder
2. Wonder Who – The Four Seasons
3. Fut – John Lennon and the Bee Gees
4. Dib Cochran and the Earwigs – Marc Bolan and David Bowie
5. Derek and the Dominoes – Eric Clapton and others
6. Steve Anglo – Steve Winwood
7. The Bunch – Fairport Convention and Friends
8. William Howard Ashton – Billy J. Kramer

Billy J. Kramer

9. Tulsa McLean – Les Gray (Mud)
10. Baron Longfellow – Andy Kim
11. New York Blondes – Blondie
12. Suzy and the Red Stripes – Linda and Paul McCartney

ELEVEN PSEUDONYMS USED BY JOHN LENNON

1. Dr Winston O'Ghurkin
2. Rev Fred Ghurkin
3. Rev Thumbs Ghurkin
4. Dr Dream
5. Dr Winston O'Reggae
6. Dr Winston O'Boogie
7. Kaptain Kundalini
8. Hon John St John Johnson
9. Dwarf McDougal
10. Dr Winston and Booker Table and the Maitre d's
11. Mel Torment

ESSENTIAL ROCK MUSIC REFERENCE BOOKS

1. Encyclopedia of Rock, Vols. 1, 2 and 3 – Edited by Phil Hardy and Dave Laing (Panther Books, UK)
2. NME Book of Rock 2 – Edited by Nick Logan and Bob Woffinden (Star Books, UK)
3. Lillian Roxon's Rock Encyclopedia (original edition) – Lillian Roxon (Grosset and Dunlap, USA)
4. The Book of Golden Discs – Edited by Joseph Murrells (Barrie and Jenkins, UK)
5. Rock On – Norm N. Nite (Popular Library, USA)
6. New Rock Record – Terry Hounsome and Tim Chambre (Blandford Press, UK)
7. Guinness Book of British Hit Singles – Jo and Tim Rice, Paul Gambaccini and Mike Read (Guinness Books, UK)
8. Rock Family Trees – Pete Frame (Omnibus, UK, Quick Fox, USA)
9. NME Guide to Rock Cinema – Fred Dellar (Hamlyn, UK)
10. British Beat – Chris May and Tim Phillips (Socion, UK)
11. The Record Research Series – Joel Whitburn (Record Research Inc, USA)
12. The Rolling Stone Illustrated History

of Rock – Edited by Jim Miller (Pan, UK, Random House/Rolling Stone Press, USA)

Add to this list a dictionary, an atlas and a thesaurus . . .

BOOKS BY ROCK STARS

While unbelievers may sometimes doubt that rock stars are capable of reading, let alone writing something so demanding of long term concentration as a complete book, several artists have been able to convince publishers of the value of their literacy, among them the following . . .

1. Jim Carroll – *The Basketball Diaries*
2. Dory Previn – *Midnight Baby*
3. Patti Smith – *Babel*†
4. Ed Sanders – *The Family, Tales of Beatnik Glory*
5. Bob Dylan – *Writings and Drawings*†
6. Ian Hunter – *Reflections of a Rock Star*
7. Mick Farren – *Watch Out Kids*
8. Alan Hull – *The Mocking Horse*†

9. Peter Hammill – *Killers, Angels, Refugees*†

Peter Hamill

10. Woody Guthrie – *Born To Win*
11. Al Kooper – *Backstage Passes*
12. John Lennon – *In His Own Write*†
13. John Lennon – *A Spaniard In the Works*†
14. Jim Morrison – *The Lords and the New Creatures*†
15. Marc Bolan – *The Warlock of Love*†

16. Phil Lynott – *Songs For While I'm Away,*† *Philip*†
17. Richard Meltzer – *The Aesthetics of Rock*
18. Robert Palmer – *Deep Blues*
19. Debbie Harry and Chris Stein – *Making Tracks*

† Denotes poetry.

10 MUSICAL ROCK WRITERS

1. Chrissie Hynde (Pretenders, *New Musical Express*)
2. Mick Farren (Deviants, solo, *New Musical Express*, *Trouser Press*)
3. Robert Palmer (Insect Trust, *New York Times*, *Rolling Stone*)
4. Nick Kent (Subterraneans, *New Musical Express*)
5. Lenny Kaye (Patti Smith Group, *Creem*)
6. Bob Geldof (Boomtown Rats, *New Musical Express*)
7. Mark Perry (Alternative TV, *Sniffin' Glue*)
8. Charles Shaar Murray (Blast Furnace and the Heatwaves, *New Musical Express*)
9. Kris Needs (Vice Creems, *Zigzag*)
10. Giovanni Dadomo, Dave Fudger, Pete Makowski (Snivelling Shits, *Sounds*)

Dishonourable mention: Steve Harley, worked at the printers which produced *Melody Maker*, but has never, to our knowledge, been a rock journalist, despite his claims to the contrary.

W. H. SMITH TOP TEN ROCK BOOKS FOR 1981

1. *Guinness Book of British Hit Singles* by Tim and Jo Rice, Paul Gambaccini and Mike Read (Guinness Superlatives)
2. *Guinness Book of Hits of the Seventies* by Tim and Jo Rice, Paul Gambaccini and Mike Read (Guinness Superlatives)
3. *Twenty-Five Years of Rock* by John Tobler and Pete Frame (W. H. Smith)
4. *Shout* by Philip Norman (Elm Tree Books)
5. *Elvis We Love You Tender* by Dee Presley (New English Library)
6. *Adam and the Ants* by Fred and Judy Vermorel (Omnibus Press)
7. *Genesis: I Know What I Like* by Armando Gallo (Sidgwick and Jackson)
8. *Status Quo: The Authorised Biography* by John Shearlaw (Sidgwick and Jackson)
9. *NME Encyclopedia of Rock* edited by Nick Logan (Salamander)
10. *Rock Family Trees* by Pete Frame (Omnibus Press)

List provided by Adrian Scott, Rock Book Buyer for W. H. Smith & Son, the largest bookstore chain in the UK.

B. DALTON'S TOP TEN MUSIC BOOKS OF 1981

1. *The Rolling Stones Book* – David Dalton (Random House)
2. *Growing Up with the Beatles* – Ron Schaumberg (Putnam)
3. *The Book of Rock Lists* – David Marsh and Kevin Stein (Dell)
4. *David Bowie: An Illustrated Record* – Roy Carr and Charles Sharr Murray (Avon)
5. *Full Moon* – Dougal Butler (Wm. Morrow)
6. *The Lords and the New Creatures* – Jim Morrison (Simon and Schuster)
7. *The Rolling Stone Illustrated History of Rock and Roll* – edited by Jim Miller (Random House)
8. *The Beatles in Their Own Words* – Miles (Putnam)
9. *The Beatles: An Illustrated Record* – Roy Carr (Crown)
10. *Rolling Stone Interviews* – edited by Ben Fong-Torres (St Martin's Press)

List supplied by Mike Crouchet, trade buyer for B. Dalton, one of the leading US bookstore chains.

ROCK BIOGRAPHIES BY GEORGE TREMLETT

Claiming to have been one of the first British rock writers, George Tremlett interviewed many up and coming stars in his role as reporter for *New Musical Express* and numerous other music magazines around the world. Having access to original interview material, during the 1970s Tremlett embarked upon a spectacularly successful series of paperback rock biographies, before apparently winding up his pop career in 1976 in favour of an executive position on the Greater London Council. The impact of his books, whatever the subsequent sneers from supposedly more creative writers, was enormous – in one calendar year, he is said to have sold more than one million books in Britain.

1. *The Osmond Story*
2. *The Rolling Stones Story*
3. *The David Essex Story*
4. *The Marc Bolan Story*
5. *The Who*
6. *The Slade Story*
7. *The Paul McCartney Story*
8. *The Cliff Richard Story*
9. *The John Lennon Story*
10. *The Alvin Stardust Story*
11. *The David Bowie Story*
12. *The Rod Stewart Story*
13. *10 CC*
14. *The Queen Story*
15. *The Slik Story*

It may be of interest to note that all but the last of these books concerned pop and rock stars whose names are still very familiar. Whether the lack of success which greeted Slik (and therefore the book about them) was in any way responsible for the move into Local Government – as a Conservative, by the way – is not known. Mr Tremlett was sent a letter inviting him to make a retrospective comment on each of his books and place them in order of merit, but regrettably he declined to respond.

RARE RECORDS

The following list was compiled by David Hughes of Collector's Auctions & Sales, 6 Wendover Drive, Frimley, Surrey GU16 5QP, UK, who will be pleased to consider additional names on his mailing list. The records listed are the most valuable to have passed through the auction in 1980 and 1981, and unless otherwise indicated, are singles.

1. The High Numbers – I'm The Face. (This group later became The Who.)	£61.00
2. Marc Bolan – The Third Degree. (An obscure pre-fame Bolan artefact.)	£56.50
3. Marc Bolan – The Wizard. (A slightly less obscure pre-fame effort.)	£46.00
4. P. P. Arnold – Everything's Gonna Be Alright. (Promotional copy.)	£44.00
5. Blinky and Edwin Starr – Oh How Happy. (Only promo copies pressed with original catalogue number, later reissued with different number.)	£43.00
6. Genesis – A Winter's Tale. (Promotional copy of early rare single.)	£40.00
7. Chubby Checker – Two Hearts Make One Love. (Promo issue of obscure cult disc much prized during Northern Soul period of later 1970s.)	£40.00
8. Genesis – A Silent Sun. (Promo copy of first single by group.)	£35.00
9. Genesis – When The Sour Turns To Sweet. (Promo copy of group's final Decca 45.)	£35.00
10. Genesis – The Knife. (Promo copy with rare picture sleeve.)	£35.00
11. The High Numbers – I'm The Face. (See No. 1.)	£34.00
12. Temptations – Why You Wanna Make Me Blue. (Promo copy on Stateside label.)	£32.00
13. Marc Bolan – Hippy Gumbo. (Acetate.)	£31.00
14. Jimmy Page – She Just Satisfies. (Very early item by Led Zeppelin leader.)	£30.00
15. Free – Keep In Touch. (Not the English band but a Dutch group.)	£30.00
16. Beatles – Lady Madonna. (Promo copy, of which few were apparently produced.)	£28.00
17. Bluesology – Come Back Baby. (Elton John was a member of this band.)	£28.00
18. Bluesology – Mr. Frantic. (See above.)	£28.00
19. Ruth Brown – Lucky Lips. (An Atlantic record released on British Columbia.)	£25.25
20. Jesse Lee Turner – Little Space Girl.	£25.00
21. Tyrannosaurus Rex – One Inch Rock. (Promo of original Regal Zonophone issue.)	£22.00
22. Genesis – Happy The Man. (Promo copy of group's second Charisma single.)	£22.00
23. Fut – Have You Heard The Word. (Alleged to be John Lennon with the Bee Gees. Issued in 1969 on the Beacon label.)	£22.00
24. Tina Britt – The Real Thing.	£22.00
25. Dubs – Gonna Make A Change. (1955 classic doo wop single.)	£22.00
26. John's Children – Orgasm (LP). (Group later included Marc Bolan.)	£21.00
27. Elgins – Heaven Must Have Sent You. (Promo copy of early Tamla Motown disc.)	£20.00
28. Dorsey Burnette – Jimmy Brown. (Promo copy of obscure and unlikely Motown item.)	£20.00

The fact that all but one of these items are singles indicates the superior investment value of the 45 rpm disc compared to the LP.

13. BIRTHS & DEATHS

BIRTHDAYS – JANUARY

1. Country Joe McDonald (1942)
2. Roger Miller (1936)
3. John Paul Jones (1946), Stephen Stills (1945), George Martin (1926), Phillip Goodhand-Tait (1945)
4. Arthur Conley (1946)
5. Judge Dread (1940)
6. Syd Barrett (1946), Wilbert Harrison (1929), Nino Tempo (1937), Doris Troy (1937)
7. Kenny Loggins (1948), Mike McGear (1944)
8. Elvis Presley (1935), Robbie Krieger (1946), David Bowie (1947), Shirley Bassey (1937)
9. Crystal Gayle (1951), Jimmy Page (1944), Joan Baez (1941), Scott Walker (1944), Les Paul (1916)
10. Donald Fagen (1946), Rod Stewart (1945), Jim Croce (1943), Ronnie Hawkins (1943), Johnny Ray (1927)
11. Slim Harpo (1924)
12. Maggie Bell (1945), Long John Baldry (1941), Charlie Gracie (1936)
13. Marsha Hunt (1947)
14. Jack Jones (1938), Allen Toussaint (1938)
15. Ronnie Van Zant (1948), Captain Beefheart (1941)
16. Sandy Denny (1947)
17. Mick Taylor (1948), Chris Montez (1943), Francoise Hardy (1944)
18. Elmore James (1918), Bobby Goldsboro (1941), David Ruffin (1941)

Bobby Goldsboro

19. Robert Palmer (1941), Dolly Parton (1946), Phil Everly (1939), Janis Joplin (1943)
20. Paul Stanley (1950), Eric Stewart (1945)
21. Edwin Starr (1942), Richie Havens (1941)
22. Sam Cooke (1931)
23. Millie Jackson (1944)
24. Neil Diamond (1941), Warren Zevon (1941), Jack Scott (1936), Ray Stevens (1939), Jools Holland (1956)
25. Joe Strummer (1945)
26. Eartha Kitt (1928), Huey 'Piano' Smith (1934)
27. Bobby Bland (1930), Kevin Coyne (1944), Nick Mason (1945)
28. Acker Bilk (1929), Rick Wright (1943)
29. David Byron (1947), Handsome Dick Manitoba (1954), Tommy Ramone (1952)
30. Phil Collins (1951), Marty Balin (1942), Steve Marriott (1943)
31. Phil Manzanera (1951), Johnny Rotten (1956), Chuck Willis (1928)

FEBRUARY

1. Ray Sawyer (1939), Don Everly (1937)
2. Graham Nash (1942), Roberta Flack (1937)
3. Melanie (1947), Johnny 'Guitar' Waston (1935)
4. John Steel (1945)
5. Al Kooper (1944), Alex Harvey (1934), Barrett Strong (1941)
6. Natalie Cole (1950), Fabian Forte (1943), Mike Batt (1950), Dave Berry (1941)
7. Dave Davies (1947), King Curtis (1934), Alan Lancaster (1949)
8. James Dean (1931), Tom Rush (1941), Terry Melcher (1942)
9. Carole King (1941), Barry Mann (1942), Jimmy Pursey (1955)

Carole King

10. Clifford T. Ward (1946), Ral Donner (1943)
11. Gene Vincent (1935), Bobby 'Boris' Pickett (1940), Gerry Goffin (1939)
12. Ray Manzarek (1935), Steve Hackett (1950), Gene McDaniels (1935)
13. Peter Tork (1944), Peter Gabriel (1950)
14. Tim Buckley (1947), Eric Andersen (1943)
15. Mick Avory (1944)
16. Sonny Bono (1935), The Kalin Twins (1939)
17. Gene Pitney (1941), John Leyton (1939)
18. John Travolta (1954), Yoko Ono (1933)
19. Smokey Robinson (1940), Lou Christie (1943), Tony Iommi (1948)
20. Walter Becker (1950), Buffy St. Marie (1941), Alan Hull (1945)
21. Nina Simone (1933), David Geffen (1943)
22. Guy Mitchell (1927)
23. Johnny Winter (1944)
24. Nicky Hopkins (1944), Paul Jones (1942)

25. Stuart 'Woody' Wood (1957), George Harrison (1943), Elkie Brooks (1943)
26. Johnny Cash (1932), Fats Domino (1928), Sandie Shaw (1947), Bob Hite (1943)
27. Steve Harley (1951), Neil Schon (1954)
28. Brian Jones (1942), John Fahey (1939), Joe South (1940)
29. Jimmy Dorsey (1904)

MARCH

1. Roger Daltrey (1945), Harry Belafonte (1925), Mike D'Abo (1944)
2. Karen Carpenter (1950), Eddie Money (1948), Lou Reed (1943), Rory Gallagher (1948)

Karen Carpenter

3. Don Gibson (1928)
4. Quincey Jones (1933), Chris Squire (1948), Bobby Womack (1944)
5. Andy Gibb (1958), Eddie Grant (1948), Eddie Hodges (1947), Tommy Tucker (1939)
6. Kiki Dee (1947), Doug Dillard (1937), Dave Gilmour (1946)
7. Peter Wolf (1946)
8. Randy Meisner (1947), Gary Numan (1958), Mickey Dolenz (1946)
9. Robin Trower (1945), Lloyd Price (1933)
10. Tom Scholz (1947), Dean Torrance (1940)
11. Harvey Mandel (1945), Nina Hagen (1955)
12. James Taylor (1948)
13. Mike Love (1941), Neil Sedaka (1939)
14. Loretta Lynn (1940), Jona Lewie (1947), Phil Phillips (1931)
15. Ry Cooder (1947), Sly Stone (1944)
16. Jerry Jeff Walker (1942)
17. Paul Kantner (1942), John Sebastian (1944), Nat 'King' Cole (1919)
18. Wilson Pickett (1941)
19. Derek Longmuir (1952), Clarence 'Frogman' Henry (1937)
20. Jerry Reed (1937)
21. Ray Dorset (1946)
22. George Benson (1943), Jeremy Clyde (1944), Keith Relf (1943), Tony McPhee (1944)
23. Chaka Khan (1953)
24. Billy Stewart (1937)
25. Elton John (1947), Aretha Franklin (1942), Johnny Burnette (1934)
26. Steven Tyler (1948), Teddy Pendergrass (1950), Diana Ross (1944)
27. Tony Banks (1950)
28. Charlie McCoy (1941), Rufus Thomas (1917)
29. Lonnie Donegan (1931), Eden Kane (1942)

Lonnie Donegan

30. Eric Clapton (1945), Graeme Edge (1944), Frankie Laine (1913), Jim 'Dandy' Mangrum (1948), Willie Nelson (1937)
31. John D. Loudermilk (1934), Herb Alpert (1935), Richard Chamberlain (1935)

APRIL

1. Ronnie Lane (1946), Rudolph Isley (1939)
2. Marvin Gaye (1939), Leon Russell (1941), Larry Coryell (1943)
3. Jan Berry (1941), Tony Orlando (1944), Jeff Barry (1937), Richard Manuel (1943)
4. Muddy Waters (1915), Major Lance (1941)
5. Agnetha Faltskog (1950), Jane Asher (1946), Dave Swarbrick (1941)
6. Michelle Phillips (1944), Bob Marley (1945), Merle Haggard (1937)
7. Janis Ian (1951), Bobby Bare (1935), John Oates (1949)
8. Steve Howe (1947), Roger Chapman (1944)
9. Carl Perkins (1932)
10. Glen Campbell (1936), Bobby Hatfield (1940)
11. Robert Fripp (1945)
12. David Cassidy (1950), Herbie Hancock (1940), Tim Buckley (1947)
13. Al Green (1946)
14. Ritchie Blackmore (1945), Buddy Knox (1933)
15. Allan Clarke (1942), Marty Wilde (1939)
16. Dusty Springfield (1939), Jimmy Osmond (1963), Stefan Grossman (1945)
17. Billy Fury (1941)
18. Hayley Mills (1946), Connie Stevens (1938)
19. Alexis Korner (1928), Alan Price (1942), Mark Volman (1944)
20. Johnny Tillotson (1939)
21. Iggy Pop (1947), John Weider (1947)
22. Peter Frampton (1950)
23. Roy Orbison (1936)

24. Barbra Streisand (1942), Robert Knight (1945)
25. Bjorn Ulvaeus (1945), Albert King (1924), Jerry Leiber (1933)
26. Duane Eddy (1938), Bobby Rydell (1942)
27. Ace Frehley (1950), Ann Peebles (1947), Pete Ham (1947)
28. Vincent Crane (1945)
29. April Stevens (1936), Tommy James (1947)
30. Bobby Vee (1943), Johnny Horton (1927)

MAY

1. Judy Collins (1939), Rita Coolidge (1945), Little Walter Jacobs (1930)
2. Link Wray (1929), Lesley Gore (1946), Hilton Valentine (1943)
3. Frankie Valli (1937), Pete Seeger (1919), Mary Hopkin (1950)
4. Tammy Wynette (1942)
5. Bill Ward (1948), Ian McCulloch (1959)
6. Peggy Lee (1920)
7. Jimmy Ruffin (1939), Jim Lowe (1927), Pete Wingfield (1948)
8. Toni Tennille (1943), Gary Glitter (1940), Rick Nelson (1940)

Rick Nelson

9. Billy Joel (1947), Ritchie Furay (1944), Tommy Roe (1942), Sonny Curtis (1937)
10. Jay Ferguson (1947), Dave Mason (1945), Donovan (1946), Larry Williams (1935), Sid Vicious (1957), Bert Weedon (1921), Graham Gouldman (1946), Jackie Lomax (1944)
11. Eric Burdon (1941)
12. Burt Bacharach (1929), Stevie Winwood (1948), Ian MacLagen (1946)
13. Stevie Wonder (1950), Ritchie Valens (1941), Mary Wells (1943), Joe Brown (1941), Paul Thompson (1951)
14. Jack Bruce (1943), Bobby Darin (1936), Troy Shondell (1944), Gene Cornish (1945)
15. Mike Oldfield (1953), Eno (1948), Trini Lopez (1937)
16. Jonathan Richman (1951), Hazel O'Connor (1955)
17. Taj Mahal (1942), Jesse Winchester (1944)
18. Rick Wakeman (1949), Rodney Dillard (1942), Toyah Willcox (1958), Joe Turner (1911)

Toyah

19. Pete Townshend (1945), Joey Ramone (1952), Mickey Newbury (1940)
20. Joe Cocker (1944), Cher (1946)
21. Leo Sayer (1948), Ronald Isley (1941)
22. Bernie Taupin (1950)

23. Albert Hammond (1942)
24. Bob Dylan (1941)
25. Paul Weller (1958), Miles Davis (1926)
26. Stevie Nicks (1948), Mick Ronson (1947)
27. Cilla Black (1943)
28. Gladys Knight (1944), John Fogerty (1945), Prince Buster (1939)
29. Gary Brooker (1945), Frances Rossi (1945)
30. Dobie Gray (1944)
31. John Bonham (1948), Peter Yarrow (1938), Mick Ralphs (1944)

JUNE

1. Ron Wood (1947), Pat Boone (1934)
2. Charlie Watts (1941), Jimmy Jones (1937), Sammy Turner (1932)
3. Michael Clarke (1944), Deniece Williams (1951), Suzy Quatro (1956), Curtis Mayfield (1942), Ian Hunter (1946)

Ian Hunter and Mott the Hoople

4. Cliff Bennett (1940), Gordon Waller (1945)
5. Albert Lee (1944)
6. Bob Seger (1946), Gary 'US' Bonds (1939), Edgar Froese (1944)
7. Clarence White (1944), Tom Jones (1940), Dean Martin (1917)

8. Bonnie Tyler (1953), Boz Scaggs (1944), Nancy Sinatra (1940), Julie Driscoll (1947)
9. Jon Lord (1941), Jackie Wilson (1934), Johnny Ace (1929)
10. Howlin' Wolf (1910), John McLaughlin (1942)
11. Joey Dee (1940), Lynsey De Paul (1950)
12. Roy Harper (1941), Reg Presley (1943), Rockey Burnette (1953)
13. Dennis Locorriere (1949), Bobby Freeman (1940)
14. Rod Argent (1945), Alan White (1949)
15. Noddy Holder (1946), Waylon Jennings (1937), Harry Nilsson (1941), Johnny Halliday (1943)
16. Lamont Dozier (1941), Ian Matthews (1945)
17. Barry Manilow (1944), Chris Spedding (1944)
18. Paul McCartney (1942), Richard Perry (1942)
19. Nils Lofgren (1952)
20. Alan Longmuir (1949), Lionel Ritchie (1949), Anne Murray (1945), Chet Atkins (1924), Brian Wilson (1942)
21. Ray Davies (1944), O. C. Smith (1932)
22. Todd Rundgren (1948), Kris Kristofferson (1936), Peter Asher (1944), Howard Kaylan (1945)
23. Adam Faith (1940), June Carter (1929)
24. Mick Fleetwood (1947), Colin Blunstone (1945), Jeff Beck (1944), Arthur Brown (1942)
25. Carly Simon (1945), Eddie Floyd (1936)
26. Georgie Fame (1943), Mick Jones (1955)
27. Bruce Johnston (1944)
28. John Martyn (1946)
29. Little Eva (1945), Ian Paice (1948), Colonel Tom Parker (1910)
30. Florence Ballard (1944)

Adam Faith

JULY

1. Evelyn 'Champagne' King (1960), Delaney Bramlett (1939), Debbie Harry (1945)
2. Marvin Rainwater (1925)
3. Fontella Bass (1940)
4. Bill Withers (1938), Jeremy Spencer (1948)
5. Robbie Robertson (1943), Smiley Lewis (1920)
6. Jet Harris (1939), Gene Chandler (1937), Bill Haley (1925)
7. Ringo Starr (1940), Rob Townsend (1947), Joe Zawinul (1932)
8. Billy Eckstine (1914)
9. Mitch Mitchell (1946)
10. Arlo Guthrie (1947)
11. Tab Hunter (1931)
12. Walter Egan (1948)
13. Roger McGuinn (1942)
14. Woody Guthrie (1912), Vince Taylor (1942)
15. Alicia Bridges (1953), Linda Ronstadt (1946)
16. Maria Muldaur (1945)
17. Spencer Davis (1941), Geezer Butler (1949)
18. Brian Auger (1939), Screamin' Jay Hawkins (1929), Martha Reeves (1941), Dion Dimucci (1939), Lonnie Mack (1941)
19. Brian May (1947), Bernie Leadon (1947), George Hamilton IV (1937)
20. John Lodge (1945), Carlos Santana (1947), Paul Cook (1956)
21. Cat Stevens (1947), Kim Fowley (1942)
22. Don Henley (1946), Thomas Wayne (1941), Chuck Jackson (1937)
23. George Clinton (1940), David Essex (1947), Tony Joe White (1943), Andy Mackay (1946)
24. Heinz (1942)
25. Steve Gibbons (1948)
26. Roger Taylor (1949), Mick Jagger (1943)
27. Bobbie Gentry (1944)
28. David Porter (1940)
29. Harold Melvin (1938)

30. Paul Anka (1941), Davy Jones (1945), Marc Bolan (1947), Kate Bush (1958). Buddy Guy (1936)
31. Nico (1944)

AUGUST

1. Ramblin' Jack Elliott (1931), Jerry Garcia (1942)
2. Andrew Gold (1951), Garth Hudson (1937), Andy Fairweather-Low (1946)
3. Jim Capaldi (1944)
4. Timi Yuro (1941), Al Wilson (1943)
5. Wardel Piper (1954), Samantha Sang (1953)
6. Mike Sarne (1940), Isaac Hayes (1938)
7. Stan Freberg (1926), Andy Fraser (1952)
8. Joe Tex (1933)
9. Edwin Hawkins (1943)
10. Ronnie Spector (1943), Ian Anderson (1947)
11. Eric Carmen (1949)
12. Buck Owens (1929), Ron Mael (1948)
13. Craig Douglas (1941), Feargal Sharkey (1958)
15. Dan Hicks (1942), Jim Webb (1946)
16. Kevin Ayers (1945)
17. Mae West (1892)
18. Carl Wayne (1944), Johnny Preston (1930)
19. John Deacon (1951), Johnny Nash (1940), Billy J. Kramer (1943), Ginger Baker (1939), Ian Gillan (1945)
20. Robert Plant (1948), Jim Reeves (1924), Phil Lynott (1951)
21. Kenny Rogers (1938), Jackie De Shannon (1944), James Burton (1939)
22. Dale Hawkins (1938), John Lee Hooker (1917)
23. Keith Moon (1946)
24. John Cippolina (1943), David Freiberg (1938), Ken Hensley (1945)
25. Gene Simmons (1949), Wayne Shorter (1933)
26. Jack Nitzsche (1937)
27. Daryl Dragon (1942), Simon Kirke (1949), Tommy Sands (1937), Willy De Ville (1950)

28. Clem Cattini (1939)
29. Michael Jackson (1958)
30. John Phillips (1935), Dale Hawkins (1938)
31. Rick Roberts (1949), Bob Welch (1945), Van Morrison (1945), Jerry Allison (1939)

Van Morrison

SEPTEMBER

1. Barry Gibb (1946), Conway Twitty (1938), Bruce Foxton (1955)
2. Jimmy Clanton (1940)
3. Al Jardine (1942), Gary Leeds (1944), Steve Jones (1955)
4. Gary Duncan (1946), Greg Elmore (1946)
5. Freddie Mercury (1946), Loudon Wainwright III (1946), Buddy Miles (1946)
6. Roger Waters (1943), Jimmy Reed (1925), Buster Bloodvessel (1958)
7. Buddy Holly (1936)
8. Peter Sellers (1925), Bill Parsons (1934)
9. Otis Redding (1941), Billy Preston (1946), Inez Foxx (1942)
10. Joe Perry (1950), Bill Medley (1940), Jose Feliciano (1945), Danny Hutton (1946)
11. Mike Oldfield (1952)

12. Barry White (1944), Maria Muldaur (1943)
13. Mel Torme (1925), David Clayton-Thomas (1941)
14. Paul Kossoff (1950)
15. Jimmy Gilmer (1940)
16. B. B. King (1925), Kenny Jones (1948)
17. Hank Williams (1923)
18. Frankie Avalon (1939), Jimmie Rodgers (1933), Dee Dee Ramone (1952)
19. Nile Rodgers (1952), Brian Epstein (1934), Mama Cass Elliott (1941), Twiggy (1949), Brook Benton (1931), Lol Creme (1943), John Coughlan (1946)
20. Freda Payne (1940)
21. Leonard Cohen (1934), Jesse Ed Davis (1944), Betty Wright (1953)
22. Debby Boone (1956)
23. Bruce Springsteen (1949), Ray Charles (1930), Tim Rose (1940), Duster Bennett (1946)
24. Linda McCartney (1942), Gerry Marsden (1942)
25. Roy Buchanan (1939)
26. Olivia Newton-John (1948), Bryan Ferry (1945), Marty Robbins (1925), John Zacherle (1918)
27. Shaun Cassidy (1928), Meat Loaf (1947), Don Nix (1941)
28. Ben E. King (1938), Helen Shapiro (1946)
29. Jerry Lee Lewis (1935), Freddy King (1934)
30. Johnny Mathis (1935), Frankie Lymon (1942)

Frankie Lymon

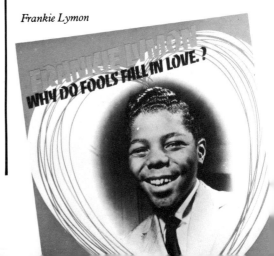

OCTOBER

1. Scott McKenzie (1944)
2. Don McLean (1945), Mike Rutherford (1950), Gordon 'Sting' Sumner (1951)
3. Lindsay Buckingham (1949), Eddie Cochran (1938), Chubby Checker (1941), James Darren (1936)
4. Patti LaBelle (1944), Leroy Van Dyke (1929)
5. Steve Miller (1943), Brian Connolly (1949), Bob Geldof (1954), Russell Mael (1953)

Steve Miller

6. Millie Small (1947)
7. Gary Puckett (1942), Kevin Godley (1945)
8. Johnny Ramone (1951), Pete Drake (1933)
9. Jackson Browne (1948), John Entwistle (1944), John Lennon (1940)
10. Grace Slick (1939), Kirsty MacColl (1959), Midge Ure (1955)
11. Daryl Hall (1946)
12. Rick Parfitt (1948)
13. Marie Osmond (1959), Paul Simon (1941), Lenny Bruce (1925), Chris Farlowe (1940)
14. Justin Hayward (1946), Cliff Richard (1940)
15. Richard Carpenter (1945), Barry McGuire (1935), Marv Johnson (1938)
16. Emile Ford (1937)
17. John Prine (1945)
18. Chuck Berry (1926)
19. Peter Tosh (1944)
20. Tom Petty (1953), Wanda Jackson (1937)
21. Eric Faulkner (1955), Steve Cropper (1941), Manfred Mann (1940)
22. Annette Funicello (1942), Eddie Brigati (1946)
23. Ellie Greenwich (1939)
24. Bill Wyman (1936), Edgar Broughton (1947)
25. Jon Anderson (1944), Helen Reddy (1942)
26. Leslie West (1945)
27. Floyd Cramer (1933), Simon Le Bon (1958)
28. Wayne Fontana (1945), Hank B. Marvin (1941)
29. Denny Laine (1944), Peter Green (1946), J. P. 'Big Bopper' Richardson (1932)
30. Frank Ifield (1937), Tim Schmit (1947)
31. Bernard Edwards (1952), Tom Paxton (1937), Russ Ballard (1947), Kinky Friedman (1944)

NOVEMBER

1. Ric Grech (1945)
2. Keith Emerson (1944), Bruce Welch (1941)
3. Brian Poole (1941), Lulu (1948), Adam Ant (1954)
4. Minnie Riperton (1948)
5. Art Garfunkel (1941), Ike Turner (1931), Peter 'Herman' Noone (1947), Gram Parsons (1946)
6. Glenn Frey (1946), P. J. Proby (1938), Doug Sahm (1941)
7. Johnny Rivers (1942), Joni Mitchell (1943), Mary Travers (1937)

Johnny Rivers

8. Leif Garrett (1961), Roy Wood (1946), Bonnie Bramlett (1944), Bonnie Raitt (1949)
9. Richard Greene (1942)
10. Screaming Lord Sutch (1940), Tim Rice (1944), Greg Lake (1946)
11. LaVern Baker (1929), Mose Allison (1927)
12. Les McKeown (1955) Neil Young (1945), Booker T. Jones (1944), Brian Hyland (1943), Mort Shuman (1932), Dickey Betts (1943)
13. Peter Sarstedt (1943)
14. Stephen Bishop (1951), Freddie Garrity (1940)
15. Anni-Frid Lyngstad (1945), Clyde McPhatter (1933), Petula Clark (1933)
16. Chi Coltrane (1948)
17. Gordon Lightfoot (1938), Bob Gaudio (1942), Gene Clark (1941)
18. Hank Ballard (1936), Kim Wilde (1960)
19. Bob Seger (1947)
20. Joe Walsh (1947)
21. Dr John (1940)

22. Peter Skellern (1947)
23. Ed Cassidy (1930)
24. Bev Bevan (1944), Donald 'Duck' Dunn (1941), Troy Seals (1948)
25. Tina Turner (1943)
26. John McVie (1945), Garnett Mimms (1937)
27. Jimi Hendrix (1942), Al Jackson (1935)
28. Randy Newman (1943), Bruce Chanel (1940)
29. Denny Doherty (1941), John Mayall (1933), Felix Cavaliere (1944)
30. Paul Stookey (1937), Roger Glover (1945)

DECEMBER

1. Lou Rawls (1936), John Densmore (1944), Jermaine Jackson (1954), Gilbert O'Sullivan (1946), Bette Midler (1945), Sandy Nelson (1938)
2. Tom McGuinness (1941)
3. Ozzy Osbourne (1948), Andy Williams (1931)
4. Dennis Wilson (1944), Freddy Cannon (1940), Chris Hillman (1942)
5. Jim Messina (1947), Little Richard (1932), John Cale (1940)
6. Jonathan King (1944), Rick Buckler (1955), Eddie Tenpole (1955), Len Barry (1942)
7. Harry Chapin (1941)
8. Gregg Allman (1947), Jim Morrison (1943), Jerry Butler (1939)
9. Donny Osmond (1959), Joan Armatrading (1950), Junior Wells (1932)

The Osmonds

10. Chad Stuart (1943)
11. David Gates (1939), Brenda Lee (1944)
12. Paul Rodgers (1949), Dionne Warwick (1940), Frank Sinatra (1915), Jeff Lynne (1947), Connie Francis (1938)
13. Alvin Stardust (1942), Ted Nugent (1948)
14. Charlie Rich (1932)
15. Dave Clark (1942), Carmine Appice (1946)
16. Benny Andersson (1946), Alan Freed (1922), Tony Hicks (1943)
17. Paul Butterfield (1942), Tommy Steele (1936), Dave Dee (1940)
18. Keith Richard (1943), Chas Chandler (1938)
19. Maurice White (1941), Zal Yanovsky (1944), Phil Ochs (1940), Alvin Lee (1944)
20. Peter Criss (1945), Bo Diddley (1928)
21. Carl Wilson (1946), Frank Zappa (1940)
22. Maurice Gibb (1949), Robin Gibb (1949), Rick Nielsen (1947)

23. Johnny Kidd (1939)
24. Lee Dorsey (1924), Mike Curb (1944), Jan Akkermann (1946)
25. Jimmy Buffett (1946), Alice Cooper (1945), O'Kelly Isley (1937), Noel Redding (1945), Pete Brown (1942)
26. Phil Spector (1939)
27. Mike Pinder (1941), Lenny Kaye (1946), Scotty Moore (1931)
28. Edgar Winter (1946), Johnny Otis (1924)
29. Yvonne Elliman (1951), Ray Thomas (1942), Rick Danko (1942), Marianne Faithfull (1946)
30. Patti Smith (1946), Del Shannon (1938), John Hartford (1937)
31. Donna Summer (1948), John Denver (1943)

Del Shannon

148

ROCK'N'ROLL DEATHS – TRAFFIC ACCIDENTS

James Dean	Sept. 1955
Eddie Cochran	Apr. 1960
Johnny Kidd	Oct. 1960
Johnny Horton	Nov. 1960
Richard Farina	Apr. 1966
Martin Lamble (Fairport Convention)	Jun. 1969
Duane Allman	Oct. 1971
Berry Oakley (Allman Brothers)	Nov. 1972
Clarence White	Jun. 1973
Duster Bennett	Apr. 1976
Marc Bolan	Sept. 1977
Chris Bell (Big Star)	Dec. 1978
Jacob Miller (Inner Circle)	Mar. 1980
Tommy Caldwell (Marshall Tucker Band)	May 1980
Harry Chapin	Jul. 1981

Marc Bolan's crashed Mini

ROCK'N'ROLL DEATHS – MURDER

Sam Cooke	Dec. 1964
Little Walter Jacobs	Feb. 1968
James 'Shep' Sheppard (Shep and the Limelites)	Jan. 1970
King Curtis (Curtis Ousley)	Aug. 1971
Al Jackson (Booker T. and the M.G.s)	Oct. 1975
Sal Mineo	Feb. 1976
John Lennon	Dec. 1980
Samuel George (Capitols)	Mar. 1982

ROCK'N'ROLL DEATHS – OVERDOSES

Brian Epstein	Aug. 1967
Frankie Lymon	Apr. 1968
Jimi Hendrix	Sept. 1970
Janis Joplin	Oct. 1970
Danny Whitten (Crazy Horse)	Nov. 1972
Billy Murcia (New York Dolls)	Nov. 1972
Robbie McIntosh (Average White Band)	Sept. 1974
Nick Drake	Nov. 1974
Tim Buckley	Jun. 1975
Paul Kossoff (Free)	Mar. 1976
Gary Thain (Uriah Heep)	Mar. 1976
Tommy Bolin (Deep Purple)	Dec. 1976
Keith Moon	Sept. 1978
Sid Vicious	Feb. 1979
Bon Scott (AC/DC)	Feb. 1980
Ian Curtis (Joy Division)	May 1980
Malcolm Owen (Ruts)	Jul. 1980
John Bonham (Led Zeppelin)	Sept. 1980
Tim Hardin	Dec. 1980
Mike Bloomfield	Feb. 1981
John Belushi	Mar. 1982

Tommy Bolin's funeral

ROCK'N'ROLL DEATHS – DROWNED

Johnny Burnette	Aug. 1964
Brian Jones	Jul. 1969

ROCK'N'ROLL DEATHS – ELECTROCUTED

Les Harvey (Stone The Crows)	May 1972
John Rostill (Shadows)	Nov. 1973
Keith Relf (Yardbirds)	May 1976

ROCK'N'ROLL DEATHS – HEART ATTACKS

Hank Williams	Jan. 1953
Bert Berns (Owner of Bang Records)	Dec. 1967

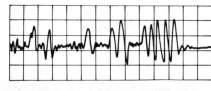

Jim Morrison	Jul. 1971*
Gram Parsons	Sept. 1973
Mama Cass (Elliott)	Jul. 1974
Paul Beaver (Beaver and Krause)	Jan. 1975
Florence Ballard (Supremes)	Feb. 1976
Freddie King	Dec. 1976
Elvis Presley	Aug. 1977
Jimmy McCulloch (Wings)	Jan. 1979
Bob Hite (Canned Heat)	Apr. 1981
Roy Brown (writer of 'Good Rockin' Tonight')	May 1981
Alex Harvey	Jan. 1982
Joe Tex	Aug. 1982

ROCK'N'ROLL DEATHS – AVIATION

Glenn Miller	Dec. 1944
Buddy Holly, Ritchie Valens, The Big Bopper	Feb. 1959
Patsy Cline	Mar. 1963
Jim Reeves	Jul. 1964
Otis Redding, The Bar-Kays	Dec. 1967
Jim Croce	Sep. 1973
Ronnie Van Zant, Steve and Cassie Gaines (Lynyrd Skynyrd)	Oct. 1977
Randy Rhoades (Blizzard of Ozz)	Apr. 1982

ROCK'N'ROLL DEATHS – MEDICAL

Chuck Willis	Apr. 1958
Stuart Sutcliffe (Beatles)	Apr. 1962
Alan Freed	Jan, 1965
Nat 'King' Cole	Feb. 1965
Woody Guthrie	Oct. 1967
Clyde McPhatter (The Drifters)	Jun. 1971
Bobby Darin	Dec. 1973
Mike Patto (Patto)	Mar. 1979
John Glascock (Jethro Tull)	Nov. 1979
Bob Marley	May 1981
Lester Bangs	April 1982
Neil Bogart	May 1982
James Honeyman-Scott	Jun. 1982

Jim Morrison's tomb

ROCK'N'ROLL DEATHS – SUICIDE

Johnny Ace	Dec. 1954*
Bobby Fuller	Jul. 1966
Joe Meek	Feb. 1967
Al Wilson (Canned Heat)	Sept. 1970
Graham Bond	May 1974
Pete Ham (Badfinger)	Apr. 1975
Phil Ochs	Apr. 1976
Terry Kath (Chicago)	Jan. 1978*
Donny Hathaway	Jan. 1979
Larry Williams	Jan. 1980

ROCK'N'ROLL DEATHS – OTHER

Tammi Terrell

Sandy Denny (Fairport Convention)
Bill Haley
Kit Lambert (former manager of the Who)

James Dean's Porsche

Marvin Gaye and Tammi Terrell

Mar. 1970	Brain tumour under suspicious circumstances
Apr. 1978	Died after falling down stairs
Jan. 1981	Natural causes
Mar. 1981	Died after falling down stairs

14. YOU DON'T SAY

WHAT A COINCIDENCE (OR NOT)

1. Following the release of David Bowie's LP 'Low', Nick Lowe released an EP entitled 'Bowi'.

2. Following the release of Fleetwood Mac's multi-million selling LP 'Rumours', British group the Rumour (who originally backed Graham Parker), released the multi-thousand selling 'Max'.

3. On the same day in 1981, Cliff Richard released a single whose A-side was 'Dreaming', and whose B-side was a remake of a song he had recorded many years before called 'Dynamite', while American teenage disco star Stacy Lattisaw released a single with an A side was called 'Dynamite' and a B-side was titled 'Dreaming'. Despite the titular similarities, none of the songs bore any musical relation to any of the others.

4. The week after the Searchers released a single called 'Changin'' in 1980, US disco aggregation Change released a single called 'Searchin''.

5. Emile Ford's million-selling 'What Do You Want To Make Those Eyes At Me For' replaced Adam Faith's 'What Do You Want' atop the UK singles chart in December 1959 – the only occasion in chart history that the title of a number one record has included the full title of its predecessor.

6. Procol Harum's 'Salty Dog' made the charts three times in a five week period in 1969. On each occasion it entered at No. 44 only to drop out the following week.

7. Personnel changes in Wings during 1974 saw Geoff *Britton* making way for Joe *English* and Jimmy *McCulloch* replacing Henry *McCullough*.

EVEN MORE OF A COINCIDENCE

1. In 1979 Cliff Richard (real name Harry Webb) had his first number one for eleven years. After a month at the summit he was toppled by Gary Numan – real name Gary Webb!

2. In 1981, both the Police and Shakin' Stevens had number one singles in England. Police drummer Stewart Copeland once released a green vinyl 10-inch album under the alias Klark Kent. Shakin' Stevens was born Michael Barratt but changed his name by deed poll several years ago – to Clark Kent!

3. During the summer of 1960 two versions of 'Look For A Star' battled it out in the American top thirty. One was by an American called Garry Miles whilst the other was by a new young British singer called Garry Mills!

4. Of the 8,000 records which have been hits in Britain in the last thirty years only two have had the title 'Automatic Lover'. One is by the Vibrators and the other by Dee D. Jackson. The songs are completely different and neither was influenced by the other, yet they were both hits at the same time in the spring of 1978.

HIT RECORDS WHICH SHARE THE SAME BACKING TRACK

1. Out Of Time – Chris Farlowe/Rolling Stones

Farlowe's only (British) number one came in the shape of this gift from the Rolling Stones in 1966. The record's basic track was a Rolling Stones demo over which Farlowe laid a vocal track. Mick Jagger produced. A slightly different version by the Stones appeared shortly afterwards on the album 'Aftermath'.

Nine years later Farlowe's hit was re-issued and immediately found itself in competition with freshly-recorded interpretations by Dan McCafferty and Kris Ife. Decca then rushed out a Rolling Stones version which was trailed in the press as being 'previously unreleased'. It was in fact the very same instrumental demo utilized by Farlowe with Jagger's original vocal over the top. The competition effectively killed the chance of any of the versions being a big hit. But for a two week period both the Stones and Farlowe's versions of 'Out Of Time' were in the chart.

2. Let's Do The Latin Hustle – Eddie Drennon & BBS Unlimited/M & O Band

The two versions of 'Latin Hustle' climbed the charts simultaneously, splitting sales almost evenly. The M and O Band's cover was, however, drawing a lot of comment based around its backing track which seemed too accurate a remake of the original to be true. It was, and after a short legal tussle decided in Drennon's favour it was admitted that maybe, just maybe, the original backing track – which was being used as a guide – had somehow found its way on to the M & O Band record.

UNACCOMPANIED VOCAL HITS – UK

Hit records totally lacking instrumental backing.

Title – Artist (Date entered chart)	Highest Chart Position
1. Highway Code – Master Singers (14 April 1966)	25

2. Weather Forecast – Master Singers (17 November 1966)   50
3. Amazing Grace – Judy Collins (5 December 1970)   5
4. Gaudete – Steeleye Span (8 December 1973)   14
5. After The Goldrush – Prelude (26 January 1974)   21
6. After The Goldrush – Prelude (22 May 1982)   28

Honourable mentions
● Airwaves' beautiful accapella rendering of 'New Day (You Are The New Day)' has twice come within an ace of the chart.
● The New Seekers' 1978 hit 'Anthem (One Day In Every Week)' – total duration 3 minutes and 10 seconds – is unaccompanied until 44 seconds from the end.

CHICAGO LP TITLES

During the late sixties and early seventies, a group variously known as Chicago Transit Authority, CTA, and finally Chicago, released a series of albums whose titles were amazingly uninventive, and who at least at the start of their recording career, seemed unable to appreciate the virtue of brevity.

Title	Number of Albums	Release Date
Chicago Transit Authority	2	1969
Chicago	2	1970
Chicago III	2	1971
Live At Carnegie Hall	4	1971
Chicago V	2	1972
Chicago VI	1	1973
Chicago VII	2	1974
Chicago VIII	1	1975
Chicago IX – Chicago's Greatest Hits	1	1975
Chicago X	1	1976
Chicago XI	1	1977
Hot Streets	1	1978
Street Player	1	1979
Chicago XIV	1	1980
Chicago XV	1	1981
Chicago XVI	1	1982

RECORDS WHICH TOOK MORE THAN TWENTY YEARS TO BECOME HITS

UK

41 years: Lullaby Of Broadway – Winifred Shaw

Miss Shaw, known variously as Winifred, Winnie and Wini, appeared in many Hollywood musicals and dramas in the thirties. The best-known of these was *Gold Diggers of 1935* from which came the Academy Award winning 'Lullaby Of Broadway', a British hit in 1976.

38 years: The Trail Of The Lonesome Pine – Laurel and Hardy

From the 1937 movie *Way Out West*, this was a smash hit when issued as a single in 1975. Only Queen's epic 'Bohemian Rhapsody' stood between it and the number one spot that Christmas.

35 years: As Time Goes By – Dooley Wilson

Another recording from the golden era of Hollywood, 'As Time Goes By' was featured in the 1942 movie *Casablanca*. It was a hit in 1977 complete with Humphrey Bogart's classic 'Play it again' dialogue.

US

29 years: Shaving Cream – Paul Wynn

Made little impression when originally released in 1946. It was reissued on a whim in 1975. Somehow juvenile vocalist Wynn's name was omitted from the reissue which instead bore the name Benny Bell. The record reached number 30 in an eleven week chart run.

OLDEST CHART DEBUTANT

US

The oldest first time chartmaker in the history of *Billboard*'s singles chart is one Nathan Birnbaum, better known as comedian George Burns. Burns was born on 20 January 1896 and made his chart debut on 19 January 1980 – just one day short of his 84th birthday – with 'I Wish I Was Eighteen Again'. The record reached No. 49 on the chart. A similarly named album peaked at No. 93.

UK

Actor Walter Brennan's only British hit was 'Old Rivers'. It entered the chart on 28 June 1962 when Brennan was 67 years and 337 days old. Brennan appeared in well over 100 films and won three Academy Awards. He also starred in several TV series' most notably *The Real McCoys*. He died in 1975.

POSTHUMOUS CHART DEBUTANTS – UK

In the last thirty years over 2,500 artists have known the thrill of making their British chart debut. Three have made their first chart appearance posthumously – a state which left them ill-equipped to make personal appearances to boost their sales.

1. Stan Laurel (died 1965) and Ollie Hardy (died 1957)

Laurel and Hardy became the first posthumous chart debutants in 1975 when 'The Trail Of The Lonesome Pine' reached number two selling over 250,000 copies.

2. Dooley Wilson (died 1953)

Wilson will forever be known for his role in *Casablanca*. And it's with a song from that movie that he scored his only hit in 1977. That song was of course 'As Time Goes By', which he appears to play in the film. Not so – Wilson couldn't play a note. The singing, however, is his.

3. Red Sovine (died 1980)

Sovine was a longtime truckers' favourite in the States with his sickly monologues. In 1980 he wrapped his car around a tree and died from the injuries he received. The following year his 1975 recording of 'Teddy Bear' was a big hit in Britain.

4. Ritchie Valens (died 1959)

In March 1959, Ritchie Valens, who had died one month earlier in the same plane crash which claimed the lives of Buddy Holly and Big Bopper, entered the British charts for his first and only week with 'Donna'.

ODDLY-SHAPED RECORDS: THE FIRST IN EACH CATEGORY

Square	It Takes Two To Tango – Richard Myhill (UK, 1978)
Oblong	Rolling On – Cirrus (UK, 1978)
Triangular	¡Gimmix! Play Loud – John Cooper Clarke (UK, 1978)

Septagonal (7-sided)	Girl (How Am I Gonna Win You) – T. J. Thorpe and the CB Band (UK, 1979)

Not only shaped like a 50p piece, but selling for one too!

Star	You Stepped Into My Life – Wayne Newton (USA, 1979)
Tear	A Heartbreaker – Cryers (USA Promo, 1979)
Shamrock	Loneliness – Horslips (UK, 1979)

Heart	Baby Of Mine – Alan Price (UK, 1979)
Police Badge	Can't Stand Losing You. – Police (USA, 1979)
Strawberry	Do You Love What You Feel – Rufus (USA Promo, 1979)

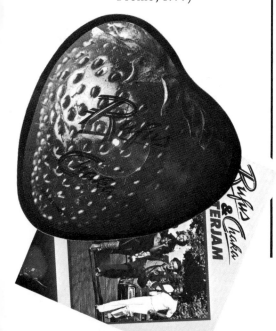

Telephone	La Bombe Humaine – Telephone (France, 1979)
Car	Drive My Car – Perfect Stranger (USA, 1981)

As *The Rock Lists Album* went to press a rash of unusually-shaped records were released in America. Amongst them were a bell-shaped single from Mystic, hexagonal singles from Rock Motion and Tim Hogan, an octagonal disc by Nick Paine and a blob-shaped 45 by Azra.

FORMER OCCUPATIONS OF 20 ROCK STARS

1. Eddie Money – Policeman
2. Leo Sayer – Magazine illustrator
3. Marc Bolan – Fashion model
4. Chrissie Hynde – Waitress, shop assistant, journalist
5. Joe Cocker – Gas fitter
6. Cliff Richard – Office clerk
7. Keith Emerson – Bank clerk
8. Elvis Costello – Computer operator
9. Bill Withers – Computer operator, aircraft mechanic, milkman
10. Gene Pitney – Tobacco picker
11. Steve Harley – Printer
12. Syreeta – Typist
13. Elvis Presley – Truck driver
14. Jimi Hendrix – US Air Force
15. Wattie (The Exploited) – British Army
16. Rod Stewart – Gravedigger
17. Deborah Harry – Secretary, Playboy Bunny
18. Brian Poole – Butcher
19. Kiki Dee – Shop assistant
20. Phil Spector – Stenographer

HUSBAND AND WIFE RECORDING ARTISTS

1. The Captain and Tennille
2. Jane Birkin and Serge Gainsbourg
3. Sonny and Cher
4. John and Michelle Phillips
5. John Phillips and Genevieve Waite
6. Kris Kristofferson and Rita Coolidge
7. Booker T. Jones and Priscilla Coolidge
8. George Jones and Tammy Wynette
9. Johnny Cash and June Carter
10. Phil and Ronnie Spector
11. Johnny Dankworth and Cleo Laine
12. Paul and Linda McCartney
13. John Lennon and Yoko Ono
14. Tony Hatch and Jackie Trent
15. James Taylor and Carly Simon
16. John Dummer and Helen April

CHIPS OFF THE OLD BLOCK

1. Pat and Debbie Boone
2. Marty and Kim Wilde
3. Johnny and Rocky Burnette
4. Dorsey and Billy Burnette
5. Andre and Lovely Previn
6. Johnny and Rosanne Cash
7. June and Carlene Carter
8. Shirley Jones and Shaun Cassidy
9. Nat and Natalie Cole
10. Lemmy Kilmister and Paul Inder
11. Doris Day and Terry Melcher

Doris Day and Terry Melcher

12. Judy Garland and Liza Minelli
13. Marnie Nixon and Andrew Gold
14. Rex and Noel Harrison
15. Otis and Dexter Redding
16. Dean and Dino Martin
17. Ed Cassidy and Randy California
18. Freddy and John Lennon
19. Jerry and Gary Lewis

20. Marion, Paul and Barry Ryan
21. Frank and Nancy Sinatra

Frank and Nancy Sinatra

22. Pops and Mavis Staples
23. Rufus and Carla Thomas
24. George Jones, Tammy Wynette and Tina Jones
25. John and MacKenzie Phillips
26. John and Julian Lennon

ROCKIN' SISTERS

1. Sister Sledge
2. The Nolan Sisters
3. The Roches
4. Rita and Priscilla Coolidge
5. Carly and Lucy Simon
6. Loretta Lynn and Crystal Gayle
7. Carlene Carter and Rosanne Cash
8. Ann and Nancy Wilson (Heart)
9. Doreen and Irene Chanter
10. Kate and Anna McGarrigle
11. Surprise Sisters
12. Veronia and Estelle Bennett (Ronettes)
13. Mary and Betty Weiss (Shangri-Las)
14. Mary Ann and Margie Ganser (Shangri-Las)
15. Dionne and Dee Dee Warwick
16. Dolly and Stella Parton
17. Liza Minelli and Lorna Luft
18. Kaye Sisters
19. Patience and Prudence McIntyre

20. Pointer Sisters (Anita, Bonnie, June and Ruth)

ROCKING BROTHERS

1. Don and Mick Addrisi
2. Billy and Bobby Alessi
3. Dec and Con Cluskey (The Bachelors)
4. Randy, Robbie and Tim Bachman (BTO)
5. Carl, Dennis and Brian Wilson (Beach Boys)
6. Paul McCartney and Mike McGear
7. Barry, Maurice, Robin and Andy Gibb
8. Randy and Mike Brecker
9. Brook Brothers
10. Jackson and Severin Browne
11. Bob and Richard Hite
12. Albert and Joe Bouchard
13. George Young (Easybeats), Angus and Malcolm Young (AC/DC)
14. Johnny and Edgar Winter
15. Pete (Chicago) and Tim (Stone Canyon Band) Cetera
16. Dave and Ansell Collins
17. John and Tom Fogerty
18. Ray and Dave Davies
19. Steve and Muff (Mervyn) Winwood
20. Mark and David Knopfler (Dire Straits)
21. Phil, Derek and Ray Shulman (Gentle Giant)
22. Maurice and Verdine White (Earth, Wind and Fire)
23. Don and Phil Everly
24. David and Shaun Cassidy
25. Gibson Brothers
26. Gerry and Freddy Marsden (Gerry and the Pacemakers)
27. Eddy and Rudy Grant
28. Alex and Les Harvey
29. Rudolph, Ronald, O'Kelly, Ernie and Marvin Isley
30. Michael, Jermaine, Jackie, Marlon and Tito Jackson
31. Carlos and Jorge Santana (Malo)
32. Michael and Rudolf Schenker
33. Ron and Russell Mael
34. Gavin and Iain Sutherland

35. Alan, Wayne, Merrill, Jay, Donny and Jimmy Osmond
36. Matthew and Mark Andes
37. Harold and Herbie Kalin
38. Eden Kane, Peter, Robin and Clive Sarstedt
39. Jimmy and David Ruffin
40. Alex, James and Livingston Taylor
41. Eddie and David Brigati
42. Duane and Gregg Allman
43. King Brothers
44. Jimmy and Jack McCulloch
45. Art and Aaron Neville
46. Eddie and Brian Holland
47. Harry and Tom Chapin
48. Keith and Tim Atack (Child)
49. Mick and Chris Jagger
50. Mark and Bob Mothersbaugh (Devo)
51. Jerry and Bob Casale (Devo)
52. Chris, Lorin and Peter Rowan
53. Ali and Robin Campbell (UB40)
54. England Dan and Jimmy Seals
55. Dave and Tom Farmer (Blackfoot Sue)
56. Paul and Barry Ryan
57. Edgar and Steve Broughton
58. David and Howard Bellamy
59. Mark and Tim Gane (Martha and the Muffins)
60. Danny and Nick Talbot (Merton Parkas)
61. David Sylvian and Steve Jansen (Japan)

BROTHER AND SISTER RECORDING ARTISTS

1. Cindy and Ricky Wilson (B52s)
2. Inez and Charlie Foxx
3. Steve and Cassie Gaines (Lynyrd Skynyrd)
4. Nino Tempo and April Stevens
5. Gladys and Bubba Knight
6. Mike and Sally Oldfield
7. Suzi and Mike Quatro
8. Michael and LaToya Jackson
9. Donny and Marie Osmond
10. Keith and Jane Relf
11. Mike Mansfield and Elkie Brooks
12. James and Kate Taylor

15. A DISTINCT LAPSE OF TASTE

THE BOTTOM THIRTY: THE WORLD'S WORST RECORDS

A regular feature of Kenny Everett's Capital Radio show during the early part of 1980 was 'The World's Worst Records' spot. Generally speaking, the records nominated for this category were of two sorts; below-par efforts by established artists (Jim Reeves, Elvis Presley, etc) and one-off chart shots from celebrities whose talents clearly did not include singing (William Shatner, Tommy Vance, etc.). After inflicting a large number of historically incompetent offerings on his listeners, Everett invited them to vote for 'The Bottom Thirty' – the world's worst records. From the thousands of votes cast the following chart emerged.

1. Dance With Me – Reginald Bosanquet

Reginald Bosanquet and Kenny Everett

2. If You Walked Away – Jag
3. Unhappy New Year – Steve Dahl
4. Lucy In The Sky With Diamonds – William Shatner
5. The Perfect Human Face – Terry Costello
6. Teddy Bear – Red Sovine
7. Snowmobile Romance – Mrs Oliver Schoenke
8. You Have Got The Gear – Jack Warner
9. Just Like That – David Hamilton
10. True Or False – Simon and Garfunkel
11. Where Is Love – Leonard Nimoy
12. A World Without Sunshine – Derrick Roberts
13. Only You – P. J. Proby
14. Old Tige – Jim Reeves
15. You Done Stomped On My Heart – Melody Suggs
16. Hurt Me – Jess Conrad
17. Summertime – Tommy Vance
18. Help – Cathy Berbarian
19. Mother Went A Walking – Pat Campbell
20. Is There Another Way To Love You – Tony Blackburn
21. Trees – Sam Finch
22. Iggi Nagga – Nick Cochrane
23. Searching For My Baby – Nola Campbell
24. Benny's Theme – Paul Henry
25. It's Legal – Shirley Anne Field
26. Still Love You (In My Heart) – Helpless Hew
27. Old MacDonald – Elvis Presley
28. Hot Lips Baby – Herbie Duncan
29. Tchaikovsky Piano Concerto No. 1 – Neasden Connection
30. I Remember Natalie – Bob Monkhouse

THE 10 WORST SONGS RECORDED BY ELVIS PRESLEY

1. Fort Lauderdale Chamber Of Commerce (from *Girl Happy*)
2. There's No Room To Rhumba In A Sports Car (from *Fun In Acapulco*)
3. Song Of The Shrimp (from *Girls!Girls!Girls!*)
4. Do The Clam (from *Girl Happy*)
5. The Bull Fighter Was A Lady (from *Fun In Acapulco*)
6. Thanks To The Rolling Sea (from *Girls! Girls! Girls!*)
7. Petunia, The Gardener's Daughter (from *Frankie and Johnnie*)
8. Adam And Evil (from *Spinout*)
9. Singing Tree (from *Clambake*)
10. Long Legged Girl (With The Short Dress On) (from *Double Trouble*)

List submitted by Richard Wootton.

ELVIS PRESLEY IMITATORS

1. Stan Freberg
2. Ral Donner
3. Shakin' Stevens
4. Les Gray
5. Pat Boone
6. Cliff Richard
7. P. J. Proby
8. Jimmy Ellis
9. Freddie Starr
10. Danny Mirror

Some of these names became famous as singers whose style aped 'The King's'. Others, like Freddie Starr and Stan Freberg, were comedians whose impersonations were partly visual and partly vocal.

RUDEST RHYTHM AND BLUES SONGS

1. It Ain't The Meat (It's The Motion) – The Swallows
2. Work With Me, Annie – Hank Ballard and the Midnighters
3. Keep On Churnin' ('Til The Butter Comes) – Wynonie Harris
4. Somethin's Wrong With My Lovin' Machine – Robert Henry
5. Shake Your Moneymaker – Elmore James
6. I Want A Bowlegged Woman – Bullmoose Jackson
7. Big Ten-Inch Record – Bullmoose Jackson
8. Sixty Minute Man – The Dominoes
9. Don't Stop Dan – The Checkers
10. I Wanna Hot Dog For My Roll – Butterbeans and Susie

List submitted by Richard Wootton.

BALD ROCK STARS/HITMAKERS

1. Errol Brown (Hot Chocolate)
2. Ed Cassidy (Spirit)
3. Telly Savalas
4. Angry Anderson (Rose Tattoo)
5. Lol Coxhill
6. Albie Donnelly (Supercharge)
7. Ringo Starr (circa 1976)
8. Douglas Trendle aka Buster Bloodvessel (Bad Manners)
9. Sal Solo (Classic Nouveaux)
10. Isaac Hayes

Sal Solo

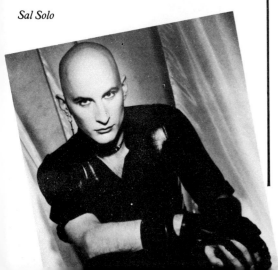

RUDE HITS

Contrary to popular supposition, BBC Radio One does not ban records. The contents of programmes are selected by individual producers upon whose discretion the Corporation relies – as a result, some records are not played because they are quite obviously offensive, while others are omitted simply because a producer either dislikes them or, more often, feels that they are inferior. While not every record listed below was judged too offensive to be heard on the radio, the vast majority could claim this dubious privilege, although they still became hits.

Artist	Title	Year	Highest Chart Position
Sex Pistols	Friggin' In The Rigging	1979	3
Ivor Biggun	Winker's Song (Misprint)	1978	22
Ivor Biggun	Bras On 45	1981	50
Max Romeo	Wet Dream	1969	10
Jasper Carrott	Magic Roundabout	1975	5
Judge Dread	Big 6	1972	11
Judge Dread	Big 7	1972	8
Judge Dread	Big 8	1973	14
Judge Dread	Big 10	1975	14
Judge Dread	The Winkle Man	1976	35
Judge Dread	Up With The Cock	1978	49
Jane Birkin and Serge Gainsbourg	Je T'aime . . . Moi Non Plus	1969	1
Donna Summer	Love To Love You Baby	1976	4
Dead Kennedys	Too Drunk To Fuck	1981	36

FAMOUS ROCK STAR HAIRCUTS

1. Wendy O. Williams (Plasmatics)
2. Phil Oakey (The Human League)
3. Peter Gabriel (Genesis)
4. Grace Jones
5. Split Enz
6. Brian Setzer (The Stray Cats)
7. Wattie (The Exploited)
8. Bob Marley
9. Eugene Reynolds (The Revillos)
10. The Wild Thing

Haircuts pointed out by Nigel Dick, who is probably only jealous.

Phil Oakey

PATTI SMITH'S ROCK STAR BOY FRIENDS

1. Allen Lanier (Blue Oyster Cult)
2. Paul Simonon (The Clash)
3. Jim Carroll
4. Tom Verlaine (Television, now solo)
5. Fred 'Sonic' Smith (MC5, Sonic's Rendezvous Band)
6. Sam Sheppard (Holy Modal Rounders, playwright)

DOIN' TIME

(Rock and blues stars who have spent time in jail).

1. Chuck Berry
2. Jerry Lee Lewis
3. John Phillips
4. Johnny Cash
5. Leapy Lee

6. Sid Vicious
7. John Lydon
8. Paul McCartney
9. Frank Zappa
10. Hugh Cornwell
11. Peter Yarrow
12. Leadbelly
13. Little Willie John

PARODY HITS AND GREAT PARODIES

Artist	Title	Song Parodied
The Detergents	Leader Of The Laudromat	Leader Of The Pack
Billy Howard	King Of The Cops	King Of The Road
Judge Dread	Je T'Aime	Je T'Aime (Moi Non Plus)
Laurie Lingo and the Dipsticks	Convoy GB	Convoy
Yin and Yan	If	If
Father Abraphart and the Smurps	Lick A Smurp For Xmas	Christmas in Smurfland
Hylda Baker and Arthur Mullard	You're The One That I Want	You're The One That I Want
Alberto y Los Trios Paranoias	Heads Down No Nonsense	Mindless Boogie
Billy Connolly	D.I.V.O.R.C.E.	D.I.V.O.R.C.E.
Edgar Broughton	Apache Dropout	Apache
Billy Connolly	No Chance	No Charge
Billy Connolly	In The Brownies	In The Navy
Steve Dahl	Ayatollah	My Sharona
Stan Freberg	Rock Island Line	Rock Island Line
Stan Freberg	Heartbreak Hotel	Heartbreak Hotel
Stan Freberg	Sh-Boom	Sh-Boom
Wurzels	Combine Harvester	Brand New Key
Wurzels	I Am A Cider Drinker	Una Paloma Blanca
Wurzels	Farmer Bill's Cowman	I Was Kaiser Bill's Batman
Wierd Al Yankovic	Another One Rides The Bus	Another One Bites The Dust
Bruce Baum	Marty Feldman Eyes	Bette Davis Eyes
The Fools	Psycho Chicken	Psycho Killer
Vince Vance and the Valients	Bomb Iran	Barbara Ann
Little Roger and the Goosebumps	Gilligan's Isle	Stairway to Heaven

14. Buddy Miles
15. Keith Richards
16. Mick Jagger
17. James Brown
18. Phil Ochs
19. Freddy Fender
20. Chrissie Hynde

A LIST OF UNLISTABLE LISTS

1. Mafia owned record companies
2. Rock stars with silver noses
3. Records hyped into the charts (Insufficient space)
4. Homo-, Bi-, and A-sexual rockers
5. Groupies who are also rock stars

Alberto y Los Trios Paranoias

ACKNOWLEDGEMENTS

It's impossible to do a book of this sort without being indebted to a large number of people for their invaluable help. We would therefore like to express our thanks for 'services rendered' to the following: to fellow-listers Bert Muirhead, Nigel Dick, Andrew Doe, Keith Beach, Mike Howard, Patrick Humphries, Collin Hill, Peter O'Brien, Rocky Prior, Keith Lambourne, John Platt, Richard Hoare, Howard Mylett, Stuart Coleman, Fred Dellar, Andy Peebles, Mike Read, Paul Gambaccini, Steve Wright, Richard Wootton, Adrian Scott, Kevin Howlett, Todd Slaughter and Paul Grein.

We would also like to thank: Ad Roland, Tivi Broklund, Alf Martin of *Record Mirror,* Peter Wilkinson of *Music Week,* Paul Bridge of *Cashbox,* David Kent, Paul Lowe, Randi Cushnir, Brian Southall, Robbie Irwin, Fred Bronson, Dafydd Rees, Barry Lazell, Herbie Flowers, Tony Burrows, Stuart Grundy, Hal Blaine, Jan Martin, Kenny Everett, Pete Frame, Jo Gurnett, Don Bustany and the Fabulous Fiona, all of whom supplied information, permission and/or pictures. We'd like to thank MPL, for supplying Linda McCartney's photograph of George Martin and Paul McCartney featured on page 13, Decca, EMI, CBS, WEA, Atlantic, RCA, Phonogram, Polydor, Stiff Records, A&M, Island, The Human League, Apple, Motown, Towerbell, Polygram, K-Tel and Virgin for supplying illustrations. It has not been possible in all cases to trace the copyright sources, and we would be glad to hear from any such unacknowledged copyright holders.

To Nicky Hayden, Sandra Wake and Terry Porter, who commissioned the book; to Debbie Geller who cajoled — nay, bullied — the authors into action whenever necessary; to Lisa Hardy who held the whole thing together and to Robin Allen who designed the book with equal measures of flair and skill, thanks to you all.

Finally, a big raspberry to time, which refuses to stand still and is even now displaying an eagerness to make as many lists as possible out-of-date by publication date.

JOHN TOBLER and ALAN JONES
September 1982